A HISTORY OF OVERSEAS CHINESE
IN AFRICA TO 1911

A HISTORY OF OVERSEAS CHINESE IN AFRICA TO 1911

LI ANSHAN

DIASPORIC AFRICA PRESS
NEW YORK

This book is a publication of

DIASPORIC AFRICA PRESS
NEW YORK | WWW.DAFRICAPRESS.COM

Copyright © Diasporic Africa Press 2012

All rights reserved. No part of this publication may be reproduced or distributed in any form or by any means, or stored in a database or retrieval system, without the prior written permission of the publisher.

Library of Congress Control Number: 2012934961

Anshan, Li, *A History of Overseas Chinese in Africa to 1911*.
Includes index.

ISBN-13 978-0-9660201-0-6 (pbk.: alk paper)

Special discounts are available for bulk purchases of this book. For more information, please contact us at sales@dafricapress.com.

Diasporic Africa Press uses environmentally friendly book materials, including recycled text paper that is composed of at least 30 percent post-consumer waste, whenever possible.

Printed in the United States of America on acid-free paper.

事实

CONTENTS

FOREWORD i

INTRODUCTION 1

CHAPTER I 17
*The Development of Early
Sino-African Relations*

CHAPTER II 55
The Beginning of Overseas Chinese

CHAPTER III 95
*The Establishment of Overseas
Chinese Communities*

CHAPTER IV 131
Oppression, Discrimination, and Protest

NOTES 171

INDEX 199

FOREWORD

Thoughts on the Use of Chinese Documents in the Reconstruction of East African History[1]

John Shen

For a long time, scholars have known that the ancient Sino-East African trade relationship produced valuable accounts of East Africa in the Chinese imperial archives. Particularly, the historical documents compiled during the Tang, Sung, and Ming dynasties contain several insightful snapshots of East Africa over the span of 800 years. Unfortunately, due to the difficulty of translating ancient Chinese texts, scholars have not been able to utilize these documents fully. In other cases, scholars have misused the translations to derive conclusions that may not be supported by the original text. In this prefatory essay I propose to re-examine the original Chinese sources and the way these sources have been used by subsequent scholars. Furthermore, I shall explore the real or potential contribution of these texts to our understanding of East African coastal history, since that history is integral to historic Africa-China relations and the later presence of overseas Chinese in Africa.

The primary source of Chinese knowledge about East Africa during the Tang dynasty (618–907) comes from *Ching-hsing Chi* ("Record of Travels") and *Yu-yang Tsa-tsu* ("Assorted Dishes from Yu-yang"). During the Sung dynasty (960–1279), most of the information is recorded in *Chu-fan-chih* ("Gazetteer of Foreigners") and *Ling-wai Tai-ta* ("Information from Beyond the Mountains"). Finally, the record of the Ming (1368–1644) naval expedition into the western Indian Ocean is preserved in *Wu-pei-chih* ("Notes on Military Preparedness"),

Hsing-ch'a Sheng-lan ("Triumphant Vision of the Starry Raft"), and *Ming Shih* ("History of the Ming Dynasty").

These documents in the imperial archive served as the basis of the Chinese understanding of East Africa. Frequently, parts of original Chinese sources were repeated by Court scholars who attempted to write a comprehensive history of an entire dynasty or even history since the beginning of time. Except for *Hsing-ch'a Sheng-lan* written by Fei Hsin in 1436, other works were compiled by court scholars who relied on Chinese travelers or Arab traders. Most likely, the earlier information came from the Arab merchants who were the major traders of the Indian Ocean.

During the Ming dynasty, however, a Court eunuch, Cheng Ho (Zheng He), led seven imperial expeditions during the period of 1405 to 1433 CE, which brought about the first direct official contact between China and East Africa. According to J. J. L. Duyvendak, an eminent sinologist, the Yung-lo Emperor commissioned these expeditions because he was motivated by "the real need of overseas products felt particularly at Court, and the desire to increase his own prestige, and reestablish the overseas renown of the Chinese Empire."[2] It was also rumored that the Yung-lo Emperor, who usurped the throne at the beginning of the fifteenth century, sent these expeditions to bring back his predecessor, who had been deposed and had fled overseas. However, this excuse is transparent because the scale of some expeditions—no fewer than 62 vessels carrying 37,000 soldiers—would be excessive for the purpose of finding a former emperor. Unfortunately, all the official records about Cheng Ho's extraordinary voyages were destroyed. As a result, our chief understanding of these expeditions today comes from Ma Huan, a Muslim interpreter, and Fei Hsin, a member of the scholar class who served as a junior officer on some of Cheng Ho's voyages.

The obliteration of documents from Cheng Ho's voyage illustrates a deeper problem with Chinese historiography: the vulnerability of historical documents to distortion by secondary handlers. Frequently, historical records from both local and national levels were compiled by Court officials to form an encyclopedia for posterity. Incidentally, Court officials often formed a group to compete with the Court eunuchs for the Emperor's favor. Therefore, when the official faction or the eunuch clique lost favor, documents by the losing side or about the defeated group were sometimes destroyed or altered. The officials particularly despised Cheng Ho, whose successful voyage found favor in the Emperor's eyes, and in 1480 the officials of the Military Department conspired to destroy records about Cheng Ho's voyage in order to prevent other eunuchs from following Cheng Ho's example.

Yet, despite the occasional distortion of records, Chinese scholars generally transcribed and transmitted historical documents with a high degree of fidelity. For instance, parts of the observations of Tu Huan in *Ching-hsing Chi* ("Record of Travels") were reiterated in secondary sources such as *T'ung Tien* ("Comprehensive Institutes"), *T'ung Chih* ("Historical Collections"), *Wen-hsien T'ung-k'ao*, *T'ai-p'ing Huan Yu Chi* ("General Description of the World Compiled in the T'ai-p'ing Reign-Period"), and *Hsin Tang-Shu* ("New Tang History"). Through the years the primary source, *Ching-hsing Chi*, was lost, so that the only way to reconstruct the observations of Tu Huan was to consult secondary sources. Even after more than 1000 years of transcription, the reiterations of Tu Huan's observations in the secondary sources are still very consistent with each other, attesting to the accuracy of transcription.

Although scholars have attempted to reconstruct a historical connection between China and East Africa since the early seventeenth century, this relationship has only been studied on a firm scholarly basis within this century. In fact the earliest translation of a Chinese historical text into English was *Chau Ju-Kua: His Work on the Chinese and Arab Trade in the Twelfth and Thirteenth Centuries, Entitled Chu-Fan Chi* by Friedrich Hirth and W.W. Rockhill. In the late 1930s, Chang Hsing-lang compiled all the previous records relating to East Africa as part of *Chung-Hsi chiao-t'ung shih-liao hui-p'ien* ("Comprehensive discussion of Chinese relations with the West").

Then Duyvendak translated many of the important documents into English in *China's Discovery of Africa*, a series of lectures given at the University of London. Since then, Duyvendak's translations of *Yu-yang Tsa-tsu*, *Chu-fan-chih*, and *Ling-wai Tai-ta* have become the standard translations for all subsequent sinologists and East African scholars. A decade later Teobaldo Filesi reexamined all the available Chinese translations from the perspective of an Africanist and concurred with much of Duyvendak's translation. More recently Paul Wheatley compiled a comprehensive list of Chinese documents, separating the primary sources from their reiterations in the secondary sources. As it happens, however, the most widely disseminated and frequently cited translation of these key texts for Africanists occurs in G. S. P. Freeman-Grenville's *The East African Coast: Select Documents from the First to the Earlier Nineteenth Century.*

As the result of these scholarly studies, different interpretations of the same Chinese sources were created. For instance, the same portion of *Yu-yang Tsa-tsu* was interpreted differently by Hirth, Duyvendak, and Freeman-Grenville. In 1911 Hirth first translated a certain phrase as "[t]heir women are clear-skinned and well behaved. The people of this country make their own countrymen prisoners whom they sell to strangers at prices many times more than they would fetch (at home)."[3] In 1949 Duyvendak translated the same text as "[t]heir women are clean and of proper behavior. The inhabitants themselves kidnap them, and if they sell them to foreign merchants, they fetch several times their price."[4] Finally, in 1962 Freeman-Grenville conflated the two interpretations to read: "Their women are clean and well-behaved. The people of the country themselves kidnap them and sell them to strangers at prices many times more than they would fetch at home."[5]

Although Hirth's and Duyvendak's versions of *Yu-yang Tsa-tsu* appear to be the same, they reflect substantial differences. Since Hirth dissociates the description of women from the description of kidnapping, he interprets the kidnapping of their own countrymen as a general statement that includes both men and women. In contrast, Duyvendak indicates that the passage focuses on the kidnapping of women only. While Duyvendak interprets the kidnapping of women as conditional by using the word "if," Hirth translates the event as customary.

These disagreements exist because Chinese, similarly to Greek, has neither punctuation nor spacing. Thus it is difficult to distinguish where one sentence ends and the next sentence begins. In some instances scholars must also read other texts to reconstruct the original meaning of certain words because they have fallen into disuse. Although Duyvendak's translation conforms to the Chinese grammatical rules better than that of Hirth, the different opinions demonstrate the subjective nature of translating these texts—or any texts for that matter.

Unfortunately, Freeman-Grenville's treatment of Duyvendak's translation epitomizes the careless transmission of Chinese sources. Freeman-Grenville, who to the best of my knowledge does not read Chinese, uses the translation of F. Hirth and W. W. Rockhill "with certain emendations as proposed by J. J. L. Duyvendak."[6] Apparently,

Freeman-Grenville simply grafted pieces of Duyvendak's translation (in boldface here) to Hirth's original translation (italicized here), without acknowledging the disagreement between Hirth and Duyvendak. Thus: "**Their women are clean** *and well-behaved. The people of the country* **themselves kidnap them and** *sell them to strangers at prices many times more than they would fetch at home.*" Scholars who subsequently use the Freeman-Grenville edition of *Yu-yang Tsa-tsu* would not know that conflicting interpretations exist. While Duyvendak included the original text on controversial translations in order for the readers to know the interpretive nature of translated work, Freeman-Grenville failed to include any reference to these problems of translation or to the original texts.

Methodologically, Freeman-Grenville's inadequate treatment of the original Chinese documents is potentially problematic for future scholars. By conflating Hirth's translation with that of Duyvendak, Freeman-Grenville essentially implies that there is a definitive translation. David Henige criticizes this type of textual intrusion where the textual editor "puts more of himself or herself into the text (and not merely into the footnotes) than rightfully belongs there."[7] Furthermore, Freeman-Grenville's exclusion of the Chinese original text should alarm historians because it could be easily misinterpreted. As Henige states, "translation is less important, on purely intellectual grounds, than the original, which, no matter how obscure its language or elliptical its expression, can alone constitute the primary source and so should not be allowed to become less accessible than a translation."[8]

Unfortunately, the errors in the transmission and translation of Chinese sources into English have prevented scholars of East Africa from using this valuable information. Furthermore, when scholars seek to use these translations as an integral part of their interpretations, poor translations become the weak points of their arguments. For example, James de Vere Allen uses several Chinese translations to help create his provocative hypothesis to explain the origins of Swahili people. However, he bases some of his argument on suspicious translated passages from Freeman-Grenville. If the translations included in Freeman-Grenville's compilation are proven wrong in the future, Allen's thesis could also be weakened or even toppled.

Of course, and more fundamentally, Allen himself is guilty of misusing Chinese sources. Allen claims that Tu Yu mentioned Mualien as a town occupied by the representative of three religions, Monophysite

Christianity, Islam, and a local traditional religion. Allen concludes that:

> *if Mualien is Berbera, it is important because the description of the population following its traditional belief-system refers to their 'incestuous habits,' the Chinese term used—so Wheatley tells us—for incest with a member of an older generation. This seems applicable to a society with the political-marital customs ascribed to the rulers of Great Shungwaya.*

However, according to Wheatley's translation, incest was prevalent among the followers of Mazdaism, not the traditional religion. In addition, Wheatley derives his conclusion by examining the writings of Tu Yu in *T'ung Tien*, which never mentions local traditional religion. While Allen may have a legitimate reason for interpreting Ziemziem as a local traditional religion, his failure to explain this interpretation in the text or in the footnote again shows poor scholarship. Consequently, the evidence for Great Shungwaya is gravely weakened because the original text does not support Allen's assertion.

Furthermore, Allen's use of Chinese sources to explain the origin of Swahili people is faulty. Allen constructs his theory for the origin of Shungwaya by connecting the description of the pastoral Po-pa-li in *Yu-yang Tsa-tsu* to the urbanized Tiung-lji in *Chu-fan-chih*. In order to reconcile seemingly incompatible images, Allen patches the two descriptions together with this critical link:

> *Suppose that some of Tuan Ch'eng-shih's herders decided, about the end of the eighth century, to establish coastal settlements and take up trade instead of herding (pastoralists often do this in exceptionally dry periods, and we know from the Rhodah Nilometer and other sources that in eastern and northeastern Africa the eighth century was by far the driest in the Christian era, so pastoral groups may well have been dislodged and forced to take up alternative livelihoods all over this region). If it was these pastoralists who first decided to found coastal settlements, they might well have invited the collaboration of iron-workers, probably drawn from neighboring agriculturalists; and it could have been these iron- workers who introduced baked flour-cakes to their diet.*

Allen attempts to prove this critical link in roundabout ways, using conjecture on conjecture. However, Allen evades the "delicate question of why the Arab sources on tenth- to fifteenth-century East Africa made no reference to Shungwaya."[9]

Allen's selective use of evidence shows that the methodology of some historians is still the biggest barrier to the proper use of Chinese accounts. While the Chinese sources provide invaluable snapshots of East Africa during different time periods, Allen misuses them by forcibly linking them together. Consequently, Justin Willis characterizes the Chinese accounts as more akin to "fifth-hand sailor yarns" than the Arab descriptions. However, it is not entirely the fault of the translations, but the desire of authors like Freeman-Grenville and Allen to substantiate their arguments that have given Chinese sources such a dubious reputation. Perhaps out of the desire to avoid controversies, East African scholars have only used Chinese sources in limited ways. For instance, Gervase Mathew utilizes Chinese documents to discuss common knowledge such as the importation of ivory, rhinoceros horns, tortoise-shells, and ambergris. He also concedes that "Chinese geographers had a detailed knowledge of Po-pa-li, a country on the western sea, and had heard of the customs of the black and ferocious inhabitants of Mo Lin."[10] However, Mathew qualifies the Chinese accounts as "probably hearsay, gathered in India or Indonesia."[11] Such limited application of Chinese reference exemplifies the current status of Chinese documents in East African history—inconsequential. In the case of Gervase Mathew, his treatment of Chinese sources does not do justice to the wealth of information stored in the original texts because he relies upon the translations of Wheatley which are accurate but limited in scope. Clearly, the shortage of reliable translations has seriously hampered the use of Chinese records in reconstructing the history of the East African coast.

So far the contribution of Chinese sources has been mixed. The excellent work of Duyvendak and Wheatley coexists with the faulty scholarship of Freeman-Grenville and Allen. This phenomenon reveals a deeper problem behind the use of Chinese documents—the lack of systematic translation and organization of sources. Since none of the earlier translators intended to create a comprehensive translation of the original Chinese texts, scholars were forced to search through bits and pieces of translations from various sinologists. For instance, Duyvendak translated some of the Chinese sources to reconstruct the early relationship between China and Africa. Consequently, he presented only the few translations that were relevant to his topic. Wheatley categorized the Chinese sources, giving scholars an overview of the original texts and subsequent reiterations. Though not nearly as organized as Wheatley, Chang Hsing-lang gathered the most Chinese sources in his comprehensive record of the Chinese relationship with East Africa. Unfortunately, Chang Hsing-lang's work in Chinese is unknown and inaccessible to most East African scholars. This lack of reliable translations forces scholars to rely upon third- or fourth-hand translations such as *The East African Coast*, which may not resemble the original text nearly well enough. In the midst of this translation confusion, historians can pick and choose any versions of the originals. Consequently, less meticulous scholars can always find one translation that will substantiate their presuppositions.

In order to combat this confusion, a comprehensive translation of Chinese originals should be initiated. By gathering the works of Duyvendak and Chang Hsing-lang, a scholarly apparatus on the caliber of Wheatley could categorize and translate Chinese sources systematically. By providing original text and annotations along with the translations, Chinese sources will become accessible to scholars. Conceivably, such a comprehensive translation project would contribute to research in Chinese and East African foreign relations, as well as to the trade patterns in the Indian Ocean. Furthermore, it will eliminate the confusion surrounding the use of Chinese sources. While the Chinese sources say much about East Africa, they also provide us with an insight to the Chinese images of East Africa. Particularly, the East Africans' lack of Chinese "moral virtue" fed into the justification for the Chinese condescending attitude toward East African slaves. Finally, Sinocentrism culminated in China's self-adulation when Malindi sent an emissary with a giraffe to the Ming Emperor via Cheng Ho's imperial fleet in 1419.

Ever since the earliest records, the Chinese gave much attention to the outward signs of "moral virtue." In *Yu-yang Tsa-tsu*, the scholar notes "barbaric" characteristics such as the semi-nakedness of the inhabitants. Perhaps the author describes native women as clean and of proper behavior in order to counter the Chinese perception that East African women are sexually "immoral" because of their "barbarian" origin. Also, in *Ching-hsing-chih*, Tu Huan was so appalled by the inhabitants' incestuous customs that he says that "[t]hey are [in this respect] the worst of the barbarians."[12] Within the Chinese world view, these descriptions of the East Africans further substantiate the Sinocentric attitude of these Chinese scholars/tradesmen by focusing on the "moral weaknesses" of the "barbarians."

As the result of the strong ethnic chauvinism toward the outside world, Chinese sources often describe East Africans in an unfavorable light. Since most East Africans were brought to China as slaves, they often received names such as: *kuei-nu* ("devil-slaves"), *yeh-jen* ("wild men"), *hei-hsiao-ssu* ("black servants"), *fan-hsiao-ssu* ("barbarian servants"), or *fan-nu* ("barbarian slaves"). Not only did the Chinese use extremely derogatory names toward East Africans, but they also described and treated them like beasts. One source compared the East Africans to devils, calling them the "ugliest people in the world."[13] Furthermore, the *P'ing-chou-k'o-t'an* writes:

> *In Kuang-chou most of the wealthy people keep devil-slaves. They are very strong and can lift (weights of) several hundred catties. Their language and tastes are unintelligible. Their nature is simple and they do not run away. They are also called 'wild men'. Their color is black as ink, their lips are red and their teeth white, their hair is curly and yellow. There are males and females. They live in the mountains (or islands) beyond the seas. They eat raw things.*

This patronizing description of the East Africans, repeated throughout the Chinese sources, is no different from the racist depictions of Reginald Coupland in *East Africa and its Invaders* (New York, 1965). Certainly, the description of East Africans reveals a racial hierarchy in the Chinese worldview that resembles the European theory of racial hierarchy in the nineteenth century.

In the same vein of self-righteousness, the Chinese exhibited unabashed self-adulation when the Ming Emperor received a giraffe from Malindi. Why a giraffe? The word for "giraffe" in the Somali language is "girin," which is very similar to "k'i-lin" in Chinese. "K'i-lin" happens to be an animal in Chinese mythology that appears only during times of peace and harmony. It symbolizes Heaven's favor upon the virtue of the Emperor, the ruler of the entire universe. Coincidentally, the superficial description of the giraffe also matches that of the "k'i-lin," which is supposed to have "'the body of a deer and tail of an ox,' to eat only herbs and to harm no living being."[14] By offering a giraffe,

Malindi unwittingly conformed to the category of a tributary state, recognizing the dominion of the Ming Emperor. Furthermore the Yung-lo Emperor probably received the giraffe as a sign of heaven's legitimization of his usurped throne.

Predictably, the state officials capitalized on this opportunity to adulate the Emperor. When the Emperor received the animal at the Feng-t'ien gate, all the officials prostrated themselves and offered congratulations. Members of the Imperial Academy, the Han-lin, and the Court painters eagerly submitted flattering poems and paintings to the Emperor. In response, the Emperor said:

> *This event is due to the abundant virtue of the later Emperor, my father, and also to the assistance rendered me by my Ministers. That is why distant people arrive in uninterrupted succession. From now on it behooves us ever more than in the past to cling to virtue and it behooves you to remonstrate with us about our shortcomings.*"[15]

Indeed the presentation of the giraffe to the Ming Emperor symbolizes the height of Sinocentrism. For a short time China indulged in self-adulation because the presence of the "k'i-lin" proved that China had attained perfect virtue, perfect government, and perfect harmony in the Empire.

The Chinese historical documents have the potential to confirm findings from other sources such as Arabic accounts of the coast, archeological evidence, or oral traditions. For example, Al-Idrisi (1110–1165) recorded that Arab merchants lured children of Zanj with dates in order to enslave them. Concurrently, *Ling-Wai Tai-ta* (1163 CE) also recorded the enslavement of black *yeh-jen* ("wild men") through the enticement of food. Clearly, the verification provided by this Chinese documentation strengthens the case for this particular practice of enslavement during the twelfth century. At the same time, scholars of eastern Africa must be cautious about the cultural context surrounding Chinese documents. Ultimately, a thorough understanding of the collection, editing, and presentation process of Chinese historical documents, along with a critical analysis of their characteristics (i.e. eyewitness, secondary report, or compilation at a distant time) will render these sources useful to the reconstruction of East African history and the history of Chinese in Africa.

INTRODUCTION

CHINA'S STUDY OF the history of overseas Chinese has gradually advanced, and has clearly shown several unique characteristics. First, scholars in disciplines other than history are adopting multidisciplinary research methods, tools, and perspectives from sociology, economics, political science, and law. To a large degree, this phenomenon is dictated by the scope of the study. Second, an increasingly international trend can be gauged by the many international overseas Chinese research magazine articles and publications in recent years, and the many symposiums held at locations such as California (United States), Shantou (China), Hong Kong, and Manila (Philippines). Third, there is growing attention towards concepts and theories related to overseas Chinese: e.g., "overseas Chinese," "Chinese," "ethnic Chinese," "Chinese merchant," and the issues of integration, assimilation, identification, and Chinese networks. There are also a greater number of in-depth studies on pressing and practical topics that affect overseas Chinese, such as economic, education, and political involvement issues. Lastly, from regions with large concentrations of overseas Chinese, similar research is beginning to span outward to all regions around the world.

We can say that indirect Chinese knowledge about Africa began in the Han Dynasty. Starting from the Tang Dynasty, exchanges between the East and the West grew more frequent, and the Chinese knowledge of Africa also grew from indirect to direct. However, Chinese immigration to Africa in large numbers did not occur until the late Qing Dynasty. Based on the current available historical documents, as early as the mid-seventeenth century, the Dutch colonialists shipped thousands of prisoners as slaves from Batavia (present-day Jakarta, Indonesia) to Mauritius and South Africa's Cape Colony. The Chinese were among the prisoners. According to foreign researchers, as early as 1593, Chinese individuals were shipped to South Africa by the Portuguese. In 1654, three Chinese were shipped from Indonesia's Batavia to Mauritius. In 1660, a Chinese named Wan Shou was exiled to the Cape of Good Hope in South Africa as a prisoner by the Dutch East India Company. These are likely the earliest Chinese living in Africa.

What cannot be overlooked is that China's research into the history of overseas Chinese in Africa is still very weak. Thus far, there have been dedicated publications on the overseas Chinese living on other continents. But the study of overseas Chinese in Africa appeared to be marginalized. The few research articles and historical data compilations were mostly limited to the early Chinese laborers in South Africa and translation work by others.

In view of this, with my very limited ability, I wish to give my best in helping fill this gap. Worthy of note is that the meanings of the terms "Chinese" and "overseas Chinese" used throughout this book are similar to academia's general understanding of these terms. That is, "overseas Chinese" refers to those still retaining Chinese nationality while "Chinese" refers to the Chinese people living in Africa and holding the nationality of their residing country. And the descendants of these two groups of people are called "ethnic Chinese." With the exception of special circumstances, this book in general does not distinguish between these two terms. This introduction, following an overview of the historical documents on overseas Chinese in Africa, will cover the following source materials used in this study: (1) unpublished government files; (2) local official documents; (3) published government documents; and (4) and local newspapers.

Analysis of the History of Overseas Chinese in Africa

The most important element in historical research is the use of historical documents. The available sources of China's domestic historical documents include the following. The first is the official files. In general, Chinese immigration to the African continent and its neighboring islands originated in the Qing Dynasty. Hence, archives kept by the Ministry of Foreign Affairs of the Qing Dynasty are vital in the study of early Chinese immigration to Africa (especially those contracted Chinese laborers who went to South Africa during 1904–1910).

In addition to the files kept by the First Historical Archives, which include data stored by the China Ministry of Foreign Affairs and Customs, a significant amount of information has already been published in the *Foreign News*. Thus, the *Foreign News* becomes one of the most important historical documents in studying early Chinese laborers. The *Foreign News* printed its first issue in January 1902 and ended its last issue in 1911. It was published once every ten days, with a total of three hundred issues. Three columns of the *News* that are most important in the study of the early Chinese laborer include "Clerical," "Translation Category," and "Negotiation Record." Each issue of the *Foreign News* included a "Clerical" column that published a variety of official documents or important decrees and circulars. This column once published important documents such as, "British South Africa Recruiting Chinese Indentured Laborers Mining Contract,"[1] "British South Africa Recruiting Cantonese Worker Mining Contract,"[2] and, "British South Africa New Prohibiting Chinese Indentured Laborers Law."[3] There were also a large number of translations, which were mainly translated from major newspapers in Britain, the United States, and Japan. Translations can be grouped into three categories. First category centers on China's foreign relations and other countries' China policy. According to my own count, there are as many as fourteen major articles on South Africa's Chinese indentured laborers, recruitment, treatment, and China's government policy. The earliest translation came from the British newspaper *The Guardian*, whose editorial article titled, "Banning Chinese Indentured Laborers in Africa," attacked the import of labor from China.[4] In addition, most issues of the *Foreign News* included the "Negotiation Record" column. In it, there were "Chinese Indentured Labor News" and "Overseas Chinese News" sections. In these sections, there were numerous news articles on early Chinese indentured laborers in South Africa, reporting on their local lives and the harsh regulations set against them.[5]

Among all the published historical documents, Sections I, IV, and IX of *A Compilation of Historical Documents on Chinese Indentured Laborers Abroad*, edited by Chen Hansheng, are of particular importance. Section I, "Chinese Official Document Collection," encompasses four volumes. Volume IV, Part XIII, titled, "Chinese Indentured Laborers in South Africa," contains 154 historical documents, which include collections such as foreign affairs correspondences, government notes, diplomatic documents, telegrams, official ordinances, official reports to superiors, signature records, official reports to peers, etc. Among the listed types, three contain the largest collections: official reports to peers (43 articles), foreign affairs correspondences (41 articles), and diplomatic documents (34 articles).⁶ The data include the exchanged correspondences between the Qing Dynasty Ministry of Foreign Affairs and Britain on the subject of Chinese indentured laborers going to South Africa for gold mining, the negotiations between Chang Deyi and the British Foreign and Commonwealth Affairs Office, reports to the Ministry of Foreign Affairs regarding Chinese indentured laborers going to South Africa from prominent local politicians (such as Zhili governor Yuan Shikai), reports and letters to the Ministry of Foreign Affairs regarding transporting Chinese indentured laborers, treatment and compensation, and living conditions from Liu Yulin (China's South Africa First Consul General) and Liu Yi (China's South Africa Acting Consul General). Although these documents focused mainly on Chinese indentured laborers in South Africa, there were also individual, direct references to the living conditions of the Chinese in South Africa at the time. For instance, in the document, "Consul General Liu Yi's Report to Ministry of Foreign Affairs on Prohibition of Opium Smoking by Overseas Chinese," the state of opium usage at the time by overseas Chinese in Transvaal and Cape Town was cited: "Each province has over a thousand population; thirty to forty percent of them smoke opium."⁷

Section IV of *A Compilation of Historical Documents on Chinese Indentured Laborers Abroad*, "A Comprehensive Book of Chinese Indentured Laborers Going Abroad," included four parts. Part I contained a collection of writings on Chinese people. In it, there were excerpts from the English publication, "Chinese Migrations with Special Reference to Labor Conditions," by Chen Da. Published in 1923, the book was intended as a report to the U.S. Department of Labor. Chapter 8 of *Chinese Indentured Laborers in Transvaal, South Africa*, carried out relatively detailed research and made an attempt to include many government documents, including treaties, contracts, conventions, and reports.⁸ Part II of the book included works by foreign writers. One of these was the renowned *Chinese Coolie Emigration to Countries within the British Empire*, by Ms. Campbell, published in 1923. Chapter 4 of *The Experiment of Transvaal*, has a rich collection of documents, British parliamentary documents being the majority. It demonstrated the author's solid historical background. This book later became one of the important reference books in the study of Chinese indentured laborers in South Africa.[9]

Section IX of *A Compilation of Historical Documents on Chinese Indentured Laborers Abroad*, "Chinese Indentured Laborers in Africa," collected three types of articles.[10] Included in the first type were British editorials, both pro- and anti-recruitment positions on the subject of Chinese indentured laborers in South Africa. All articles of this type were collected from the *Foreign News*. The second type of articles were book collections. There were translations of Leon Slawecki's *French Policy towards the Chinese in Madagascar* (University of Chicago, 1971), *Chinese Indentured Laborers in Transvaal*, the writings of Zhang Zhilian regarding Chinese indentured laborers in Africa, and the writings of Chen Zexian regarding recruitment of Chinese indentured laborers in the unrestricted area of the British, French, Belgian, Portuguese, Spanish, and German colonies. Among them, Zhang Zhilian's work is particularly valuable. In his research effort, he conducted a broad search. He then combed through and organized the collected data. Zhang provided invaluable materials for the study of Chinese indentured laborers recruited to African colonies by the European powers. With rigorous research and clear references, he provided an accurate account of his data sources.[11] The third type of article was travel journals, and there was only one such article. It was "South Africa Travel Journal" by Xie Zixiu, who was from Kaiping, Guangdong Province. Xie arrived at South Africa in October 1903. His stay there coincided with the arrival of Chinese mining workers in South Africa. In order to investigate the true working conditions of these Chinese indentured laborers, Xie resigned from his Chinese Association Secretary post in Johannesburg and worked in the Office of the British Royal Advisors. "What propelled me was the desire to investigate," he wrote, "not greed or salary."[12]

In *Tongzhi Treaty, Guanxu Chao Dong Hua Records, Guanxu Treaty, Foreign Custom Treaty, New Compilation of Foreign Treaties, The Stories of Treaties with Various Nations* by Lu Yuanding, and *A Compilation of Old Foreign Treaties*, edited by Wang Tieya, there were a small number of references on this subject. These references included official reports to emperors, treaties, etc. Examples are "'China–UK' [and] 'China–France' Drawing Recruitment Contract Treaty," "Ministry of Foreign Affairs nominating Liu Yulin, to the Emperor, for the British South Africa Consul General Post" and "China–UK Worker Protection

Bylaws." In addition, a number of correspondences regarding recruitment of Chinese indentured laborers to work in South African goldmines were kept in Kailuan Records. This was because the Kaiping Mining Company was also involved in the recruitment of labor.[13] The second issue of *Bei Guo Chun Qiu*, published in 1960, included several correspondences and contracts which were valuable references in studying the history of Chinese indentured labor recruitment by the Committee of South Africa Transvaal Mining Affairs (later renamed to the Office of Transvaal Mining Affairs) during 1904–1906.[14] In *Collections of Historical Sino-African Relations (1500–1918)* by Ai Zhouchang, Part IV, "Chinese Indentured Laborers and Overseas Chinese," also compiled a number of historical documents, mostly obtained from *History of Chinese Going Abroad Compilation* and the second issue of *Bei Guo Chun Qui*.[15]

Among the official data recorded during the Republic Period, there were the files kept in China's Second Museum Archives, bulletins and magazines issued by the government, such as *Foreign Bulletins*, published by the Ministry of Foreign Affairs (monthly publication, founded in 1921, Beijing), *Ministry of Foreign Affairs Bulletins* (monthly publication, founded in 1928, Nanjing), *Foreign Affairs Weekly* (founded in 1934, Nanjing), *Foreign Affairs Bulletins* (semi-monthly publication, founded by the Wang Puppet Regime in 1940, Nanjing). The information regarding overseas Chinese in Africa in these publications was provided by the local Chinese consulates. It was mostly about local Chinese activities or the negotiations between the Chinese consul and the local government. For instance, every issue of the *Foreign Affairs Weekly* had a "Consul News" column, which included newsletters from the Johannesburg consul general and Cairo consul general, reporting on local Chinese celebrations, news on establishing cultural organizations, and various overseas elementary school education events.

Publications from the National Government Overseas Chinese Affairs Commission (renamed to the Central Overseas Chinese Affairs Commission, under the direct jurisdiction of Kuomintang in 1932) was also a source for the study of overseas Chinese in Africa during that period, such as *Central Overseas Chinese Affairs Monthly Magazine*, *Overseas Chinese Weekly News*, *Overseas Chinese Affairs Monthly News*, *Overseas Chinese Affairs Weekly Magazine* and *Overseas Chinese Affairs Seasonal Magazine*, etc. The last two were published by the Wang Puppet Government. In addition to providing statistics of overseas

Chinese populations, these publications also contained integrated articles. *Overseas Chinese Weekly News* was founded in 1932 and overseen by the Education Department under the Overseas Chinese Affairs Commission. In Volume 1, Issue 2, there was an article written by He Changqi, "Recent Observation of Overseas Chinese Affairs in South Africa." In it, he systematically depicted the various harsh regulations imposed upon Chinese by the South African government, and voiced his opinions on foreign negotiations. Issue 9 published the translation by the Chinese Consul General in South Africa, "The Law Governing Asians Renting Properties in Transvaal," which gave us a fundamental understanding of this discriminatory legislation. Issue 14 published an article by Shao Ting, Chinese vice consul at Johannesburg, detailing the negotiations between Chinese and South African governments on the subject of Asian rental property law.[16]

Overseas Chinese Weekly News had a total of forty-four issues. Its publication terminated in June 1933. It was then renamed to *Overseas Chinese Affairs Monthly News*. From the very beginning, every issue of the magazine contained statistics of local overseas Chinese populations, information on overseas Chinese schools and community organizations, etc. This magazine included articles that provided us extremely valuable data for understanding overseas Chinese in Africa. For instance, the November–December combined issue in 1936 included an article by an author writing as "Yu Yu." In the article, a relatively detailed introduction was given on Lourenço Marques, a Portuguese colony in what is now Mozambique. The articles were partitioned into eight sections: "Introduction," "Overseas Chinese' Reasons for Immigration," "Current Business State of Overseas Chinese," "Farming State of Overseas Chinese," "Education State of Overseas Chinese," "Relations between Overseas Chinese and Government," "Overseas Chinese Organizations and Such," and "Ending."[17] There was also information in several official and semi-official publications, such as *Overseas Chinese Warriors*, *Overseas Chinese Pioneers*, and *Overseas Chinese Communication*. However, one must comb through and organize the large amount of data. For instance, in Issue 8 of the *Overseas Chinese Warriors*, there was an article by Chen Yimei, a Mauritius Chinese, entitled "Patriotic Fever of Overseas Chinese in Mauritius." Chen frankly depicted how the Mauritius Chinese, through a variety of means, supported China's war against Japan during World War II.

Information posted by the Taiwan Kuomintang government is yet another often-overlooked type of official historical document. For instance, in *Revolution Literature*, compiled by the Kuomintang Party History Committee, there were descriptions on various Kuomintang overseas branches. Included in Part II of *Chinese Kuomintang Abroad*, compiled and written by the Kuomintang Central Third Group, was an article, "Development Summaries of the Party Affairs in Madagascar." Also, in the book *Overseas Chinese Chorography*, published in 1956 and compiled by the semi-official Taiwanese organization Overseas Chinese Chorography, there was also coverage on the state of the overseas Chinese in Africa, especially the Chinese in South Africa. *Overseas Chinese Economic Annual Chronicle*, compiled by the Taiwan Overseas Chinese Committee, was founded in 1958 and is still in publication today. In it, there was a valuable collection of articles containing overseas Chinese economic information. Several books on Kuomintang party history also had relevant historical data.[18]

Memoirs of many overseas Chinese and historical figures about their personal experiences were also important historical documents. And there was the previously mentioned *South Africa Travel Journal* by Xie Zixiu, *Memoir of the Overseas Chinese Situation in South Africa* by Ye Xun,[19] and *My Personal Witness in Mauritius* by Liu Xinlin.[20] These documents were accounts of the author's personal experiences and memoirs, thus they held historical value. In the books of Feng Ziyou, there was also mention of early overseas Chinese's contributions towards China's revolution. For instance, in *Informal History of the Revolution*, Feng Ziyou described how pioneer revolutionist Yang Quyun, after the failed Guangzhou Uprising, went to Johannesburg and Pietermaritzburg, South Africa to establish the Revive China Society.[21] The Chinese leader in South Africa, Lian Zikuang, once submitted a report to the Taiwan Kuomintang Central Committee on early activities among Chinese in South Africa in support of Chinese revolution. The report was valuable in understanding the viewpoint of the Chinese in South Africa around the time of the Xinhai Revolution.[22] In addition, in magazines such as *Xinmin Repository*, *Eastern Magazine*, *South University and Overseas Chinese*, there were letters and articles written by overseas Chinese in Africa, depicting their own personal encounters.

Eastern Magazine was a cornerstone in China's domestic study of international affairs. It also contained information on overseas Chinese in Africa. In Volume 1, Issue 10, there was an article, "British South Africa's New Regulation Restricting Entrance of Chinese Indentured Laborers," offering a comprehensive introduction to the restriction laws governing the local Chinese by the Cape Town government in 1904. In the same issue, there was yet another article reproduced from a *Foreign Times* editorial. That was probably the first serious reaction towards the event by China's domestic intellectual community. The author's analysis of South Africa's harsh regulations was incisive. He sharply criticized the Qing Dynasty government's policy of abandoning its citizens: "It is unpredictable what the newly arrived Chinese indentured laborers will face. The longtime local Chinese residents are not living in peace and comfort. If this is not our government's fault, whose fault is it? The government cannot deny its own crime in abandoning its citizens."[23] In my historical research on overseas Chinese in Africa, this source provided me the earliest domestic statistics on the subject. The magazine's early issues also included "Various Overseas Chinese Communities: Recent News" and "Overseas Chinese Business" columns. For instance, in "Various Overseas Chinese Community: Recent News," Volume VII, Issue 6, there was the news that Liang Cuixuan, a representative of the South Africa Transvaal Chinese Organization, which was formed to oversee the benefit of its community and resist harsh government regulations, was jailed and forced into hard labor for his role in the resistance.

South University and Overseas Chinese was a domestic specialized magazine focusing on issues related to overseas Chinese, hosted by Ling Nan University, which was located in Guangzhou at the time. Although the magazine mainly focused on overseas Chinese in America and South Asia, it also included communications and articles related to overseas Chinese in Africa. For instance, Volume 8, Issue 3 included a letter written by Li Shuyao to the Minister of Farming and Mining. Mr. Li at the time was sent to South Africa to attend an international geology conference. He was heartbroken upon witnessing how the local Chinese were mistreated by whites, and could not keep his silence. He wrote to the minister, pleading for him to "consult with the Ministry of Foreign Affairs and manage to negotiate."

South Sea Study (founded in 1928), *South Sea Intelligence*, and *South China Intelligence* (founded in 1934) were magazines published by Shanghai Ji Nan University, Department of South Asian Chinese Education (later renamed to the Overseas Culture Department) to study overseas Chinese. These three magazines occasionally included articles on overseas Chinese in Africa. For instance, *South Intelligence*, Volume I, Issue 3 included an article written by a Mauritius Chinese elementary school teacher Guan Zhongfang, "Research on the New Mauritius Chinese arrivals." It was the very first Chinese academic thesis on this subject.[24]

Records kept and publications produced by local Chinese community organizations were the most significant direct materials. But for various reasons, I could only access indirect materials via other publications. Several newspapers published by the overseas Chinese in Africa were the rare direct materials that documented Chinese lives. Based on my knowledge, "Voice of Overseas Chinese" founded by Chinese in South Africa on June 1, 1936 included broad news coverage that included South Africa, Mauritius, Madagascar, Réunion, Mozambique, and other East African regions. In particular, there were many Chinese newspapers in Mauritius. At its height in the 1950s, there were as many as five: *Overseas Business News* (founded on September 7, 1926), *Zhong Hua Times* (founded on August 11, 1932), *China Times* (founded on December 10, 1953), *New Business News* (founded on March 8, 1956), and *Citizen Daily News* (founded on October 31, 1958).[25] In addition, there were several magazines such as *Jing Bao*, a weekly magazine founded on April 14, 1975 by Chinese in Mauritius,[26] *Ming Feng*, a semi-monthly magazine founded on February 15, 1947 by Chinese in Madagascar,[27] and the *Three Language Magazine* founded by Chinese in Réunion.[28] The majority of the present day China's collection of Chinese in Africa newspapers was from the 1950s–1960s time period.

Domestic newspapers were also sources. Prior to 1949, few references of overseas Chinese in Africa existed. However, *Sheng Bao* published excerpts of McNeil's "Overseas Chinese." In it, there were statistics on overseas Chinese in Africa.[29] In addition, when the Spaniards came to China to recruit Chinese indentured laborers for Fernando Pó Island, *Sheng Bao* provided extensive coverage of the event. During World War II, many major domestic newspapers and newspapers in the Liberated Area frequently reported on the support overseas Chinese in Africa gave to their motherland in her plight against the Japanese. For example, *Xing Hua Daily News* and *Liberation Daily News* had respectively reported on active donations made by Chinese in Mauritius, South Africa, and Madagascar in support of the war effort, injured soldiers, and war refugees. Since the founding of the People's Republic of China, no newspapers have been published to cover overseas Chinese. *Overseas Chinese Affairs News*, a monthly publication, offered few articles on overseas Chinese in Africa.[30] *China Voice News* (trial issue published in July 1982), and *Guangdong Overseas Chinese News*, (founded in 1956, resumed publication in 1979) also had various news and reports on overseas Chinese in Africa.

Foreign historical documents mainly are composed of the following two types: (1) Direct materials, including official documents, local publications, personal observation, and memoirs, etc.; (2) Indirect materials, including mostly information referred to by foreign publications. Official documents include both unpublished government files and published official documents. I should note that due to my research experience at British Public Record Office at Kew and Ghana National Archives, I am more familiar with the file classification system in these two countries.[31] My analysis of other countries' files was based on indirect materials.

Unpublished Government Files

Such materials are kept in all countries where there were ever Chinese indentured laborers or overseas Chinese residents. Take the UK for example: There were British Foreign and Commonwealth Office documents (i.e., files assigned FO numbers) and British Colonial Office documents (i.e., files assigned CO numbers). For instance, British Foreign and Commonwealth Office document 367 (FO 367) are all in the "Africa/General Remark, 1906" category, of which the number 16 file contains the document, "Transvaal Chinese merchants' petition, September 27, 1906." It provides us information on the protest made by Transvaal's Chinese merchants to fight for their living rights. Another example is British Colonial Office document 291 (CO 291), the "Original Correspondences—Transvaal Governor addressing to British Secretary of State, 1902–1907" category. The 1904–1907 time period saw the recruitment of Chinese indentured laborers at its most active in South Africa.[32] There were materials related to Chinese labor in these correspondences.

During that time period, the British government and private companies brought in Chinese indentured laborers mainly for the railroad and other types of construction. Therefore, information contained in the British Colonial Office's files is of particular importance. Take the Gold Coast (now Ghana), for example. I made a special effort to review the Colonial Office's CO 96 documents in Public Record Office at Kew. These documents are in the British Colonial Gold Coast file category. I have seen two correspondences written by the Gold Coast Colony Governor to the British Colonial Secretary, indicating acceptance of Chinese indentured laborers. In the official files from 1879, 1889, 1895, and 1897, there were articles suggesting bringing in Chinese indentured laborers. For instance, in 1895 there was a memorandum on the issue of bringing in Chinese indentured laborers written by Gold Coast governor Maxwell on his way to take office in West Africa. Also, in 1897, there was an urgent letter written by a colonial officer named Howard Johnson to Chamberlain on the state of the Gold Coast Chinese indentured laborers.[33]

Towards the late 1890s and the 1920s, to fortify its rule in its African colonies, the French built railroads in French West Africa and French Central Africa. The French brought in Chinese indentured laborers numerous times for the construction of Dakar's various municipal projects: the Dakar–St. Louis Railroad and French Central Africa's Point Nova–Brazzaville Railroad. There were large overseas Chinese populations in Mauritius, Madagascar, and Réunion. Mauritius became occupied by the French in 1715, and remained a French-governed colony until 1810, when it was turned over to and managed by the British East India Company. In 1762, the French kidnapped a group of Chinese indentured laborers from China and shipped them to Mauritius to work in the plantations. Beginning in 1896 and up until its independence in 1960, Mauritius was reduced to a French colony. Réunion was transferred from the rule of the British to the French in 1815. To date, it remains an overseas province of France. Therefore, the files kept by France's former Colonial Department and its Overseas Department were highly valuable in the study of Chinese in Africa.

Take Madagascar, for example. Files kept by the French government include immigration data in Madagascar. For instance, among the overseas files kept by the French Archives Nationales, there were the "Madagascar Files." In it, MCE 188, MCE 208/425, MCE 214/444, and MCE 308/778 all contain information related to Chinese in Madagascar. Among them, MCE 308/778, "Immigrants: Establishing Asian and African Immigration Regulations," contains information on regulations limiting Chinese immigrating to Madagascar.[34]

Next, consider Réunion. Among the early overseas portion of the French national files, there were data on Chinese in Réunion, such as the (ANOM) C 432/34517 file, "Chinese Immigrants (1845)."[35] Undoubtedly, these official documents are helpful in our research of Chinese in Réunion.

Local Official Documents

The advantage of using local government files is the concentration and directness of the information. Take Madagascar, for example. Among the Madagascar government files, the "Civilian Cabinet Series" includes Files 358 and 372, "Chinese Immigrants: 1912–1939" and "Madagascar Chinese Events, 1932–1952," respectively. These two documents systematically introduced the state of the Chinese immigrants in Madagascar during the time period. The "Civilian Cabinet Series" contains File 362, "Kuomintang, 1932–1952." China's Kuomintang established a direct branch in 1928 in Madagascar and had since been very active. It established seventeen sub-branches and thirteen communication offices. This document should be helpful in understanding local Kuomintang activities.[36] Likewise, among the administrative information kept by the Ghana Government, there was the suggestion of bringing in miners from China. In countries and regions with a relatively large Chinese population, such as Mauritius, Madagascar, Réunion, and South Africa, government documents and files on the subject of Chinese (or Asians) are kept.

All these materials are valuable in studying the local Chinese history. For instance, *History of Chinese in West Indies* by the Chinese scholar Pennell is a classic. The book studied Chinese in Mascarene Islands, Madagascar, and South Africa. *Colour, Confusion and Concession: The History of Chinese in South Africa*, by Melanie Yap and Dianne Leong Man and published in 1996, is another valuable book that took many years to complete. Réunion's Chinese scholar Huang Suzheng also completed a book of similar influence in 1996: *Chinese History in Réunion*. The common element among these three books is their use of the vast amount of local government and community files.[37]

Published Government Documents

During 1903–1908, the British Government successively published Parliamentary documents (files numbered Cd) on issues related to South Africa Transvaal Chinese indentured laborers, comprising a total of about twenty articles. These data can be separated into two groups. The first group includes documents related to labor issues, while the other group includes legislature documents on hiring labor, transporting labor, or domestic labor (or Asians). For example, Cd.–1985, "Concerning Affairs Correspondences between Transvaal and Orange River Colony (continuation), February 1903," contains information on the South African government's explicit request to bring in a labor force, and the British government's attitude. Another example is Cd.–3994, "Concerning Correspondences Regarding Laws Governing Transvaal's Indentured Laborers, April 1908." This document is significantly valuable in our understanding of Chinese indentured laborers' treatment by the South African government.

In addition, the British Foreign Office Confidential Prints also include contents with references of Chinese in Africa (mainly Chinese indentured laborers). Careful combing is required to find these references. For example, the British Foreign Office Confidential Prints 8583 is a document on importing Chinese laborers into Transvaal. The British Foreign Office Confidential Prints 8893, yet another example, is regarding Chinese immigrants in British colonies. Countries and regions where Chinese once lived all have such publications. For instance, since the beginning of the twentieth century there have been publications in South Africa on controlling Chinese indentured laborers and on correspondences between Chinese communities and the colonial government.[38]

Local Newspapers

At the end of the nineteenth century, in addition to South Africa, other British, French, Belgian, German, Spanish, Portuguese, and Italian colonies in Africa also successively recruited Chinese laborers to build railroads or to mine.[39] Thus, several local newspapers in Africa also published news related to Chinese indentured laborers; some reproduced from publications of its ruling country. Take the Gold Coast (now Ghana), for example, at the end of nineteenth century. Due to the shortage of labor situation in the Gold Coast, its colonial government brought in a group of Chinese indentured laborers in August 1897. At the time, local newspapers such as *Gold Coast Express*, *Gold Coast Independent*, and *Gold Coast Chronicles* reported on this issue on numerous occasions. They also voiced various opinions on this action of the Gold Coast colonial government.[40] Because the majority of the local population was against this action by the colonial government, there were heated debates at the time.

Individual recollections were also important historical documents. They include both published memoirs and oral accounts. In May 1810, the British East India Company shipped fifty Chinese indentured laborers from Guangdong to Saint Helena Island. In the memoirs of then Saint Helena Island governor Alexander Peterson, he gave a description of the work done by the Chinese indentured laborers.[41] In the process of writing *Colour, Confusion and Concessions*, Melanie Yap and Dianne Leong interviewed several eyewitnesses and recorded a large number of oral accounts. There were also valuable accounts from contemporaries documenting their own observations. For example, an author writing under the name "An English Eyewitness" published an article, "John Chinaman on the Rand," in 1905. The author had visited Orange, Cape Town, Natal, and Transvaal, and lived in post British-Boer War South Africa. He understood the public opinion on Chinese indentured laborers at the time and had witnessed how South Africa goldmine owners abused these laborers. The author wrote, "In order to make the Chinese speed up retrieving gold ore from deep underground mines, the mine owners applied at will various tactics, such as fines, whipping, expulsion, coercion, etc." When Chinese indentured laborers revolted and public opinions attacked and smeared them, the author sided with the laborers: "Understandably, it was the abuse of the mine owners that led to this rebellious behavior."[42]

智慧

CHAPTER I

THE DEVELOPMENT OF EARLY SINO-AFRICAN RELATIONS

CHINESE IMMIGRATION TO Africa began in modern times. However, contacts between China and Africa started in ancient times. For the ancient Chinese, Africa was the end of the Western Zone. Contacts between China and Africa took place gradually and slowly. In their cognition of Africa, the Chinese progressed from "indirect" to "direct" knowledge and from hearsays to personal experiences. The interaction of the two peoples also evolved from private visits to official contacts. This chapter starts with the indirect knowledge Chinese had about Africa prior to the Tang Dynasty. It then summarizes the interactions between China and Africa throughout the Tang, Song, Yuan, Ming, and Qing dynasties.

INDIRECT KNOWLEDGE PRIOR TO TANG DYNASTY

Academia cannot come to an agreement on when and how the Chinese came to know about Africa. Based on the current research, there exist the following views.[1]

Prior to the Han Dynasty

Many historians set 138–126 BCE as the historical starting point of Sino-African relations. Zhang Xiang does not agree with this view because it ignored the private contacts among the civilians that took place before the official contacts. In his view, "The Sino-African history started prior to Zhang Qian's Western Zone expedition." Zhang Xiang's view was based on the fact that Da Xia had been in contact with Egypt since the sixth century BCE. "As long as commodities and information could reach Da Xia, then it could reach Egypt; and as long as the Chinese can reach Da Xia, they could receive information from Egypt." Zhang reaffirmed this belief in his article, "On Several Ancient Sino-African Relation Research Issues."[2] Certainly, his view is merely a deduction.

Sheng Fuwei set the earliest communication date between the East and the West to the Chun Qiu Zhang Guo Period. "Through grassland nomads, Egypt and the western region of China could become neighbors with each other. Therefore, the earliest interaction between China and Egypt can be traced back to the Chun Qiu (770–476 BCE) and Zhang Guo (475–221 BCE) Period." Sheng believed that due to the vast distance and transportation difficulties, trading between the two could only be conducted indirectly.[3] Sheng also pointed out that the country Dou Le mentioned in the book *Hou Han Shu Xi Yu Zhuan* was the famous harbor Adulis of ancient Aksum. Its envoy arrived at Luo Yang in 100 CE, which was an important milestone in the history of Sino-African relations. "Because of the Adulis envoy's visit to China, the Aksumite Kingdom in [what is now] Ethiopia became the first African country to establish a diplomatic tie with China."[4]

In the Han Dynasty

Based on place names mentioned in various Chinese and foreign books, Zhang Xingliang was the first to implicitly put forth the view that Africa–China relations began during the Han Dynasty.[5] Yang Renbian indicated, "For certain, Sino-African indirect trade relations had already begun during the Chinese Han Dynasty."[6] Chen Gongyuan stated, "In the second century CE (during the Han Dynasty), African ancient civilization Egypt already had indirect relations and sea trade with China."[7] Zhang Junyan wrote, "During the Dong Han Period, en route through North Africa, China established direct contact with the Roman Empire by sea."[8] The former author mentioned "indirect trade relations"; the latter emphasized "direct contact by sea." The two time periods coincide. Mr. Sun Yutang brought up this point in a 1979 article, "As far back as the Han Dynasty, through intermediaries, there were commodity trades and culture exchanges between China and Egypt. This relation began shortly after Zhang Qian went to the Western Zone as an envoy."[9] The authors of *History of Sino-African Relations* held the same view. In their opinions, although there had been indirect civilian contacts since the tenth century BCE between China and Egypt, the real starting point of Sino-Egyptian relations should still be set to the time when Zhang Qian visited the Western Zone. "That was when the Chinese learned about Alexandria of Egypt (Li Xuan) and dispatched an envoy to Li Xuan,"[10] Taiwanese scholar Fang Hao writes.[11]

According to the available data, there was evidence indicating Sino-African interactions prior to the Tang Dynasty. The evidences can be grouped into archeological affirmation (explicit and implicit) and historical documents (explicit and implicit).

Archeological Affirmation (Explicit)

In 1979, a stone with paintings from the Dong Han Period was discovered in Xu Zhou Jia Wang. On the stone, there were drawings of several "Kirins" (Qilins). Among the Kirins, there were at least three with the characteristics of an African giraffe.[12] This finding offered evidence that the Chinese were aware of certain African specialties. In 1993, while studying hairs of a female corpse from the Egyptian Twenty-first Dynasty (1070–954 BCE), Austrian scientists discovered certain unusual materials. After analysis, the materials were identified as silk fabric. At the time, China was the lone silk producer. "We can say with certainty that it was a Chinese product."[13] This suggests that Chinese specialty goods had arrived in Egypt.

Archeological Affirmation (Implicit)

In 1974, a large-scale shipping factory archaeology site from the Qing Han Period was unearthed in Guangzhou. "This was a large-scale ancient shipping factory, with three rows of ship building platforms in addition to a woodwork area. The berth and dock were combined, and composed of sleeper wood, skateboard, and wooden pier. They had the appearance of modern-day railroads. The sleeper wood had large and small types. The skateboard's width was adjustable. The two skateboards on the second building platform had a distance of 2.8 meters, which would enable the building of boats with width between 5.6 to 8.4 meters (i.e., between 2 Zhang 4 Chi to 3 Zhang 6 Chi in the Han Metric System)."[14] This is evidence that Chinese shipping technology at the time was already quite advanced. It was no accident that Fangyu became an important city in overseas trade. This archeological site implicitly offered the possibility that Chinese engaged in oceanic voyages. However, it cannot be evidence of Sino-African traffic.

Historical Documents (Explicit)

Shi Ji Da Wan Zhuan included references of Li Xun. Non-Chinese scholars Pelliot, Devondre, Felix, and several Chinese scholars thought it was Alexandria, Egypt.[15] *Qian Han Shu Di Li Zhi* included references to the "Yi Cheng Bu Kingdom." Foreign scholar Herman thought this was Ethiopia.[16] Zhang Xingliang also held the same view.[17] *Hou Han Shu Xi Yu Zhuan* included references to the "Da Chin Kingdom." A number of scholars thought it referred to the eastern portion of the Roman Empire, such as Syria, Egypt, and Asia Minor.[18] *Wei Lue Xi Rong Zhuan* included references of "Chi San" and "Wu Chi San." Some scholars thought this was Alexandria, Egypt; German scholar Rysard observed, "*Wei Lue* stated, 'West of the Sea, there exists a city named Chi San.' Chi San in ancient pronunciation can be inferred to be Di San. I dare say that this is the Chinese pronunciation of the city located on the tributary of the Nile, Alexandria. Chi San is Alexandria."[19] The above four historical documents all applied inference. The documents themselves were not sufficient as evidence of Sino-African Relations.

Historical Documents (Implicit)

Han Shu Yi Wen Zhi collected a large number of Sea Astrology books.[20] This implicitly explained the degree that Chinese were involved in and attended to ocean navigation at the time. However, it could not be used to explain Sino-African traffic by sea. From the Han Dynasty to the Sui Dynasty, there were practically no references to Africa among Chinese historical documents. But we could see a minute amount of evidence of Sino-African relations among foreign historical documents. In the sixth century, a Greek Christian clergyman named Cosmas wrote the *Christian Endemic Chronicle*. In it, he mentioned maritime traffic in the Indian Ocean at the time, "With Ceylon Island in the center, boats from India, Persia, and Ethiopia traveled around. There were many boats departing from Ceylon Island as well. There were also boats from distant places... and other trade areas." Products coming from these places included local specialties such as silk, cloves, and rosewood, etc.[21] This historical document provided evidence that Chinese merchant ships were very active in the Indian Ocean trade activities that centered around Sri Lanka.

In summary, documents from the Han Dynasty offered sporadic records about Africa, but the information was inconclusive. Thus scholars could not agree on the interpretation. Another element worthy of our attention is the lack of African references in historical documents from the Wei Jing to Sui dynasties. This implicitly tells us that the historical documents from the Han Dynasty were likely ambiguous hearsays. However, if combining these "ambiguous hearsays"[22] and the two types of archeological affirmation, we could then make the following deductions: (a) Private contacts started before official contacts; prior to the Tang Dynasty, information on Africa had already reached China; and (b) indirect contacts took place prior to direct contacts. Prior to the Tang Dynasty, specialty goods from each side had already reached the other through intermediaries.

Chinese's Knowledge about Africa during the Tang Dynasty

Based on the various historical documents from the Tang Dynasty and information unearthed in China and elsewhere, Chinese's knowledge about Africa progressed from indirect to direct. In *Chinese Historical Documents in Reference to Africa during the Tang Dynasty*[23] compiled by Zhang Xingliang, there was a chapter by Shen Fuwei on this historical period describing Sino-African relations from various viewpoints.[24] In his writing, Taiwanese scholar Chen Xingxiong analyzed various historical documents from the Tang Dynasty in detail. Chen described his personal experience of seeing the Chinese porcelains kept in the Tanzania National Museum, as well as his study of archeological findings since the 1960s. He reached his conclusion based on the summary of various historical documents. Although further exploration is needed to confirm his conclusions, Chen's research techniques do offer some novel ideas.[25]

There were three historical documents from the Tang Dynasty that directly and explicitly involved Africa:

1. *Jing Xing Ji* by Du Huan
2. *You Yang Za Zu* by Duan Chengshi
3. *Gu Jing Jun Guo Xiang Dao Si Yi Shu* by Jia Dan

Du Huan was the son of the author of *Tong Dian*, Du You. He accompanied the West Conquering Officer, Gao Xiangzhi, on a westward crusade. In 751, during the failed Battle of Dalas River, Du was captured by the Dashi people. More than ten years later, in 762, Du returned home by sea en route to Guangzhou, and published *Jing Xing Ji*. *Jing Xing Ji* has since been lost. However, over 1,500 words of the book were preserved in the Border Defense section of *Tong Dian*.[26] In it, there were descriptions of the Molin Kingdom.

> *We then visited the Molin Kindom. It was to the southwest of the Jiu Sa Luo Kingdom. We crossed a large river, walked two thousand miles and reached the kingdom. People there were black, rude, and uncivilized. There were few grains, no grass or trees. Horses ate dry fish. People ate Niao Mang which is Asian Dates. There were a lot of plagues. The kingdom was on the land route to many other kingdoms. There was one country, governed by several laws: Dashi Law, Daqing Law, and Xunxun Law. Xunxun Law was the harshest law among all foreign laws. Talking was forbidden during meals. Under Dashi Law, people punished their own family and children, even for minor faults. This was so that they themselves would not be blamed for others' crimes. People there did not eat pig, dog, donkey, or horse meat. They did not revere or worship their kings or parents. They believed in deities and ghosts. Its custom was to set aside one holiday for every seven days. On holidays, sales and banking were banned; people drank alcohol and played all day.*

Where is Molin located on a modern map? Historians have various interpretations. With the exception of a few individual scholars who believe it is located in Northwest India, the majority of scholars believe it is located somewhere in Africa:

1. Mauritania or Libya[27]
2. Morocco of North Africa[28]
3. Maghreb of North Africa[29]
4. Egyptian Coast, adjacent to the Red Sea[30]
5. Malindi in East African coast of Kenya[31]
6. Manda of Kenya (nowadays Lamu)[32]
7. Maluakon of Sudan[33]
8. Ancient Ethiopia Kingdom of Aksum[34]

To sum up, there are two points about which we are confident: First, Molin was located in northeast Africa. Second, these documents conveyed that Chinese knew about this place during the early and mid-Tang Period.

You Yang Za Zu Jing Yi by Duan Chengshi (803–863 CE?) also had a paragraph describing someplace in Africa. Duan, well-read and with an exceptional memory, wrote *You Yang Za Zu* in 850–860. In it, he recorded products and customs in the Bobali Kingdom.

> *The Bobali Kingdom was located in the South West Sea. People there did not eat grains. They only ate meat. They often stuck needles into domestic animals to retrieve blood and mix it with milk for drinking. They did not wear any clothes. People covered themselves below the waist with goatskin. Their women were fair and pretty. Men sold women to foreign merchants for high prices. They only produced Ivory and Ahmo [?] Spice. The Persians planned to invade the country and gathered thousands... The country had never been subordinated to any other countries since ancient time. In battles, they used ivory shields, wildebeest horns as protection and weapons. The Dashi [Kingdom], with twenty thousand soldiers, repeatedly attacked it.*

Regarding the location of the Bobali Kingdom, most scholars believe it is the modern-day Berbera, Somalia. Zhang Xingliang thought this view could be confirmed with Bibaluo in *Zhu Fang Zhi* from the Song Dynasty.[35] Only British scholar Freeman-Grenville held a different view. He thought the living habits and clothing of Bobali, as described in *You Yang Za Zu* by Duan Chengshi, are very similar to the Maasai living in modern-day Kenya and Tanzania.

> *The Maasai people live in modern-day Kenyan and Tanzania region... They are nomads and do not farm. In some distant and isolated area, they farm land and raise cattle. Similar to "needling domestic animals," as described in You Yang Za Su, the Maasai use arrows to puncture cattle's blood vessels in the neck, retrieve blood, then mix it with animal milk as a beverage. Cattle skins are not common, mostly used for clothing. In recent times, they are replaced by blankets. Young warriors usually are naked above the waist. Women have elegant manners. The tradition is to have a group of women marry a group of warriors. The Maasai view these traditions as very natural. The most extreme tradition is that the men and heads of the households would generously offer their wives to visiting guests as a friendly gesture. Arrows are still in use as warfare weapons. The arrows we see today have sharp iron heads. Cattle skins are used as shields.*[36]

> *Based on this argument, Freeman-Grenville thought that the Bobali Kingdom was different from Bibaluo. Its people likely are Maasai people living on the East African coast. This view has not taken root on the following grounds. First, from a human race perspective, the Maasai are a typically "black race," not consistent with the description that "women were fair," though "fair" is an ambiguous descriptor. Second, we know little about the history of Maasai migration. We only know that it was not until the sixteenth century when they crossed the equator and entered the northeast region of Tanganyika.*[37]

Tanzania National Museum curator and Tanzania archeology expert Fidelis Masao and Kenyan archeology scholar Mutolo both agree with the view that the Bobali Kingdom described in Duan Chengshi's book is Somalia.[38] In addition, *You Yang Za Zu* also mentioned the Xiaoyi Kingdom, Rengjian Kingdom, Xidang Kingdom, and Wusili Kingdom, etc. According to Zhang Xingliang's research, Xiaoyi is located in modern-day southern Egypt; Rengjian is modern-day Tunisia; Xidan is the modern-day Sudan; and Wusili is modern-day Egypt.[39]

This historical information clarifies two points. First, the Bobali Kingdom is located on the east coast of Africa. Second, Chinese during the Late Tang period had a relatively accurate knowledge of the

African region. Jia Dan (730–805 CE) enjoyed studying geography and although many of his publications were lost, seven of the "major traffic routes" identified by him were preserved in the *Xing Tang Shu Di Li Zhi*. Two of them were sea routes, with one from Dengzhou to Korea and the other from Guangzhou to the Persian Gulf via East Africa.

We traveled two hundred miles through Guangzhou Southeast Sea and arrived at Tun Men Shang. We then sailed westbound... After travelling westwards for a day, we arrived at the Wuci Kingdom where the Folici River of the Dashi Kingdom entered the sea... We arrived at the capitol of the Mao Meng Kingdom, Fuda City. Entering from the south of Brahman, passing through the Meilai Kingdom to reach the Wuci Kingdom, we traveled along the east side of the sea. The area up to the west of the west coast all belonged to the Dashi Kingdom. Its southwest tip was called the Sanlang Kingdom. Traveling northbound from the Sanlang Kingdom for twenty days, passing through over ten small kingdoms, we arrived at the She Kingdom. We then traveled another ten days, passing through six or seven small kingdoms and arrived at the Sayiquheje [Sumalier?] Kingdom, which was on the west side of the sea. Traveling westbound for six or seven more days, passing through six or seven small kingdoms, we arrived at the Meizhuan Kingdom. Traveling northwest for ten days, passing through over ten small kingdoms, we arrived at the Balihemounan [?] Kingdom. Traveling another day, we arrived back at the Wuci Kingdom and met the east coast route from which we originated.

Scholars pretty much agreed on this Guangzhou to Persian Gulf voyage route; however, they held different views on "westbound to 'Sanlang.'" Some thought "Sanlang" was "Ceylon" because of the pronunciation; some thought it was "Aden." Judging from the voyage dates and route distance, Zhang Xingliang thought it could not have been Aden. "Without a doubt, Sanlang Kingdom must be on the Southeast African coast."[40] Others who agreed with the view that Sanlang was located in Africa held the following opinions as to Sanlang's exact location:

1. Port of Dar es Salaam, Tanzania[41]
2. Seila Port, Somalia[42]
3. The African residential area between Tanganyika and Mozambique[43]
4. Zanzibar[44]

5. The modern-day Tanzania coastal region[45]

Judging from the travel itinerary in the above passage, traveling by sea from Fulila River (i.e., the Euphrates River) to the southwest, Sanlang Kingdom would have taken about forty-eight days. Based on this observation, Zhang Xingliang's view was more reliable. Sanlang should be somewhere along the east coast of Africa.

In addition to these three books, several other historical documents studying the Tang Dynasty, such as *Jiu Tang Shu*, *Ce Fu Yuan Gui*, *Tang Hui Yao*, etc., also described enslaved Africans as "curly hair black body" and "entire body pitch black except for red lips and white teeth." Since there had been busy Sino-Arabian trades during the Tang Dynasty, these statements were very convincing. The Arabian slave trade in captive Africans existed prior to the Common Era. When coming in contact with the Chinese, the Arabs brought enslaved Africans to China through three different means. First, Arab merchants used enslaved Africans as trade commodities with the Chinese. Second, Arabs might have given enslaved Africans to Chinese merchants as gifts. Third, these captive individuals might have been presented to the Chinese courts as tributes. A noteworthy point here is that some of the dark-skinned captives referenced in the sources, such as "Kunlun slave," "Sengdi slave," and "Black slave" were likely indigenous peoples from Southeast Asia, though certainly some were Africans as well.[46]

The direct evidence on Sino-African trade during the Tang Dynasty mainly came from the Tang pottery and Tang coins unearthed in Africa and the black people depicted in Tang clay figurines and paintings discovered in China. There were a large number of Chinese ceramics from the Tang Dynasty unearthed in Africa, with the majority of them centering in Fustat of Egypt. Fustat is an archeological site located in the southern suburb of Cairo, Egypt. This city was built in 642 CE by the Arabs when they defeated the Egyptians. In the subsequent five hundred years, Fustat became the Egyptian center of politics, commerce, and pottery. The city was destroyed in 1168 in the Second Crusade.[47] Researchers have been studying the artifacts unearthed in Fustat for over ninety years; over 20,000 Chinese ceramic artifacts have been unearthed. These artifacts now are scattered around the world, with the majority of them kept in Cairo's Museum of Islamic Art, Fustat's Storehouse of Unearthed Artifacts, Sweden's

Far East Museum, Italy's Faenza Ceramic Museum, Japan's Idemitsu Museum of Art, and Waseda University.

According to Chinese scholars, the ancient Chinese porcelains unearthed at Fustat share four characteristics: large quantity, long delay, fine quality, and many layers of kiln-fired glaze.[48] Among the artifacts, there are several porcelain tiles from the Tang Dynasty. For instance, in Cairo's Museum of Islamic Art, there are 42 tiles of Tang porcelain. Of the 303 ceramics artifacts kept in Japan's Idemitsu Museum, 161 are Chinese ceramics, 19 are Tang-related. Additional Tang porcelain tiles were subsequently discovered in the Aizhabu port in northern Sudan, the Manda Island of Kenya, and Comoros Islands. Although the number of artifacts discovered is small, they are nevertheless proof of Sino-African relations. These ancient Tang porcelains discovered in Africa can be sorted into four types: Yue Kiln, Xing Kiln (white porcelain), Changsha Kiln, and Tangsan Cai.[49]

In addition to ancient Chinese porcelains, five pieces of Tang coins have been unearthed in Africa. Based on Freeman-Grenville's sorting, four of the coins, made during the Tang Gao Zong Period (649–683 CE),[50] were unearthed in Kichwele, Zanzibar Island.[51] Another single coin was discovered in Mogadishu, Somalia. However, based on Chen Xingxiong's analysis, the source of this information is unclear, and thus questionable. In addition, there was speculation that Tang coins were discovered in Kilwa and Mafia Island, etc. "But records are incomplete. The information cannot be confirmed."[52]

In 1954, archaeologists unearthed the tomb of a young lady named Pei Shi from the Tang Dynasty. The tomb was located in the southern suburb of Xi An City. In the tomb, there was a 15 cm black pottery figurine, which featured a black body, curly hair, flat face, low nose bridge, wide nose wings, pink lips, white eyes, and relatively thick lips.[53] Based on these characteristics, the figurine was modeled after a typical "black" African. In ancient Chinese paintings, hints of black subjects can be found. For instance, Yan Liban's "Zhi Gong Painting" and Zhou Fanghua's "Man Yi Zhi Gong Painting," both in Taipei's National Palace Museum collection, contain black figures. However, we cannot be certain that these are "blacks" from Africa.[54] We can also see black figures on the Dun Huang Stone Paintings from the Tang Dynasty.

Based on the above historical Tang documents and unearthed artifacts, we can offer the following inferences:

1. During the Tang Dynasty, only a very few individuals under unusual circumstances were able to visit Africa. Otherwise, there would have been other records among the historical documents left behind.
2. Chinese merchant vessels had not yet reached Africa. In reference to the Sanlang Kingdom's itinerary, it appears that the author was recording other people's accounts. Otherwise, he would have described events and sceneries along the way from the Wuci Kingdom to Sanlang, instead of using a flashback writing style to record the trip from Sanlang to the Wuci Kingdom.[55]
3. The ancient Tang porcelains discovered in Africa were likely the product of indirect trade. If they were direct trade products (referred to as "Ya Cang Products" by some books), then there should have been other Chinese products, such as daily use goods, artwork, and durable goods, etc.
4. Egypt appeared to be the first stop in the indirect product trade of ancient Chinese porcelains. All ancient Tang porcelains discovered elsewhere in Africa were transported from Egypt.
5. The intermediaries between China and Africa should be the merchants in the Arabian region. They had long been utilizing the monsoon and Red Sea channel to conduct trade along the coast of East Africa, by land and by sea, in addition to establishing close contacts with the Chinese. They are fully qualified as intermediaries due to their geological location, trade experiences, business reputation, maritime knowledge, and guard against pirates.[56]

Sino-African Relations during the Song-Yuan Period

Starting from the Song Dynasty and continuing until the Yuan Dynasty, contact between China and Africa increased. This was detectable in two ways. First, maritime traffic between China and Africa is certain, demonstrated through books such as *Ling Wai Dai Da* by Zhou Qufei (1178 CE) and *Zhu Fang Zhi* by Zhao Rushi (1225 CE) of the Nan Song Dynasty, and *Dao Yi Zhi Lue* by Wang Dayuan (1349 CE) of the Yuan Dynasty. Second, private and official contact between both sides continued to develop.

Zhou Qufei from Yong Jia became an imperial-designated scholar in 1163 CE and took office in Gui Lin from 1172 to 1178 CE. In his book *Ling Wai Dai Da*, Volume II, *Overseas Countries*, and Volume III, *Overseas Countries Reached by Sea*, he categorized the seas and oceans that he knew about, such as "Jiao Zhi Sea," "South Ocean Sea," "East Ocean Sea," "Ceylon Sea," "East Dashi Sea," and "West Dashi Sea." Among them, the West Dashi Sea was the westernmost. It is the modern-day Mediterranean Sea and included maritime routes connecting to the Mulangpi Kingdom (modern-day northwest Africa and the southern region of Spain).

Names of African locations referenced in *Ling Wai Dai Da* included Wusili (Egypt),[57] Mulangpi, Kunlun Zengji, Mojia (Morocco),[58] and Tuopandi (Damietta Port in Egypt).[59] More detailed descriptions were given in the book on Mulangpi and Kunlun Zengji. The book made several references to Mulangpi: "the many Mulangpi kingdoms, numbered in the thousands." It also included a paragraph on the Mulangpi Kingdom.

Mulangpi Kingdom: There was a huge ocean west of the Dashi Kingdom. West of that sea, there were countless numbers of kingdoms. Dashi's giant ship could reach the Mulangpi Kingdom. Sailing westbound from Dashi, the voyage would take one hundred days. There are ships that can carry several thousand people on board. These ships are as immense as Mulang is on land. That is why nowadays people refer to giant ships as Mulang ships. The Mulang Kingdom has very unusual products. A grain of wheat is two inches long; melons are six feet wide. Grains are stored in underground storage and could last over ten years. It has domesticated sheep that are several feet tall, with large fan-like tails. Every spring, the sheep are cut open in the stomach, for tens of kilograms of fat to be retrieved, and then sewed back. The sheep continue to live afterwards. Without the annual cutting and sewing, those sheep would have died from obesity.

Zhang Xingliang believed "Mulangpi" was the pronunciation of Maghreb.[60] "Mulangpi is the name given to the North Africa region. It includes more than Morocco alone." At times, it also includes Western Europe.[61] Other scholars basically agree with this view. *Ling Wai Dai Da*, Volume 3, discussed the Kunlun Zengji (Cengqi) Kingdom.

The Kunlun Zengji Kingdom is in the Southwest Sea, connecting various Ocean Islands. Its skies are often covered by large birds. There are wild camels, which get swallowed by large birds during the encounter. People would pick up wings of the big birds and cut their tubes to use as water buckets. There are also camel cranes, their bodies six- or seven-feet in length. They have wings and can fly, but not high. They eat a wide range of materials. People feed them burned red hot metals. The kingdom also produces ivories and rhino horns. The island has many barbarians with pitch-black bodies, curly hair. People lure them with food, then capture them in the thousands, and sell them as slaves.

*Regarding the location of the Kunlun Zengji Kingdom, the general consensus is that it is in East Africa. But there are different opinions as to its exact location. Some scholars think it is Zanzibar, but covers a wider area than the modern-day Zanzibar. It is believed that the name was used to refer to the "Ancient East Africa Coast General Area."*⁶² *Some scholars believe it was referring to Madagascar Island and its adjacent East Africa coast.*⁶³

The information related to Africa in the *Ling Wai Dai Da* was later used in *Zhu Fang Zhi* by Zhao Rushi. Zhao Rushi, a descendent of the Song Emperor Tai Zong, held an office in the Fujian Province during the Song Jia Ding Bao Qing Period (1208–1227 CE). He had the opportunity to come into contact with merchants from various countries. While inquiring about customs of various countries, he also reviewed and compared various types of maps and books. He completed this book while in office. In his autobiography, he wrote, "Assigned to this post here recently, I spend all day reading various foreign maps... I listed names of these countries and their customs... I removed hearsays and kept facts. I thus name this book *Zhu Fang Zhi*."⁶⁴ The original book has since been lost. The current version was retrieved and reorganized from Yong Le Da Diang's 4,262 foreign terms.

There were fifty-seven countries and regions listed and described in *Zhu Fang Zhi* (not counting Okinawa). Although some information was reproduced from previous publications, a significant portion of the contents were firsthand data based on the author's interviews. Names of countries and places in Africa include Wusili, Mogalie, Bibaluo, Zhongli, Yegentuo, Zengba, Kunlun Zengji, Mulangpi, Binouye, and Tuopandi. Bibaluo is the Bobali Kingdom in *You Yang Za Su*, today's

Berbera in northeast Africa; Wusili is today's Egypt; Mulangpi was basically reproduced from *Ling Wai Dai Da*; Yegentuo Kingdom is the Alexandrian city; Tuopandi is Egypt's Damietta Port; Binouye is today's Tunisia and Libya's Tripoli region.[65] The most valuable information in *Zhu Fang Zhi* is its information on East Africa. On Zengba Kingdom, we have the following account:

> Zengba Kingdom is located south of Hucala Kingdom, in the midst of the islands, with a large mountain to its west. Its people are Dashi ethnicity and follow Dashi religion, wrapping themselves in green fabrics, wearing red shoes. Their daily diets include rice, noodles, bread, and lamb. The land is mountainous, with forests and woods. It has [a] warm climate and no cold weather. It produces ivories, gold, ambergris, and Yellow Sandalwood. Each year, people from the coast of Hucala and Dashi would send trade ships here by exchanging white fabrics, porcelains, and red copper.

Based on current scholarship, the Zengba Kingdom was the present-day Zanzibar. The "large mountain" was referring to Mount Kilimanjaro.[66] The Hucala Kingdom was Gujarat of India. The porcelains mentioned in the passage were very likely the specialty of China. Both Zhou Qufei's *Ling Wai Dai Da* and Zhao Rushi's *Zhu Fang Zhi* brought up "Kunlun Zengji." "Zeng Ji" sounded like "Zenj" in Persian, meaning "black people." The original name of East African coast was "Zenjibar." "Bar" means "coast" or "land," and thus, Zanjibar means "land of the blacks" or "kingdom of the blacks." The name originally included the entire coastline of East Africa, but today, the name only includes Zanzibar Island, Pemba Island, and several other small islands. Likewise, "Zengba" sounds like "Zenjibar."[67]

Of the Zhongli Kingdom, we have the following account:

> In the Zhongli Kingdom, people go bareheaded and barefooted. They wrap their bodies in fabrics and do not wear clothes. Only the king and high court officials wear clothes and wrap their heads to be distinguished from the commoners. The king's residences are built with bricks while commoners' houses are covered with straw. Their daily diets include bread, goat's milk, and camel's milk. There are lots of cattle, goats, and camels. This is the only kingdom in Dashi that produces mastic.

Many people here know witchcraft; they can turn human into birds, beasts, or fish. The locals are erratic, dizzy-headed, dumb, and vulgar. At the port where foreign trade ships dock, if disputes occur between the foreigners and the locals, the locals cast spells on the foreign ship to strand it. Only after mediation and conciliation, the spell and thus the ship could be released.

The restricted areas in the kingdom are very strictly guarded. Every night, countless birds land in the city suburbs and leave by daylight. People in the kingdom catch these tasty birds for food. These birds are only around in late spring and disappear by summer. This cycle is repeated year after year.

When people die, they are placed in coffins. All the friends and family come by to pay respects, each bringing a sword. The guests ask the family of the deceased: "Did someone murder him? If so, we will avenge him and kill his killer." The family then replies, "He was not murdered by others. He died of natural causes." The guests then drop their swords and cry.

Every year, large dead fish frequently wash ashore. The fish measure over one hundred feet long and over twenty feet wide. People in the kingdom do not eat the flesh of the fish; they only retrieve the fish brain and eyes for oil. The oil is then mixed with ashes to repair boats or for lighting. The poor retrieve the fishes' ribs for building homes, the backbones for doors, and the joints for mortar. The kingdom has mountains and neighbors with the Bibaluo Kingdom. The kingdom is encompassed by four thousand miles' distance, with the majority of its surrounding areas deserted. Its water produces ambergris. People do not know where the ambergris comes from. It comes in blocks and out of nowhere. Sometimes it weighs three to five kilograms; other times it weighs ten kilograms, all washed ashore. Locals then divide it up. Sometimes you can unexpectedly spot it from a boat in the ocean, too.

The word "Zhong" in "Zhongli Guo" is likely to be an error and should have been "Sheng." "Sheng Li" sounds like "Somali." Scholars in general believe that the Zhongli Kingdom is today's Somali coast, including Socotra Island.[68] The author's depiction of the Zhongli Kingdom was very detailed, including housing, buildings, products, customs, clothing, social classes, etc. This can explain three points. First, many local merchants and visiting merchants traveled to China. Second, the Zhongli Kingdom had an influential status in the East African region. Third, the Chinese were relatively familiar with this area.

Also included in *Zhu Fang Zhi* was a list of forty-seven foreign products. Among them, twenty-two were products of Central Asia and Africa. Some of the products were the specialties of the latter region. In addition, *Zhu Fang Zhi* also included descriptions of various animals unique to Africa. Other than the familiar elephants and rhinos, there were descriptions of the camel crane (i.e., the ostrich) as "six, seven foot long, have wings, can fly, but not very high," the description of the Cula (i.e., giraffe, sounding like Zarafah in Arabic) as "shaped like a camel, as big as a cattle, yellow color, front feet five feet high, rear feet three feet lower, head high up, skin one foot thick," and the description of Louzi (i.e., the zebra) as "red, white, black alternating three colors, belt-like stripes." Information in both Zhou Qufei and Zhao Rushi's books came from hearsay, or were based on indirect investigations. This is different in Wang Dayuan's book from the Yuan Dynasty. Wang went on oceanic voyages twice, first from 1330 to 1334 CE, the second from 1337 to 1339 CE. He wrote *Dao Yi Zhi Lue* in 1349, describing what he saw and heard.[69] Wang's book followed *Ling Wai Dai Da* and *Zhu Fang Zhi*, and was later followed by books from the Ming Dynasty, such as *Ying Yai Sheng Lan* and *Xing Cha Sheng Lang*. Wang's book is truly an important source of information on China's foreign traffic history. Feng Chengjun once described this book as containing "many errors and [being] difficult to follow." Bo Xihe advised others not to quote it. Su Jiqing, however, viewed these opinions as "shallow views" or "seemingly ignorant."[70]

Dao Yi Zhi Lue recorded a few country names located in North Africa and East Africa: Asili, Manali, Ceng Yaoluo, and Jia Jiang Menli. Asili is Quseir of Egypt, located on the west coast of the Red Sea;[71] the rest are Malindi of Kenya, Kilwa Kisiwani of Tanzania, and Quelimane of Mozambique.

> *Asili, located in the far southwest corner of Daguoli. It has no mountains or forests. When wind blows, sands would fly towards one's face and keep people away. Residents build bamboo shelters to protect from the wind. It has a hot climate. There is no precipitation over half of the year. People dig wells as deep as 2,000–3,000 feet for sweet tasting*

water. Locals plant wheat which prospers on underground water. An unusual custom here is that men and women braid their hair and weave cattle hair into ropes, and then connect the ropes to the end of their hair so that the hair would extend to knee length. Locals make bird feathers into clothes, make bread from wheat. People here do not know how to boil sea water to make salt. Local products include wool fabrics, which are used for trades. Locals like to use silver and iron products, and glass beads.

The above description, although not long, gives a complete picture of its location, land, products, customs, clothing, food, and trade products.

Manali, situated in the southeast of Mili, is an isolated island in (Ju) Huan Jiao. It has tens of thousands of Phoebe trees and is surrounded by waters. There are giant oysters, often ignored by the locals. Its land and mountains are barren. Its climate is volatile. Its customs change. Men and women braid their hair and wear jewelry on the arms. People wear multi-color, short shirts... Camel is a local product, nine feet tall, used by locals to carry loads. There are six-foot-high cranes, eating pebbles as meals. Upon hearing people clap, the cranes would open their wings and dance. It is quite a scene to see. What an amazing animal!

Three places were mentioned: Manali, Mili, and (Ju) Huan Jiao. Su Jiqing thought, respectively, they were Malindi, Malan (northwest of the Sabac River in East Africa), and Ungama (the Portuguese called it "Beautiful Bay"). In the passage, camels and African ostriches were also mentioned.

In describing Ceng Yaoluo, the author labeled its location as "in the southwest of Dashi" and gave a description of its unique landscape: "Its canyons have no trees. Land is pure and simple." Of its crops and products, the author writes, "The land is barren, not fit for growing grains. Therefore, potatoes are grown as the staple food. Whenever visiting trade merchants carry grains, locals would trade; but the trade profit margin is thin." The author described its people as "blunt"; of its style, "men and women with hair rolled up, wearing seamless short skirts"; of its social system as "having chiefs." Its local specialties include "ivory, ambergris, gold..." Its local products include "gear boxes, silver, five-color fabrics, etc." Scholars agree that Ceng Yaoluo is the same as Zengba and Zengbaluo. They are different translated names for Zanzibar. Its exact location is in the nowadays Kilwa Kisiwani of Kenya.[72]

In his description of Jia Jiang Menli, the author was quite impressed with the superior geographic characteristics of the place. "Traveling through the two thousand miles of Jia Li, I saw dense forests of trees and bamboos. The land is rich, with three harvests of crops every year." The author also described its local customs: "Men and women roll their hair up and dress in long shirts. Various Muslims live here." Regarding the term "various Muslims," this is Su Jiqing's explanation: "Arabian, Persian, Somali, and Indian Muslims, although sharing the same religion, hold different trades in the society, such as missionaries, merchants, explorers, etc." The author also provides us with an important piece of information: "Its local merchants frequented Peng Jia La carrying Hei Nan. Based on their sizes and heights, different amounts of money are exchanged." Hei Nan means "young black children." This is an indication that there already existed an active slave trade in the region at the time.[73] It is the first reference of Jia Jiang Menli among ancient Chinese books. Wang Dayuan was likely the first Chinese arriving at Mozambique.

In Africa, more ancient porcelains were discovered from the Song and Yuan Dynasties than from the Tang Dynasty. According to the research of Ma Wenkuan and Meng Fan, ancient Song Yuan porcelains were discovered in Egypt, Sudan, Morocco, Ethiopia, Somalia, Kenya, Tanzania, Zimbabwe, and Madagascar. There were also ancient porcelains of different time periods discovered at the same site. For example, adjacent to the famous oval-shaped archeological site of Great Zimbabwe is another archeological site whose cave revealed artifacts that included forty-three pieces of porcelain tiles from thirteen objects made in the Song Yuan Period.[74] The famous traveler Ibn Battuta wrote, "The price of porcelains in China is like the price of pottery in my country or perhaps even cheaper. This type of porcelain was transported to and sold at various Indian locations before eventually reaching the Maghreb. They are of the finest quality among all porcelains."[75]

Also, a German scholar wrote two academic essays, one published in *Tong Bao* in 1894 and another published in the American *Dong Fang Xue Hui Magazine* in 1909. In them, the author mentioned that the British unearthed coins from the Song Dynasty on Zanzibar Island in 1888 and the Germans unearthed copper coins from the Song Dynasty in Somalia in 1898.⁷⁶ The most significant revelation was that among the 176 pieces of Chinese coins unearthed in Kiwengwa, Zanzibar in 1945, four were from the Tang Dynasty, 108 were from the Bei Song Period, 56 were from the Nan Song Period, and eight were unidentified.⁷⁷ These archeological findings proved that North African merchants had traded in China's Quangzhou during the Song Period. In Tanzania's Kilwa archeological site, items unearthed there included about twenty copper coins from the Bei Song to Early Ming Period.⁷⁸

During the Song Yuan Period, contacts of both private and official nature between China and Africa became more frequent. This had much to do with the emphasis on foreign trade during the Zhao Song Period, and also the Yuan rulers' public policy to advance foreign trade. By the Yuan Dynasty, there had been three maritime routes between China and Africa:⁷⁹

1. China to North Africa: China—India—Aden—Egypt
2. China to East Africa: China—Maldives—East Africa
3. China to Madagascar, which included two different routes:
   a. China—Socotra Island—Madagascar
   b. China—Malaba Coast—Madagascar

In 1346, the famed Ibn Battuta came to China. In addition to staying in Beijing, he also visited several southern cities, such as Quangzhou and Guangzhou. He stayed in China for over a year, and was very impressed with the prosperity there. After returning home, he dictated an account of what he experienced and witnessed in China and let others organize the materials, and then published *The Journey* (from the original name, *A Gift to Those Who Contemplate the Wonders of Cities and the Marvels of Traveling*). In the book, he covered China's political system, judicial system, customs, architecture, local products, transportation, economics, and monetary system. He also gave a particularly detailed account of Beijing city's design pattern and royal infightings.⁸⁰ Bringing direct knowledge of China to North Africa, the book would have surely made a significant impact.

Meanwhile, China's understanding about Africa also deepened. Zhu Siben of the Yuan Dynasty (1273–1333 CE) made a most accurate African map at the time. In the map, southern Africa was already included, with its end pointing towards the south. Unfortunately, this map by Zhu Siben had been lost. One can only get a glimpse of it in

Guang Yu Tu, added by Luo Hongxiang of the Ming Dynasty. Another contemporary of Zhu Siben was geologist Li Zeming who drew *Sheng Jiao Guang Bei Tu*, which also included maps of Africa and Europe.[81] In the maps drawn by the Arabic and European contemporaries, the southern part of the Africa all extended towards the east. This situation continued until the mid-fifteenth century.[82]

During the Song Yuan Period, the bilateral official contacts also increased. The following is a chronology of the two parties dispatching envoys to each other:

1. Song Dynasty (1008)—China established diplomatic ties with the Fatimid Dynasty. Since then, both sides dispatched envoys to each other multiple times.[83]
2. Song Dynasty (1073)—East Africa's Yuluhedi Kingdom (i.e., Kenya's Gede, a thirteenth-century Swahili port town) dispatched an envoy to China.[84]
3. Yuan Dynasty (1282)—China dispatched an envoy A Dan to the Aluquianbo (?) Kingdom and established diplomatic ties with the Egyptian Mamluk Dynasty.
4. Yuan Dynasty (1283)—Gudanu Kingdom (i.e., Gondar of Ethiopia). "Due to merchant A. Wei et al. came to pledge allegiance on behalf of his country."
5. Yuan Dynasty (1291)—China dispatched an envoy to Madu (i.e., Ethiopia).
6. Yuan Dynasty (1328)—Yaji Kingdom (i.e., Ethiopia) dispatched an envoy to China.[85] Moreover, according to Marco Polo's account, Kublai Khan of the Yuan Dynasty had also dispatched envoy to Madagascar.[86]

In summary, we can draw the following conclusions: During the Song Yuan Period, China's understanding of Africa was enhanced. Exchanges between the two increased. The evidence is as follows:

1. More historical documents mentioned places in Africa, with more detailed and concrete descriptions of some African countries and regions.
2. Chinese scholars had a more in-depth understanding of African countries and shifted from knowing simple geographical locations

and local specialties to understanding local customs, production methods, and social systems.
3. Sino-African maritime traffic became a fact. Various trades took place with increased frequency. New maritime trade routes leading to the East African coast were established.
4. Direct, private Sino-African contacts were also realized. Wang Dayuan's visit to East Africa and Ibn Battuta's visit to China both strengthened their understanding of each other.
5. Sino-African official contact increased. Mutual, peaceful, diplomatic relations were advanced. There were historical records documenting both sides dispatching diplomats, either envoys or merchants, to the other.

Sino-African Relations during the Ming Dynasty

By the early Ming Dynasty, Sino-African relations advanced further. This is demonstrated in two ways. First is San Bao Eunuch Zheng He's visit to the "West Ocean," passing through the Indian Ocean and arriving on the eastern coast of Africa. Second, there were several significant publications on overseas traffic, including *Xing Cha Sheng Lan* by Fei Xing, *Ying Yai Sheng Lan* by Ma Huan, and *Xi Yang Fang Guo Zhi* by Fang Zhen. Because these three all accompanied Zheng He on his envoy mission trips to Africa, their books included detailed descriptions of various African countries and regions, and hold significant historical value.

Emperor Ming Tai Zu placed a strong emphasis on overseas relations. This was evident even before he founded the dynasty. In Yuan Shun Di Zhi Zheng 27 (1367 CE), when Zhu Yuan Zhang first established his base in Hangzhou and reset its political calendar, he also set up the office of Shibo Tiju Si (Maritime Trade Office). According to *Ming Shi Zhi Guan Zhi*, the responsibility of that office was to "manage foreign tributes and trade." During the Hong Wu Period, Emperor Ming Tai Zu dispatched a large number of envoys by land and sea to strengthen diplomatic ties and develop trade. Later on, due to rampant pirate activities, to curb those "criminal-minded civilians" living on the coast from conspiring with sea pirates, he ordered a ban on oceanic commerce.

After Emperor Ming Cheng Zu Zhu Li took office, sea commerce was permitted again. Overseas relations became a priority. Various favorable policies were put in place to encourage foreign merchants engaging in trade activities. As a result, more and more envoys and merchants came to China. In Yong Le 3 (1405 CE), three coastal cities—Lai Yuan Yi (Fujian Hostel), An Yuan Yi (Zhe Jiang Hostel), Huai Yuan Yi (Guang Dong Hostel)—established hostels to receive foreigners visiting China, via the office of City Boat Bureau. Meanwhile, Emperor Ming Cheng Zu also dispatched a large number of envoys to strengthen diplomatic ties with neighboring countries. From Yong Le 1 (1403 CE) to Yong Le 18 (1420 CE), there were twenty-nine such efforts via the sea routes. In addition to Yong Le 4 (1406 CE), Yong Le 8 (1410 CE), and Yong Le 17 (1419 CE), there were envoys dispatched to South Asia every year, sometimes as many as seven occurrences in one year.[87] It was no accident that six of Zheng He's seven visits to the "West Ocean" (1405–1433 CE) all took place during the Yong Le Period.

The exact times of the seven occurrences of Zheng He's oceanic voyages are listed below:

Occurrence	Chinese Calendar Year	Dates
1	Yong Le 3–5	1405–1407
2	Yong Le 5–7	1407–1409
3	Yong Le 7–9	1409–1411
4	Yong Le 11–13	1413–1415
5	Yong Le 15–17	1417–1410
6	Yong Le 19–20	1421–1422
7	Xuan De 6–8	1431–1433

Zheng He's last name at birth was Ma, and he was born in 1371 in Yun Nan Kun Yang Zhou (now part of Jing Ning county), in Bao Shang Xian He Dai village. He was kidnapped in his youth, castrated, and sent to work as an inner court servant in a royal palace. Initially, he served Yang Wang in his palace. After assisting Yang Wang in rising up to become the new emperor through a rebellion, he was given promotions. "Zheng" was the imperial last name given by Emperor

Ming Cheng Zu on New Year's Day, Yong Le 2 (1404 CE). Being tall and handsome, Zheng was chosen by Emperor Ming Cheng Zu as his envoy for the many "West Ocean" voyages. From Yong Le 3 (1405 CE) to Xuan De 8 (1433 CE), Zheng He was dispatched on seven overseas envoy missions, traveling through Southeast Asia, the South Asia peninsula, crossing the Indian Ocean to reach the Persian Gulf and Arabian Peninsula, and eventually landing on the East African coast.

The common belief is that Zheng He's fleet reached Africa on its fourth voyage. Sheng Fuwei believed that during his third trip, Zheng He dispatched a small exploration fleet to Mogadishu; thus it was during his third trip in Yong Le 7–9 (1409–1411 CE) when Zheng's fleet reached Africa. The basis for this theory is the maritime route depicted in Lu Rong's *Shu Yuan Za Ji*, Volume 3.

> *In Yong Le 7, Eunuch Zheng He, Wang Jing Hong, Hou Xian et al., commanding a fleet of 27,000 soldiers and officers and forty-seven ships, carried expensive gifts bestowed by the Imperial Court and traveled through various foreign countries in the South East and the West Oceans. In September of that year, the fleet departed from Tai Cang Liu Jia Port. It visited the Zhang Cheng Kingdom, Lin Shang, Kun Lun Shang, the Bing Tong Long Kingdom, the Zheng Da Kingdom, the Xian Lou Kingdom, Jia Ma Li Ding, Jiao Lang Shang, Zhao Wa Kingdom, Jiu Gang, Chong Jia Luo, Ji Li Di Meng, the Man Ci Jia Kingdom, Ma Yin Dong, Peng Keng, Dong Xi Zhu, Long Yua Jia Miao, Jiu Zhou Shang, A Lu, DangYang, Su Men Da La, Hua Miang Wang, Long Yu, Cui Feng Yu, Xi Lang Shang, Liu Shang Yang, Da Ge Lang, A Zhi Guo, Bang Ke Ci, Pu La Wa, Zhubu, Mu Gu Du Dong, Ci Sa, the Zuo Fa Er Kingdom, Hu Lu Mo Si, Tian Fang, Okinawa, the San Dou Kingdom, the Ni Kingdom, and the Su Lu Kingdom. The trip ended upon the emperor's order on August 15, Yong Le 22. (See Xing Cha Sheng Lan, by Fe Xing of Tai Cang, for detailed descriptions of various countries' local customs and products.)*

Lu Rong for generations lived in Tai Cang where Zheng He's fleet was stationed. Lu had served in high official positions in Nanjing and later in Beijing. The author of *Xing Cha Sheng Lan*, Fei Xing, accompanied Zheng He on this envoy trip. It is entirely possible that Lu Rong received a copy of the first edition of *Xing Cha Sheng Lan*. Thus, Lu's claim here does have a basis. Also, the above passage included the reference of "Shu Bu" (mouth of the Jubba River in present-day Somalia). According to *Ming Shi Zhubu Zhuan*, "Zhubu, adjacent to Mogadishu, during Yong Le, had sent tribute to the Imperial Court. The country has a small population and relatively honest customs. Zheng He had visited it." In the chronicles of Zheng He's subsequent four oceanic voyages, there was no mention of Zhubu. Therefore, it is likely that Zheng He's fleet already reached Somalia during his third oceanic voyage. The reference to "Pu La Wa" in the passage is present-day Barawa of Somalia. "Mu Gu Du Dong" is likely a misspelling of "Mu Gu Du Su," which is the present-day Mogadishu of Somalia.

In Yong Le 10 (1412 CE), Emperor Ming Cheng Zu ordered Zheng He to make his fourth envoy journey. After one full year of preparation, Zheng He selected a group of talented men, including the author of *Jing Yia Sheng Lan*, Ma Huan. Regarding the route of the fourth oceanic voyage, *Ming Shi Lu* had two references in Volume 1, Parts 3 and 4.

In November, Yong Le 10, Eunuch Zheng He was dispatched to offer gifts such as leno and colored silk fabrics to countries such as Man La Jia, Java, Zhang Cheng, Sumatra, A Lu, Ke Zhi, Lu Li, Nan Bo Li, Peng Heng, Ji Lang Dan, Jia Yi Le, Ji Lu Mou Si, Bi La, Liu Shang, and Sun Ta.

Based on this account, Zheng He only reached one African country, Da Bi La (i.e., Barawa) in this oceanic voyage. However, there was a different account in Ming Shi Lu, Volume 182, on visiting envoys from African countries. These envoys' visits likely followed Zheng He's return from his fourth oceanic voyage.

In November, Yong Le 14, countries Gu Li, Java, Mang La Jia, Zhang Cheng, Sumatra, Nan Wu Li, Sha Li Wan Ni, Peng Heng, Xi Lang Shang, Mu Ku Du Su, Liu Shang, Nan Bo Li, By La Wa, A Dan, Ma Lin, La Sa, Hu Lu Mo Si, and Ke Zh [?] dispatched envoys and sent local specialties such as horses, rhinos, elephants, etc., as tributes.[88]

To sum up, Zheng He in his fourth oceanic voyage visited Mogadishu, Somalia, Malindi, and Barawa. During his fifth oceanic voyage in Yong Le 15 (1417 CE), Zheng He was ordered by the emperor to escort envoys from various countries such as Mogadishu home while paying return visits to these countries and offering tributes.

According to records on a Nan Shang temple monument, "Yong Le 15, he led the fleet to the Western Zone. As tributes to the Imperial Court, the Qi Hu Lu Mo Si Kingdom gifted lions, leopards, and Da Xi horses; A Dan gifted Qi Ling [giraffes] and a long-horned Ma Ha Beast. Mogadishu gifted Hua Fu Lu [zebras] and lions. The Bu La Wa Kingdom gifted a thousand-mile camel and a Tuo Ji [ostrich]…"

The main purposes of Zheng He's sixth oceanic voyage were to escort the various countries' envoys home and to pay visits in return. After escorting the envoys of Mogadishu and Barawa home, he paid each of these two countries another friendship visit. After the death of Emperor Ming Cheng Zu in July, Yong Le 212 (1424 CE), Emperor Ren Zong Zhu Gao Ji took throne in August of the same year. The new emperor agreed with his official Xia Yuanji's view that the oceanic voyages were too costly for the country and ordered "all work related to the Western Ocean envoy mission come to a stop." Emperor Ren Zong reigned for only one year before his death. Emperor Xuan Zong Zhu Zhan Ji took the throne. Xuan De 5 (1430 CE), he ordered Zheng He to make his seventh oceanic voyage. Fei Xing, Ma Huan, and Gong Zhen accompanied Zheng on this envoy mission.

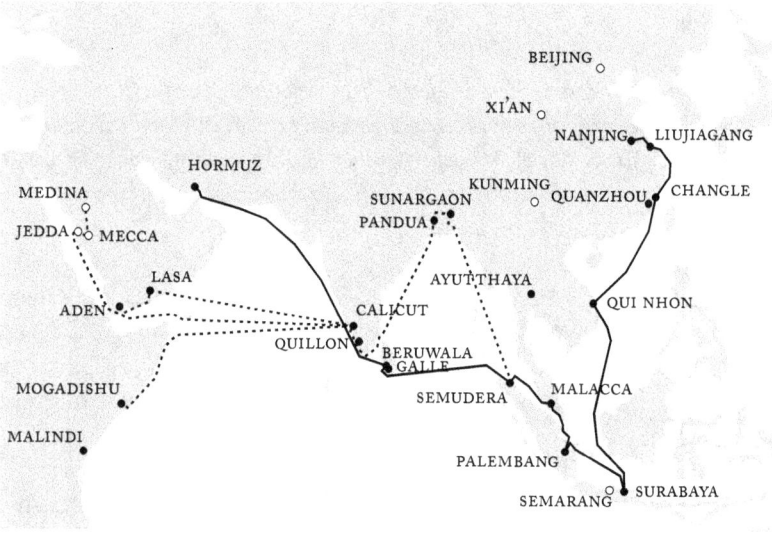

The route of Zheng He's seventh expedition, ca. 1431–1433

This time, Zheng He's fleet visited about twenty countries, including Mogadishu and Barawa. Judging from the maritime routes that Zheng He took, there were many from China to Africa via ports in the Indian Ocean. Zhang Tiesheng believed that during the Ming Dynasty, there were two maritime routes connecting China and East Africa:

1. Along South Arabian Sea coast—North coast of Somalia—Socotra Island—East African coast.
2. Across Indian Ocean—Maldive's capitol island (Male Island), or India's Xiao Ge Lang (Kuilong or locale in Sri Lanka).[89]

Some scholars believe that there were three routes:

1. Maldive—Aden Bay—Egypt.
2. Xiao Ge Lang—Mogadishu.
3. India—Hormuz—Aden—Guada Fuyijiao (?)—East Africa.[90]

Other scholars think there were five routes:

1. Sumatra –Maldives—Egypt.
2. Sumatra—Maldives—Mogadishu.
3. Xiao Ge Lang—Maldives—Mogadishu.
4. Bie Luo Li (?)—Maldives—Mogadishu.
5. Bie Luo Li—Barawa.[91]

Actually, the basic routes were the same among the various classifications. There were at least three available maritime routes from China to the East African coast:

1. China—India's Kuilong—Mogadishu.[92]
2. China—Ceylon's Bielouli (or Maldives's Male).[93]
3. China—Maldives's Male—Mogadishu.[94]

Zheng He's oceanic fleet could also have gone through Aden (or an Egyptian port) and then Guada Fuyijiao, and then sailed towards the East African coast.

The Ming Dynasty's ocean navigation publications also provided us with relatively accurate knowledge about Africa. Fei Xing, Ma Huan, and Gong Zheng all participated in Zheng He's oceanic voyages. Their publications naturally were much more detailed than their predecessors. In Fei Xing's *Xing Cha Sheng Lan*, he mentioned the Zhubu Kingdom, the Mu Gu Du Su Kingdom, and the Bu La Wa Kingdom. What is worthy of quoting is the writing regarding the Zhubu Kingdom.

> *The Zhubu Kingdom, connected to the Mogadishu's mountains, has very few villages. Towns are built with rocks. Houses are built with rocks. Local customs are honest. Men and women have curly hair. Men wrap fabrics around themselves. Women wrap their heads with fabrics, hiding body and face. Mountains are yellow and red. It may not rain for years. Grass and trees do not grow. Locals dig deep wells and fish for a living. Local specialties include lions, leopards, six- or seven-foot-tall ostriches with camel-like feet, ambergris, mastic, and amber. The locals trade for Tuzhu, silk fabric, gold, silver, porcelain, peppers, grains, etc. Its chief was moved by the gifts given by the Imperial Court, thus offered tributes in return.*"[95]

The passage included descriptions of the Zhubu Kingdom's location, residents, climate, produce, customs, and products. In the end, it also mentioned that because of the Imperial Court's gifts brought by Zheng He's fleet, the local chief was deeply moved and thus offered tributes in return, as a friendly gesture. In Volume 1 of Ma Huan's *Ying Yia Sheng Lan*, "Journey Poem" included a reference to "Da Wan Mi Xi Passage Merchant." "Mi Xi" is Egypt.[96] Gong Zheng's *Xi Yang Fang Guo Zi* mainly described the various countries in the Southeast Asia.

1.1 Cross References of Place Names Associated with Zheng He's West Ocean Voyages and Historical Documents from the Song Yuan Period[97]

Ling Wai Dai Da	Zhu Fang Zhi	Yi Dao Zhi Lue	Zheng He's West Ocean Voyage Name	Approximate location today
			Geerdefeng	Guadafuyi Horn (?)
			Sugudala (also Xuduodayu)	Socotra Island
	Bibaluo Kingdom			In the vicinity of Berbera in Northern Somali
	Zhongli Kingdom			Somali coastal region, including Socotra Island
			Mugudusu (also Mugudu)	Region around Mogadishu of Somalia
			Bulawa (also Bia)	Region around Barawa, of Mogadishu
			Mangbasa	Mombasa
			Sunla	Likely in East Africa
			Zhubu	mouth of the Jubba River, Somalia
	Zengba Kingdom	Zengbaluo		South of Somalia
		Manali	Malin (also Malindi)	Region around Malindi of Kenya (also Kilwa)

		Jia Jiang	Region around mouth of Zambezi River, Mozambique
		Menli	
Kunlun Zengji Kingdom	Kunlun Zengji Kingdom		Region around Madagascar and its adjacent African coast
Wusili Kingdom	Wusili Kingdom		Egypt
	Egentuo Kingdom		Alexandria of Egypt
Tuopandi Kingdom	Pandi		Damietta of Egypt
Moga Kingdom	Moga Kingdom		Morocco
Mulangpi Kingdom	Mulangpi Kingdom		Region around northwest Africa and south Spain
Pinuoye			Region around Tunisia and Tripoli of Libya
		Heer	Ancient town of Eyl in Somalia
		Muerlihabier	Huoerdiau (?)
		Mulywang	Mercado (?)
		Menfeichi	Mombasa
		Moerqianti	Meileika (?)
		Lasinaa	Las-Anod
		Hapuni (also Hapuer)	Hafengjiao
		Lahazila	Jialehajiaer (?)

Due to the establishment of East Africa maritime routes, Chinese porcelains were shipped to Africa in large quantities in the Ming Dynasty. The blue and white porcelain from Jing De Zheng was in the porcelain production mainstream at the time. The technology used for producing the blue and white porcelain had significantly advanced during the Yong Le Xuan De Period, regardless of glaze, color, style, or decoration. Therefore, the majority of the Ming porcelain exported to Africa was blue and white. According to Japanese scholar Koyama Fujio's calculation in 1965, among the Ming porcelain tiles discovered at the Fustat archeological site, there were 1,656 pieces of blue and white porcelain while there were very few pieces of Long Quan blue porcelain and only seven pieces of colored porcelain.[98] There were also discoveries of Ming porcelain in other regions of North Africa, East Africa, and South and Central Africa.[99]

Sino-African trades made significant progress during the Ming Dynasty. Zheng He's West Ocean voyage also undoubtedly advanced bilateral trade. According to Fei Xing's *Xing Cha Sheng Lan*, many oceanic fleets used various Chinese specialties to engage in local trade. In the Zhubu Kingdom, "locals trade for Tu Zhu, silk fabric, gold, silver, porcelain, peppers and grains." In Mogadishu, "locals trade for gold, silver, silk fabrics, rice, beans, porcelain."[100] Imports from Africa included various African local specialties, such as ivory, rhino horn, mastic, rose sandalwood, purple cane, ambergris, gold, *ischaemum vitriol*, and myrrh, in addition to African animals such as the giraffe, ostrich, and zebra.

Had Zheng He been to regions south of Kenya and Tanzania? Based on results of the current research, there had not been any direct evidence of Zheng He having been to the southern region of East Africa or South Africa. However, some western historical documents seem to offer other historical inferences. Based on records available, when Portuguese explorer Vasco da Gama crossed the Cape of Good Hope and arrived in Mozambique's coast in 1498, he had his crew offer gifts of clothes and food to the locals. They were puzzled by the locals' lack of interest in their gifts, and by accounts that at the place where the sun rose, there had been whites[101] who arrived by sailing the same type of ships.[102] In addition, anthropologists conducting research in Pate Island on the northern coast of Kenya were told by the locals that their ancestors came from Shanghai, which was also the origin of the term "Shanga."[103] Some geographic books written by missionaries who visited China during this period also mentioned Africa, certainly spreading awareness of its existence.[104]

In summary, we can make the following conclusion regarding Sino-African relations during the Ming Dynasty:

1. Relations between China, North Africa, and several East African countries became relatively close. Both sides dispatched envoys frequently and exchanged gifts.
2. Judging from their official relations, China was in a dominant and leading position, at least in its own view. The fact that some African countries taking the initiative to send envoys and gifts to China's Imperial Court seems to confirm this point.
3. Zheng He's oceanic voyage indeed carried worldly significance. Not only did it reflect China's national influence and its maritime and navigational ability, but it also elevated the occasional Sino-African private commerce relations into regular official relations.
4. Zheng He's West Ocean voyage vastly improved the Chinese's understanding of Africa. Among the historical documents that recorded the routes of Zheng He's fleet, the number of African countries and regions mentioned reached as many as sixteen.
5. Propelled by Zheng He's oceanic voyage, Sino-African trade relations were further enhanced. This is evident from the artifact unearthed in Africa and Chinese import list.

Regrettably, this type of friendly diplomatic exchange between independent countries was not able to last. After Emperor Min Ren Zong, conservative officials' attacks led China to close its door to foreigners. This then resulted in the obstruction of both diplomatic relations and overseas trade during the Late Ming Period. Thus, Sino-African relations were also affected.

What's worth mentioning here is that although there had been references of "Kun Lun Nv" (enslaved Africans) in ancient Chinese books, large numbers of enslaved African did not show up in China until Western colonialists invaded Africa and also encroached upon China. At the time, Portuguese colonialists brought many enslaved Africans to the Chinese coastal region. According to documents, in 1635 there were 7,000 residents in Macau, of which 5,100 were slaves, mostly enslaved Africans. Among Zheng Zhilong's army, there were black soldiers. In 1661, to protect the Chinese territory of Taiwan,

Zheng Chenggong led an intense battle against the Dutch colonialists. In the battle, black soldiers fought bravely, and successfully helped Zheng Chenggong defend the territory.[105]

Sino-African Relations during the Qing Dynasty

In the early Qing Period, there were some lingering Sino-African contacts. Official relations were replaced by private contact; direct commerce was replaced by indirect trade. One special characteristic of this period was that due to China's open door to the world and the introduction of missionaries, many Chinese with a strong sense of time, after witnessing the fate of other weak nations, became convinced of the need to translate and compile foreign history books. During this period, several books that introduced foreign history surfaced, including books on Africa. A noteworthy event was the invasion of Egypt, an ancient civilization, by the European powers starting from the end of eighteenth century. Chinese intellectuals were alarmed by Egypt's fate. In *Cui Xing Bao*, Issue 2, published in September 11, 1902, an article stated, "I read Egyptian history and grieved for the Pyramids. I turned around and looked at my motherland, then asked, 'When will it be her turn?'"

Furthermore, many eighteenth-century publications mentioned African place names such as the Cape of Good Hope, Mauritius, and Cape Town. Those publications include Fan Shouyi's *Shen Jian Lu*, Chen Lunjiong's *Hai Guo Wen Jian Lu*, Xie Qinggao's *Hai Lu*, and Wang Da Hai's *Hai Dao Yi Zhi*. At a later time, in *Xi Xue Dong Jian Ji*, Rong Hong mentioned his experience of seeing Chinese in Saint Helena Island. Zhang Deyi in *Hai Hang Shu Qi* described Egyptian customs. Ding Lian in *San Zhou You Ji*, the only recent Chinese book on a journey to Africa's inland, gave a detailed account of inland lives and customs.[106] Below is a summary introduction of books by Fan Shouyi, Xie Qinggao, Ding Lian, and more.

1.2 Major Books and Translated Works Published in the Qing Dynasty Regarding Africa

Author	Book	Description
Fan Shouyi	*Shen Jian Lu*	The book references South Africa.

Chen Lunjiong	*Hai Guo Wen Jian Lu*	The book references certain African regions.
Xie Qinggao	*Hai Lu*	Yang Bingnan wrote the book based on Xie Qinggao's dictated account. The book references certain African regions and islands.
Lin Zexu	*Si Zhou Zhi*	This is mainly a translated work. During a trip, the author turned over the work to Wei Yuan and asked him to continue studying foreign situations. The book references the African continent.
Wei Yuan	*Hai Guo Tu Zhi*	The book was published three times, increasing from fifty to one hundred volumes. It references the African continent.
Ma Dexing	*Chao Jin Tu Ji*	This book references Egypt.
Guo Liancheng	*Xi You Bi Lue*	This book references North Africa.
Zhang Deyi	*Heng Hai Shu Qi*	This book references Egypt.
Wang Tao	*Man You Sui Lu*	This book references Egypt.
Ding Kang	*San Zhou You Ji*	This book references the East African inland. It is the only recent Chinese book on a journey to Africa's inland.
Zou Daijun	*Xi Zheng Ji Cheng*	This book references East Africa and North Africa.
Translated by Mai Dinghua	*Recent History of Egypt*	The original author was the Japanese scholar Chai Shiro. The book was translated into several languages.
Translated by Zhao Bizheng	*Egyptian History*	The original author was the Japanese scholar Saburo Kitamura.
Unknown	*The Horrors of Egypt*	The book was published by Wen Ming Press in 1903.
Unknown	*The Horrors of Egypt*	The book was published by Xing Chan Ci in 1910.

Fan Shouyi (1682–1753 CE) was from Shang Xi Ping Yang. In Kang Xi 46 (1707 CE), he was dispatched by the Imperial Court to accompany missionary Joseph Anthony Provana and travel to Europe. They departed from Macau, passed through Batavia and South Africa's Cape of Good Hope, crossed the Atlantic, and arrived in Brazil, and then continued on to visit Portugal, Spain, Italy, and the Vatican. Fan Shouyi studied in Italy for several years and converted to Christianity. Afterwards, he returned to Portugal. In 1711, he accompanied Father Provana on a return trip to China. When their ship passed through the Cape of Good Hope, Provana became weak and sick, and died. Fan Shouyi returned to the East alone.[107] In *Shen Jian Lu*, Fan described the voyage route from Indian Ocean to Atlantic Ocean and also mentioned "Da Lang Shang" of South Africa's Cape of Good Hope.[108] Fan Shouyi is likely the first recorded Chinese visitor there.

Xie Qinggao of the Qing Dynasty (1765–1821 CE) was one of the early visitors to Mauritius. Xie Qinggao was from Jing Bao of Jia Ying Zhou (today's Guangdong Mei County). He traveled abroad with a foreign ship at the age of eighteen and spent fourteen years overseas. He went blind at the age of thirty-one. The book *Hai Lu* was written by Yang Bingnan, on Xie Qinggao's dictated account. In the book, Xie wrote about various African regions, such as Mozambique's Ma Sha Mi Ji, Mauritius's Miao Li Shi, the Cape of Good Hope's Xia Shang, and Saint Helena's San Die Li. He wrote about the voyage in the Cape of Good Hope: "The ocean was wide open and windy with violent waves. While our ship was passing through the region, it became so windy that we had to wait for the wind to die down before resuming the voyage." Xie also described Mauritius's geological location: "Miao Li Shi... All returning-home traffic in the Atlantic must pass through Ge La Ba [Jakarta], Di Wen [Timor], turn west, then go north. It takes about a month to reach this mountain." When he arrived at the Cape of Good Hope, he gave the place this description: "Miao Li Shi, an island in the Southwest Sea, with several hundred miles' circumference, and under the governance of Fou Lang Ji [France]."[109] In other Qing Dynasty publications, there were references to the voyage route between Indonesia and South Africa, and it was also mentioned that Dutch ships must dock in "Ge" on their return trip home to replace crew and resupply. The Chinese sailors on these ships would stay there temporarily before boarding and serving on another Dutch ship. Ge was Cape Town.[110]

Ding Lian, as a clerk of the Dutch Consul in Africa, toured inland East Africa with Ba Zhonghe and Yue Sile in 1877. In *San Zhou You Ji*, he gave a lively description of the political situation and local customs of the East African inland. In the book, he depicts the look of an African king: "The king was handsome and well-mannered, age twenty-eight or twenty-nine, indeed a rarity of Africa. We later learned from his followers that this was the fifteenth generation of the country's ruling family. The king enjoyed discussing history and current events with intellectuals." In the book, there is also description of the army on the eve of a battle: "Middle tents were where the king stayed, approximately 100–120 feet in each direction. There were three of them. The tents looked like palaces, very ample. There were thousands of soldiers surrounding the tents holding weapons. The soldiers were mostly black-faced with deep eye sockets, ugly looking, but intrepid. In front of the royal tent was a team of soldiers dressed in yellow. The generals were seated in the front row; the prime minister and other officials were seated in the second row, while the king sat in the third row." He describes the local salt mines as "six feet deep, two to three miles wide, twenty some people engaged in collecting salt… Salt and rocks look alike. They need to be immersed in clear water. Once all the mud is removed, the salt is then edible." On women's clothing, he writes: "wearing a copper necklace carved with floral patterns, heavy and large, some as heavy as over ten kilograms. When going out, women must wear their copper necklaces. They were not bothered by the heavy weight or by its ugly look." There are also depictions of various African villages, fighting among the villages, religions and churches, witchcrafts, etc.[111]

Other than writings of Chinese travelers, diplomats, and scholars, Sino-African interactions also took place through a third party, Western merchants and colonialists. During the eighteenth century, Madagascar's Sakalava Kingdom was at its prime. The king at the time had a firm grip of his kingdom. To gain favor with the king, French merchants gave him precious porcelains that were bought in China and also a finely carved crown that was skillfully painted in China.[112] Starting from 1760, the direct exchanges between China and Madagascar resumed in a new form. In that year, the French began shipping Chinese laborers to Madagascar's plantation. This will be covered in the next chapter.

Réunion and China's exchanges started in the 1720s. On November 3, 1724, the French warship *La Minerve* went around Africa's Cape of Good Hope, passed through Réunion Island, crossed the Indian Ocean, and arrived in Guangzhou, China in the following year. In 1727, Réunion Island's colonial director Dumas dispatched followers to the Fast East to collect precious farm seeds and seedlings and bring them back to Réunion to plant. At the time, the list of items brought from China to Réunion included tea, pepper, rhubarb, cinnamon, etc. They enriched the crops of Réunion. This was the beginning of the direct contacts between Réunion and China.[113]

In the first half of the nineteenth century, British merchants ordered a three-masted ship in Guangzhou. The ship was 160 feet long, 25.5 feet wide, weighed 800 tons, and made with teakwood. Upon its completion, the ship was named *Qi Ying Hao*. *Qi Ying Hao* sailed westbound from Hong Kong on December 6, 1849, heading towards England. There were only forty-two crewmembers, including twelve British, thirty Chinese, and a captain named Kai Lite. *Qi Ying Hao* sailed around the Cape of Good Hope on March 31, 1847. This was likely the first Chinese ship to do so. After the ship arrived at Saint Helena Island, realizing that there was not enough food onboard, Captain Kai Lite decided to change course and head for New York. When *Qi Ying Hao* arrived in New York, the newspaper reported it in a headline. To mark the accomplishment, the captain ordered his crew to fire ceremonial salutes and raise flags. New Yorkers, as many as seven to eight thousand visitors per day, went onboard to tour the ship. Later, *Qi Ying Hao* left New York, crossed the Atlantic Ocean, and docked in Gravesend, England twenty-three days later, on March 28, 1848. Its total time at sea on this voyage was 477 days.[114]

In their fight for Egypt and their desire to shorten the distance of the sea route between Europe and Asia, European powers started constructing the Suez Canal in 1859. At the time, there were already Chinese laborers participating in the construction of the canal.[115] After the Suez Canal opened for traffic in 1869, the travel distance between Europe and Asia was significantly shortened. This made Euro-Asian commerce more convenient, and control of the Sino-African trades began to shift from the Arabs to the Europeans. Tea was added to the China and North Africa trade list, while porcelain still dominated African trade south of the Sahara. Other than North Africa, the Qing Dynasty's porcelains were discovered in East, South and Central

Africa, the Saint Helena Islands in the Atlantic Ocean, Madagascar in the West Indian Ocean, and Mauritius.[116]

The above basically covers an abbreviated history of the Sino-African unofficial contacts during the Qing Dynasty. Overall, during this period, Sino-African relations made little progress. In comparison to the active trade of the early Ming Dynasty, ties regressed significantly. The new bilateral relationship has the following characteristics:

1. All official Sino-African relations ended. However, private, unofficial contacts continued.
2. Direct trade relations halted during late Ming Period, then transformed into indirect trade relations.
3. The Chinese had increased exposure to Africa through the publication of many books on African journeys and history.
4. Bilateral relations became active again in the nineteenth century. However, it was far from a resumption of the original diplomatic ties. Neither side was a sovereign as before.
5. The new interactions resumed in a totally different international environment. In this new bilateral relationship, there was an intervening third party, the European powers. Just as important was the fact that both China and Africa were facing a world about which they knew little, and felt perplexed. In a few short decades, Africa was completely divided up by European powers while the indentured Chinese laborers became the pioneers of Sino-African relations. Some of the laborers became the early overseas Chinese settlers.

CHAPTER II

THE BEGINNING OF OVERSEAS CHINESE

The Chinese I requested in 1813 never arrived, which resulted in inconveniences for the island, especially after the labor demand increased with the many arrangements made for the arrival of General Bonaparte.

—Saint Helena Governor Sir Hudson Roy, 1816

At the time, goldmines were operated in South Africa, with a total of seventy-five mines, of which sixty-four were producing gold, eleven were yet to produce gold. Now there are thirty some mines. There are over fifty thousand Chinese laborers. In the one year that I have been in Africa, I have settled all the Chinese laborers. I am departing Africa for England in July. Among the laborers, those who were not skilled were sent down to work in the mines. Each laborer receives a three-month training prior to starting work. Starting salary is set at $15 per month and gradually increased to $20 to $30 per month.

—Bo Liwen, 1906

After three years of hard labor, a typical [South African] Chinese laborer remains poor, thus has to continue the indentured labor work. Some die penniless. Compensation is given in iron coins for which exchanges are nearly impossible. Only upon the completion of a contract are the iron coins exchanged for gold coins. The goldmines vary in depth; some are 100–200 feet deep; others are 500–600 deep. Mechanical elevators are used to move workers up and down the mines. If a worker is not vigilant, he can easily fall to his death... If the foreman is not pleased with a worker, the worker is led to an isolated area where the worker is whipped and tortured while hung in the air with hands and feet bound."

—A Letter from Transvaal, Zhou Peizhi

The early overseas Chinese settlers can be grouped into two types: free immigrants and indentured laborers. There were three sources of the "free immigrants": (1) Chinese from Southeast Asia or China who boarded ships to arrive in Africa. Some of them were farmers unable to return home; others were exiled patriots who had fought to overthrow the Qing Dynasty. (2) Early stage Batavia prisoners who were exiled to Cape Town. Upon completion of their sentences, they chose to remain for various reasons. Some were ashamed of having been jailed; some adapted to the local life; some did not receive the permission to leave; some were short on return trip fares; and the rest were not able to board a return ship for other reasons. (3) Chinese laborers who decided to stay after completing their contracts. These laborers had savings and wished to remain abroad to make a living. In general, during the early stage, Chinese in Mauritius and Réunion came from Guangdong (including people from Guangfu and Kejia) and Fujian. The Chinese in Madagascar all came from Guangdong; the early stage of Chinese composition in South Africa, however, was relatively more complex, with the majority coming from Guangdong and Fujian.[1] Some of the immigrants were in farming, others in business. They gradually settled in their respective areas.

The indentured laborers are not the ancestors of the modern-day overseas Chinese in Africa; nor were they an important component of the early-stage Chinese organizations in Africa. However, judging from the numbers, indentured Chinese laborers were the majority of the early-stage overseas Chinese in Africa. Meanwhile, their experiences left a significant footprint in modern African history. Viewed from this perspective, the indentured Chinese laborers are an indispensible and important part of the overseas Chinese history in Africa.

The International Backdrop of "Indentured Laborer" Recruiting

From the viewpoint of world economic history, indentured Chinese labor was the result of a labor shortage in the capitalist economy after the abolition of slavery. During the transition period from slave trade to legal trade, the world economy went through an adjustment process. Abolishing the slave trade and slavery brought about a labor shortage that needed to be compensated in other ways or forms. Especially in the Americas, plantations required cheap labor. To solve this problem, European capitalists cast their eyes on China. Prior to the Opium War, the European powers did everything possible to plunder laborers from China. Based on statistics, from 1800 to 1850, there were 320,000 indentured Chinese laborers shipped to all over the world.[2] In The Modern World-System, Emmanuel Wallerstein marked the period 1730–1840 as "the second great expansion of the capitalist world-economy." Indeed, after three centuries of original accumulation, capitalism had stored up enough energy and began its second worldwide expansion. An important factor of European accumulation was the Atlantic slave trade, which lasted over four hundred years. The practice of trading Africans as products was a violation of a fundamental human right. It started with the Portuguese explorers plundering a group of enslaved Africans on the West African coast during the mid-fifteenth century and ended in the 1870s.[3] In this unprecedented human catastrophe, "the number of African Atlantic slaves traded reached a total of 15,400,000."[4]

During more than four hundred years, world trade expanded in both quantity and geography. Economies in Western Europe and North America rapidly expanded. Western Europe was the first to complete the transition from original accumulation to industrial revolution, and then quickly expanded to overseas. In the meantime, African progress fell behind that of other regions due to the outflow of its people into the slave system. The famous Nigerian historian Joseph Inikori once sharply pointed out that on one hand, to support capitalist production and supply the international market, these countries bought, transported, and used over ten million enslaved peoples; and on the other hand, they shipped and sold the products produced by these captive Africans. These two approaches composed a large share of the international economy at the time. In short, "The development of the Atlantic economy between 1451 and 1870 was realized by sacrificing the African economy."[5]

It is not difficult to see that the Atlantic slave trade was an important element of the Western European and North American economic development. This was demonstrated at least in the following two ways. First, slave trading and slavery were the major sources of capital during the British industrial development; the triangular trade and colonial economy had significantly stimulated various departments in England and injected new energy into the industrial revolution. Second, after the American Revolution, the economy built upon colonial slavery began to decline and its significance to England decreased. After the capitalist economy took shape, the monopoly of the plantation economy started to decline. Meanwhile, the longstanding humanitarian propaganda in England and France led to disputes in the British Parliament. In the end, the enslaved in the Americas rose up and fought for their own freedom. All of these factors led to the collapse of slavery.[6]

At the turn of the eighteenth and nineteenth centuries, the capitalist world economic system gradually incorporated Africa in its own track. In early nineteenth century, industrial revolution raised the issue of raw materials and a sales market; the slave trade gradually was replaced by "legal trade." In 1807, England was the first to abolish the slave trade. Under the cover of "abolishing the slave trade," some European merchants penetrated farther inland in Africa. Using the previously established business stops and colonies as their bases, on one hand, they sent out explorers on reconnaissance trips to find new inland business routes; on the other hand, they looked for various means to deal their competitors a blow. These merchants solicited financial backings from their government by suggesting that legal trade would prove to be "the most effective way to destroy the slave trade."[7] Through various means, European capitalists played an active role in influencing and lobbying their governments to take political and military action to merge colonies and protect their own economic interests. Because of their lobbying efforts, the pace of dividing up Africa increased.[8] Meanwhile, the focus of trade was shifted from spices, ivory, and gold to various industrial raw materials.

2.1 *Time Table of Abolishing the Slave Trade and Slavery by Countries*[9]

Country	Abolishment of slave trade (announcement date)	Abolishment of slave trade (effective date)	Abolishment of slavery (announcement date)	Abolishment of slavery (effective date)
England	1807	1808	1833	1838
France	1794,1 1818	1818	1848	
Spain	1814	1820s	1870	1872[2], 1878
Portugal	1815	1803	1854[3]	1878
Denmark	1792	1803	1885	
Holland	1814	1814	1885	
Sweden	1813	1813	1885	

Because the British government already announced the abolishment of the slave trade, it could not tolerate such "unfair competitions." Influenced by the British, the Vienna Convention held in 1815 passed a declaration on abolishing the slave trade. Through means such as gunboat diplomacy, treaty signing, large monetary donations, and debt cancellation, England successively signed the so-called slavery abolition treaties and supplemental regulations with Spain (December 1822), Holland (January 1823), Portugal (March 1823) and France (November 30, 1831). In August 1833, England announced the abolition of slavery in its territories. In the following half-century, other European and American countries also abolished slavery in tandem.

A noteworthy point is that legal trade did not uproot the slave trade; on the contrary, the two went hand in hand. Former Soviet scholar Abolamowa called the slave trade during this period, the "Smuggling Slave Trade."[10] Slave trading continued despite of laws and regulations. Why? There were three main factors. First, the American plantation economy, built upon the slave trade and slavery, was just beginning to flourish and still needed a large labor force. Second, due to the ban on the slave trade, prices of slaves skyrocketed, which provided slave merchants even more incentive to engage in smuggling. Third, back in Africa, due to the high profitability of raw materials such as palm oil, rubber, lumber, and peanuts, the plantation economy in Africa—in places such as in Nigeria, Zanzibar, and Mauritius—flourished, which led to an increased demand for labor. By the end of the nineteenth century, with the successive discovery of diamond and gold in South Africa, the situation was even more precarious.

There existed various interconnections between legal trade and the slave trade. A very prominent example, conspicuously practiced by the French and Portuguese, was to disguise slave labor as legal trade. They referred to this type of labor as "indentured labor." A laborer was set free after a certain number of service years (e.g., for the French, fourteen years; the Portuguese, five to ten years). For the French, this type of "legal" slave trade was concentrated in two areas: from the West Africa region (such as Senegal and Gabon) to the Americas, from Southeast Africa to Madagascar, Comoros, and Réunion. After serving fourteen years, an indentured laborer was then set free. The Portuguese indentured labor system mainly concentrated in São Tomé–Príncipe. The plantation economy in this region benefited from the popularity of coffee and later cocoa production in the 1850s.[11] A noteworthy point here is that the Chinese indentured laborers were successively shipped to the above regions and worked as coolies—a term used by Europeans for hired laborers from India and China.

In the second half of nineteenth century, most regions in the world were divided up by the European powers. On one hand, the vast earth offered rich natural resources, but the manpower to exploit these resources was lacking. On the other hand, gold was successively discovered in the United States, Australia, and South Africa, which resulted in European capital pouring into these regions. The labor issue could only be solved by encouraging immigration and utilizing indentured labor. After the Opium War, European countries stepped up their efforts in plundering Chinese laborers. During its peak between 1850 and 1875, as many as 1,280,000 indentured Chinese laborers went abroad, while the number was 750,000 between 1876 and 1900.[12] At the time, various European companies and their recruitment agents, through mostly deceptive and violent means, recruited Chinese laborers. They signed contracts with Chinese farmers, handcraft workers, small merchants, and refugees, and then shipped the recruits to their respective colonies to engage in various development work. The footprint of indentured Chinese laborers covered the world. They built railroads in North America, West Africa, East Africa, and Madagascar; they mined gold in the United States, Australia, South Africa, and Ghana; they worked in plantations in the Americas, Southeast Asia, and Mascarene Islands of West Indian Ocean.

Most scholars placed their research focus on the nineteenth century.[13] In reality, in the eighteenth century, Chinese were abducted through various means and sent to the European powers' African colonies (such as Mauritius) to work as coolies. Of course, this type of abduction and kidnapping was quite common in the nineteenth century. Most of these Chinese laborers signed a "contract," thus it could be said that they went of their own "free." We call this recruitment tactic "abduction" because (1) it was illegal to recruit Chinese workers from China to work in Africa. There was no consent from the Chinese government; and (2) the working conditions and compensation were far from what was promised by the employers in their contracts, and thus could not satisfy the contracted Chinese laborers.

Early-stage Indentured Chinese Laborers, 1700–1904

In the late stage of the slave trade period, some European countries started to import indentured laborers from China. After the abolishment of the slave trade and slavery, these countries viewed a weak China as the best source of cheap labor for their American and African colonies. Although 1904–1910 was the peak of indentured Chinese laborers leaving for Africa, prior to that, there had been many Chinese laborers recruited to Africa. Below, we will further examine the pattern of European powers recruiting indentured Chinese laborers to Africa from the eighteenth to twentieth centuries.

Mauritius

Mauritius is located approximately 800 kilometers east of Madagascar. In 1598, the Dutch arrived to colonize it and renamed the island to Mauritius after a Dutch Prince named Mauris. In 1715, the French occupied the island and renamed it "Francis Island." During the Anglo-French War, the British force occupied Mauritius in 1810. In the 1914 Paris Peace Treaties, the island was officially designated as a British colony. American scholar Bowman in his study of Mauritius believed that Asian Indians came to Mauritius as indentured laborers while Chinese came as free immigrants.[14] British scholar Phillip Snow, who specialized in Sino-African relations, also held the same view.[15] This view, however, was not accurate. In reality, Mauritius's early Chinese arrivals were all indentured laborers.

Beginning in 1760, the French shipped Chinese to work in Mauritius's plantations. The first Chinese workers were hostages, plundered from the Southeast Asia region by French Navy General d'Estaing during the Anglo-French War, numbered around three hundred. At first, the French wanted to force the workers to farm, but the Chinese refused by stating that they specialized in business and knew nothing about farming. The French had no choice but to ship the workers back the next year. According Zeng Fanxing, Chinese scholar and Mauritius's Minister of Culture, Art, and Entertainment, several Chinese in that original group did not actually leave the island.[16] In 1762, the French shipped another group of Chinese workers directly from China.[17]

By the 1780s, the French continued shipping laborers from China to Mauritius. In Guangzhou, the French recruitment agent Charles d'Estaing remarked:

There were over 3,000 Chinese on board the British, Dutch, and French ships heading for Francis Island in 1783. I once boarded Port Louis merchant['s]… ship at Guangzhou, heading for Francis Island to transport 132 workers, of which nineteen were craftsmen: shoemakers, blacksmiths, tailors, and carpenters. In the following year, I convinced twelve sugar industry farmers and workers to go to Francis Island with their work equipment. These workers were requested by the Governor and the General Officer.[18]

The main reason that Mauritius imported Chinese was for the development of the island's sugar cane plantations and sugar industry. Because of the plantation needs, the government actively advocated for immigration of indentured laborers. Based on scattered data, during the French colonial period, importing Chinese laborers was carried out under irregular conditions. In 1810, after the British force occupied the island, Farquhar, who had served as a British officer in the Southeast Asia, was designated as the Governor of Mauritius. He actively advocated for the policy of bringing in laborers from China. He knew, however, that the Qing Government was publically against the policy. Therefore, he advocated for using "indirect methods to recruit immigrants," in addition to colluding with Qing officials.[19]

A labor shortage forced the British to cast their sights on India and China. In 1829, the British colonial government in Mauritius brought in the first group of indentured laborers, including four hundred Chinese workers and four hundred Indian workers.[20] However, Chinese workers' resistance forced the government to send them back at the plantation owners' expense. This led to plantation owners' loss of interest in employing indentured Chinese laborers in the subsequent ten years. In 1840, the Indian government was displeased with the labor recruitment tactics and stopped providing indentured laborers to Mauritius. As a result, the plantation owners had to go to Southeast Asia to recruit overseas Chinese again. In 1843, Mauritius brought in one thousand Chinese coolies from the Straits Settlements.[21] From December 29, 1840 to July 5, 1843, Mauritian agents in Singapore recruited three thousand Chinese laborers on behalf of many Mauritian companies. Li Zhuofan explained this by quoting a copy of a government document: "From 1840 to 1844, a total of eight to nine thousand Chinese immigrants were recruited from Calcutta, Singapore, or other ports in the Straits."[22] In merely several years, overseas Chinese became the majority among the Mauritian farm workforce.[23] There were a few more rounds of recruitments later on, but due to the difficulty of meeting the needed female quota, the effort was abandoned. Afterwards, all the Mauritius Chinese immigrants came mainly of their free.

Réunion

Réunion is a volcanic island located in the West Indian Ocean, 676 kilometers southeast of Madagascar, very close to Mauritius. In 1513 Portuguese voyager Mascarene arrived here and named the island "Mascarene Island." The island has been a French colony since the French occupation in 1643 (with the exception of the period from 1810 to 1815 when the island was briefly occupied by British forces). In 1649, it was renamed to Bourbon Island; and renamed again to "Réunion" in 1793. During the period of the slave trade, the French shipped a large number of enslaved Africans from the African continent to the island to work on the plantations. After France abolished the slave trade in 1817–1818, the supply of enslaved Africans dwindled. In 1829, the Réunion government decided to bring in Asian immigrants. It is very likely that the indentured Chinese laborers were introduced in this period; however, the majority of the labor force during this period came from India. Two years later, the government issued an order for "Indian and Chinese laborers and other free Asian civilians," with the following key regulations:

1. Employment contracts must be turned over to be reviewed by a special committee before becoming effective.
2. The contract period was set to five years.
3. Monthly salary had to be more than ten francs.
4. Employer must provide food supplements and medical benefits.
5. Employers must pay for contract workers' return trips.

This was the earliest immigration law regulating Asian laborers in the West Indian Ocean region. In 1843, Réunion government issued an order to bring in one thousand Chinese laborers as an experiment. Three years later, Governor Ge Liebo announced an end to bringing in new indentured Chinese laborers.[24] During this period, Réunion continued dispatching personnel to Southeast Asia and mainland China to recruit Chinese laborers directly; there were two such recruitment efforts in 1844. In early 1845, recruiters from Réunion arrived in Xia Men and contacted Connerly of the local British merchant firm Deji. In June, through the Deji firm, by means of recruiting indentured laborers, 180 coolies were recruited; they boarded a French ship leaving Xia Men for Réunion. On October 4 of the same year, another group of Chinese laborers arrived in Réunion. In 1846, Réunion recruited one more group of indentured Chinese laborers numbered in the two hundreds; the group also departed from the port of Xia Men. All of the laborers signed five-year contracts with their employers, with a monthly compensation of four silver coins. According to the research by Chen Zexian, "This was the first documented occurrence of Western capitalist countries recruiting laborers to go abroad from Xia Men."[25] Since then, the French colonial government successively recruited laborers from Asia in 1848 and 1852; however, the employers and the colonial government kept no records of the laborers' nationalities and names, only their assigned worker numbers and tasks, thus no one knows the nationalities of these laborers.[26]

In 1849, the French government publicized the Réunion census after the abolition of slavery. At the time, there were 31,291 whites and 66,621 colored residents, which included 590 Chinese. In 1882, the French recruited another 2,010 Chinese laborers to Réunion from Shanghai.[27] Starting from 1885, Réunion government resumed recruiting indentured Chinese laborers; this time, the recruitment continued until 1901. In 1901, 812 Fu Zhou workers boarded a German ship and arrived in Réunion.[28] They were the last group of indentured Chinese laborers recruited by Réunion. Until 1901, there had been a total of 3,000 Chinese laborers recruited from Fujian.[29] The whereabouts of the indentured Chinese laborers in Réunion in the nineteenth century upon contract completion could be grouped into three categories: some went back to China directly; some relocated to Mauritius or other parts of Africa; some stayed behind and married local women.

Saint Helena

Saint Helena Island is a volcanic island, like Réunion, located in the south Atlantic Ocean, 1,840 kilometers from Africa's west coast. In 1502, the Portuguese arrived on the island and named the island after Emperor Constantine's mother, Saint Helena. In 1633, the Dutch occupied the island and made it the base of West Africa's slave trade. In 1657, the island fell into hands of the British and became a territory of the British East India Company, specializing in supplying inter-continental ships traveling between Europe and Asia. With the exception of a few whites, the majority of the island's residents were enslaved Africans. After England abolished the Atlantic slave trade, supplying labor became increasingly difficult. In 1810, the governor of Saint Helena Island asked the East India Company's Business and Management Office, based in Guangzhou, to recruit a team of Chinese craftsmen and farmers. At the time, the Qing Dynasty government had a ban on its citizens traveling abroad; therefore, this type of recruitment could only be carried out illegally and underground.[30]

In May 1810, British East India Company shipped fifty Chinese laborers from Guangdong to Saint Helena Island and was very pleased with the laborers' performance. As a result, the company brought in another one hundred and fifty Chinese laborers. Alexander Peterson, governor of Saint Helena Island at the time, gave a description of the different types of tasks performed by the Chinese laborers. Most of these Chinese were hired to carry out farm work, such as building fences, smoothing farmland, burning wild land, driving carriages, planting and reaping potato crops, and various other jobs. "Some became experts in farming." The British East India Company paid each Chinese laborer one cent per day and supplied the workers with food. In addition to handcrafts and farm work, these laborers also participated in some military training activities.[31]

In 1815, the British exiled French Emperor Napoleon I, who was defeated in the Battle of Waterloo, to Saint Helena Island. Because the island was converted from a midway supplier for ships into a prison for important criminals, the British had to station a large military force on the island. The island required new barracks, forts, and other buildings; guarding soldiers also required multitudes of supplies. Thus, Sir Hudson Roy, governor of the island, again requested help from East India Company's Business and Management Office based in Guangzhou. On May 7, 1816, Roy complained to a special committee of the British Lower House:

The Chinese I requested in 1813 never arrived, which resulted in inconveniences for the island, especially after labor demand increased with the many arrangements made for the arrival of General Bonaparte. The inconvenience has been alleviated by the measure authorized by your committee to have each passing ship drop off a few Chinese workers. We hope this measure will continue until we receive a total of one hundred and fifty workers. We at the base look forward to reaching this ideal number. Without the intervention of your committee, it will be inconvenient and also improper.

The special committee was not very enthusiastic about his demand, which fueled Roy's impatience. This loner governor sent yet another letter to the British Lower House in the following year. In the letter, his worker demand increased from one hundred and fifty to three hundred and fifty, and he also expressed the urgency of the matter. He explicitly stated that Saint Helena Island needed twenty carpenters, ten masons, fifty plasterers, six blacksmiths, and farm workers who could grow crops, raise domestic animals, and garden. Compensation was set to $15 per month per person for the fifty carpenters; $6 per month per person for the three hundred farmers. All the Chinese laborers would receive a four-month advance. Due to the illegal nature of this type of overseas recruitment, the activities could only take place underground. In 1820, the British Business Office in Guangzhou recruited twenty Chinese laborers for Saint Helena Island; the laborers were discovered and retained by the Qing officials onboard a ship. In the end, to resolve the matter, the British Business Office had to pay the fine of 1,000 silver.[32]

Life was hard for the Chinese laborers working on the island. The island was hot, humid, and rugged. Most whites could not tolerate the extreme heat; therefore, the island had few white residents and only a small rotating crew of white managers. After arriving on the island, the majority of the Chinese laborers were disappointed; they could only tolerate their condition in silence. Like most of the Africans and a small number of Indians and Malaysians, the Chinese laborers worked from sunrise to sunset. Occasionally, they also had to perform tasks similar to a soldier's duties, such as pulling cannons and transporting firearms. Alexander Peterson, governor of Saint Helena Island, once remarked, "To put it simply, employing them is similar to employing Indian Artillery." The Chinese laborers were under the supervision of the Europeans, engaging in heavy and monotonous labor, but their final whereabouts have been lost to history.

Madagascar

At the end of the eighteenth century and the beginning of the nineteenth century, it was suggested the French government introduce Chinese laborers to Madagascar. The early Chinese in Madagascar came from Mauritius and Réunion, and could not be counted as indentured Chinese laborers. Occasionally, however, the French would ship Chinese laborers from China's neighboring ports to Madagascar. For instance, in 1865, a ship leaving Macau for France carried an unspecified number of coolies to Madagascar.[33] The indentured Chinese laborers arrived separately in four groups. The first arrived on the island in 1896 when the French officially established the Madagascar Colony. At the time, the employment of indentured Chinese laborers was mainly for building the Tamatave–Antananarivo Road.

2.2 *Arrival and Departure Records of the First Groups of Indentured Chinese Laborers in Madagascar*[34]

Group No.	Arrival Date	Departure Date	Group Size	Notes
1	May 10, 1896	February 5, 1897	499	
2	August 25, 1896	May 20, 1897	614	
3	April 5, 1897	December 20, 1897	1,023	285 were sent back on September 2, 1897 due to feigned sickness.
4	August 11, 1897	May 19, 1898	867	55 were sent back on September 2, 1897 due to feigned sickness.

In the beginning of the twentieth century, the Madagascar colonial government brought in two more groups of indentured Chinese laborers. The first group was brought in mainly for paving the Diego-Suarez Road in 1900. According to a telegram sent by the island governor to the colonial ministry, five hundred laborers were needed with the following employment conditions:

1. The maximum length of employment was two years.
2. Monthly compensation was set to be 20 pesos per person for the laborers and 30 pesos per person for the translators and foremen.
3. Compensation started from the departure date, with one month's advance.
4. Free healthcare benefits.[35]

This group of Chinese laborers departed on February 10, 1900 and arrived at Diego-Suarez in April of the same year. Due to difficulty in acclimatization, this group of indentured Chinese laborers did not work out as well as anticipated.

In 1901, the governor of Madagascar once again decided to bring in indentured Chinese laborers. After months of difficult negotiations with the French Colonial Ministry, consent was finally given. The French Colonial Ministry then signed an agreement with a merchant in Tamatave. According to "Instructions on the Recruitment and Utilization of Chinese Laborers in this Colony," published in the Independent Madagascar Public Notes and issued on May 8, 1901 by Governor Gallieni, the contract for employing Chinese laborers was as such:

1. Each Chinese laborer was employed for three years, starting from the arrival date in Tamatave.
2. Each laborer received 25 francs per month; a foreman received 30 francs.
3. Each laborer received food, clothing, housing, and healthcare supplements.
4. Upon contract completion, return trip fares were provided to each laborer.

A total of 764 of Chinese laborers plus a translator arrived in Tamatave on June 27, 1901. They were likely recruited by Francis Vichi, a French merchant who lived in China for a long time and had significant recruitment experience. According to data collected by Chinese scholar Chen Zexian, in 1901, on behalf of Madagascar's colonial government, Vichi made a request to the Fu Zhou Administration of Foreign Affairs, asking to recruit laborers in Fu Zhou. With the consent of Qing Dynasty officials,[36] and the help of Gao Jin, the French consul at Fu Zhou and local Catholic missionaries, Vichi and the recruiters he employed, by means of deceptive tactics, successively recruited over three thousand people between 1901 and 1902 and let them board French steamships in groups, going to Madagascar and Réunion.[37]

The original intent for recruiting this group of indentured Chinese laborers was to have them build the Antananarivo Railroad. But in the end, only 280 Chinese were involved in the construction of the railroad. The remaining Chinese were dispatched to various regions in the colony. The distribution of the indentured Chinese laborers by region is shown below.

Tamatave	100 people
"Large Enclosure"	26 people
Mahajanga	50 people
Ambatondrazaka	19 people

Fianarantsoa	200 people
Antananarivo–Moramanga Railroad	280 people
Arivonimamo (?)	39 people
Betafo	20 people
General farming	22 people[4]

The Chinese laborers participating in the railroad construction faced harsh realities. Among them, four died before work even started, and most of them fell ill during the construction. Their fatality rate was as high as 76.9 percent in the ten months' construction period. Governor Gallieni admitted this rate was higher than those for workers from other countries.[38] This was due to acclimatization, harsh working environment, and poor treatment of workers. Most of the Chinese laborers fell ill; some used escape as a means of resisting. In the end, the colonial government had no choice but to send back most of the Chinese laborers.

Tanganyika

In 1886, Tanganyika became a German colony. In 1891, the German East African colony was established. The new governor, Baron Von Soden, formulated a regulation for recruiting East Asian laborers. The regulation called for sending East Asian laborers to various regions of Tanganyika. The laborers would work on officially designated tasks under the supervision of the Germans. In 1892, the German East Africa Special Permission Company and German East Africa Plantation Company joined forces to recruit laborers from British Straits Settlements and from Shantou, China. However, the German and British firms entrusted with the German companies' task were locally notorious. As a result, the Germans' recruitment attempt in Shantou was opposed by locals and subsequently failed. In the end, 240 male laborers were recruited from Singapore, 243 male laborers from Java, and 24 female laborers from Java. This group of laborers departed from Singapore on July 25, 1892, boarding the British steamship Flint Marshall and heading for the coast of East Africa. On August 10 of the same year, several Western newspapers (such as the German

Berlin Daily and Business News) published news on the arrival of the first group of East Asian laborers in the German East African Colony.

In September 1892, Germans in East Africa recruited a group of Chinese laborers through coolie dealers in Macau and shipped them to Tanganyika on board a British steamship. In the subsequent years, the German East Africa Plantation Company successively recruited several groups of Chinese laborers from Shantou (in 1896), Macau (in 1902), and Singapore (in 1907) to work as coolies on Tanganyika plantations. At the time, China's Jiaozhou Bay had become a German concession territory. Germans in the territory also joined in on the recruitment of indentured Chinese laborers for the German East African colony. For instance, in 1905, sixty hardy young men were recruited from inner Shandong Province and sent to Tanganyika to work as policemen.[39]

The main reason for Germans to recruit Chinese laborers was to build railroads, which has long been ignored by scholars. Germans built two railroads in Tanganyika: (1) A railroad from Tanga in the north to Moshi, with a total length of 220 miles. Its construction started in 1891, continued intermittently, and was completed twenty years later in 1911; and (2) a railroad from Dar es Salaam to Kigoma by Lake Tanganyika, with a total length of 780 miles. Its construction started in 1904 and completed in 1914. There has been no historical documentation on Chinese laborers' roles in the construction of these two railroads, though there were scattered reports in early newspapers in Hong Kong. In addition, overseas Chinese Qu Zhengmin collected data based on his own personal experiences in East Africa and his interaction with the locals.

Africans who live by the Tanga–Moshi Railroad mentioned that at the turn of the century, a "large number" of Chinese construction workers lived at the foot of Udzungwa Mountain and taught the locals farming and tea planting. The two groups got along well, and there is still a "Shanghai Village" ("Kijiji Shanghai" in the Kiswahili language) in that region today.[40] Zhang Shuchuan, from Shandong Gaomi, was employed in the Johannesburg area as a translator and missionary during the Guangxu Period. He once mentioned that the British and Germans simultaneously recruited laborers in the Jiaozhou Bay area to go to Africa. In addition, a Scot named Murray, who served as chief engineer of the Railway Administration after the independence of Tanzania, was invited to participate in the construction negotiation of Tanzania–Zambia Railroad between China and Tanzania. Murray mentioned that there had been thousands of Chinese laborers building railroads for the German government. Unfortunately, no records were kept by the Railway Administration.

In 1891, the Germans started constructing the Tanga–Moshi Railroad. In the beginning, they trained workers at the construction site. With the exception of German engineers, everyone else was African. Due to the rugged and dangerous terrain, construction work was very difficult and progress was slow. At the time, the British were also building railroads in Kenya by recruiting well-trained Indian technicians and supplementing with African laborers; their progress was fast: it took only nine years to complete the 870-mile railroad. To increase speed, the Germans recruited Chinese laborers from various parts of the Far East in 1898. During the Bei Fa Period, a group of Chinese carpenters came to work in East Africa; they met several laborers and foremen who had participated in railroad construction during the period of German rule. Some of them married local women, had no intention of returning to China, and planned on spending their old age in East Africa. In summary, with certainty, there were approximately two thousand Chinese who participated in the railroad construction. The fact that the Chinese once were building railroads in German East Africa has long been forgotten.

French West Africa

In French West Africa, the center of administration was established in Dakar, Senegal. Dakar was an important slave exporting port in the slave trade period. During the nineteenth century, the majority of colonial activities in French West Africa concentrated in the Senegal region and from here the activities spanned to other colonies. In 1854, Napoleon III of France named Faidherbe as governor, and had him expand the colonies in West Africa. Faidherbe initiated many massive construction projects. A group of laborers were specifically recruited from China to participate in municipal construction in Dakar, working as plasterers, bricklayers, and carpenters.

In 1879, upon order from the French government, Shi Keqing, French consul at Guangzhou, made a request to the Chinese officials, asking that French merchants, on behalf of the French colonies, be allowed to recruit Chinese laborers from various commercial ports in the south. From 1880 to 1882, French merchants successively recruited a large number of Chinese laborers in Guangzhou, Shantou, and Shanghai and sent them to Senegal, Réunion, and other places. In 1881, both the Dakar–Saint Louis Railroad and the Kankan–Conakry Railroad construction sites broke ground simultaneously. Due to the construction of these two railways, the French government and the Senegal colonial government came to confront the labor issue. In 1883, to advocate for importing labor from Asia, a Sino-French Trading Company was formed to facilitate the import of indentured Chinese laborers. In the meantime, the French also drafted a large number of laborers from its many colonies (such as Morocco and French West Africa) by force.

Chinese laborers arriving in Senegal were forced to participate in the construction of the Dakar–Saint Louis Railroad. This railway was 264 miles long; it served both as the lifeline connecting two important cities and also as the transportation route for exporting peanuts, a major economic crop, from Niort. The construction was undertaken by a large railroad corporation, Badi Niort Company. Funding was mostly provided by the French government, with the Senegal bank providing a portion. Constructing railroads was the main source of profit for the Badi Niort Company; projects obtained through its close ties with the government often brought in high profit margins. This time was no exception. The project was approved by the French Parliament, and the government guaranteed that after completion of the railway, the Badi Niort Company would receive compensation of 1,200 francs per mile.[41] The railway construction was paid for with lives of numerous railway laborers, and was completed in 1885.

Those Chinese laborers lucky enough to survive likely went on to participate in the construction of the Kankan–Conakry Railroad, which was 555 miles long and an important transportation route for penetration into inland West Africa. Because of the length of this railway and the complicated terrain that it traversed through, construction progress was relatively slow. In 1899, the French colonial government brought in another group of indentured Chinese laborers. This group appeared to be sent from the Indo-China region. By 1900, 217 miles of the Kankan–Conakry Railroad was completed. A large number of the railroad construction laborers died from extremely difficult working conditions, mistreatment by foremen, acclimatization, poor diet, and diseases. The railway was completed in 1904. Due to the high fatality rate, the policy of importing indentured laborers from China was judged to be a failed experiment by the French.[42]

British West Africa

British West Africa also brought in Chinese laborers in the nineteenth century. At the time, the British Gold Coast Colony was in its last phase of conquering the Asante Kingdom; and the colony itself had many labor needs, such as constructing railroads, transporting goods, exporting products, and mining. These needs caused a labor shortage. To solve this problem, from 1875 to 1889, the colonial government repeatedly issued laws to regulate labor. This included the Labor Law in 1875, the Public Labor Law in 1889, the Law Governing Owners, Servants, and Foreign Employees in 1893, and the Roadway Law in 1894.[43] These laws gave the colonial government the direct ability to recruit labor and thus alleviate the labor shortage problem. By the mid 1890s, due to the needs for skilled laborers in gold mining, Gold Coast governor Maxwell proposed introducing Chinese laborers. He believed that the Chinese miners were more diligent than local miners, thus would benefit the development of the local gold mining business.[44] Discussions on this proposal were in local newspapers such as the Gold Coast Express, the Gold Coast Independent, and the Gold Coast Chronicles. There were various views on this government proposal; some claimed that Chinese laborers were not welcomed in other colonies, thus the Gold Coast did not want them; others claimed that British technicians who had worked with the Chinese laborers were dissatisfied with their performance.[45]

In reality, in the 1870s and 1880s, there were suggestions to import Chinese miners. The British colonialists, in view of the goldmines' great potential in the colony, thought that by introducing Chinese laborers, the landscape of this colony could be altered. For instance, in 1883, Richard Burton and V. L. Cameron suggested the introduction of Chinese laborers after inspecting the Vasseur gold mine in the Gold Coast Colony.[46] At the time, the British saw the transformation in the U.S., Canada, Australia, and the Americas after introducing Chinese laborers. It appeared to be a superstition associated with Chinese laborers. In the same year, Ellis wrote in his book, "As long as an energetic governor would introduce Chinese laborers, the landscape of the Gold Coast will be entirely different than what it is today."[47]

Regardless of the strong local opposition and British colonial administration's grave doubts, the Gold Coast government decided to import a group of Chinese laborers. Governor Maxwell was the plan's architect. His real aim was to use it to test the possibility of importing Chinese laborers on a large scale to expedite gold production in the colony, because at the time, production of the Vasseur and Akim (Akyem) goldmines had already attracted attention from several large British corporations.[48] To get London's approval, Maxwell made a special trip back to England to lobby. He also met with members of the Liverpool Commerce Committee and reached a consensus with them. This plan eventually received the approval of the colonial administration and a nod from the British business community.

In July 1897, sixteen Chinese miners and technicians traveled through the Straits Settlements and Liverpool and arrived at the port of Winneba.[49] Chinese laborers were assigned to work in the Vasseur and Akim mines with the local miners. There was little information on their work situation and living conditions. However, local newspapers revealed the following two points. First, the workers were regretful and homesick shortly after their arrival.[50] Second, they had difficulty with acclimatization and often fell ill.[51]

In September 1897, shortly after returning to England, Governor Maxwell died. The death of the architect and advocate of the plan to introduce Chinese miners put an end to the project. The Chinese minors boarded a steamboat heading for England in November 1897. Maxwell's successor, Governor Frederick Hodgson, adopted an entirely different labor policy. According to some scholars, the British West African colonial government recruited Chinese laborers to work in Sierra Leone. Campbell, in her 1923 book, wrote: "Everyone knew that there was a labor surplus in South China; thus at different points of time, there were individuals considering introducing indentured laborers to the west coast of Africa. Sir Jones already imported many Chinese in Sierra Leone."[52] Due to lack of data, this subject will have to be studied in the future.

The Congo Free State

Starting from the 1870s, Belgian King Leopold II, through means of deception and bribery, signed over four hundred treaties of an enslaving nature with the kings and chiefs in the Congo River region. Later on, he occupied these regions as his own territory. In the 1884 Berlin Conference, the region east of the Congo River was given to Leopold II and the Congo Free State was born with Leopold II as its head. In 1887, Leopold II dispatched followers to China to negotiate labor recruitment. Since China had signed treaties with Belgium, the Qing government felt that Belgium should be allowed to recruit on behalf of its own colonies, but not for the Congo Free State, and thus refused Leopold II's request.

In 1892, through its agents in China, the Congo Free State established contacts with Macau-based Portuguese labor traders and entrusted them to recruit labor on its behalf. The Portuguese recruitment agents provided the following contract conditions while recruiting in inland Guangzhou:

1. Those who wished to work in the Congo Free State must sign a three-year contract with the employer.
2. During the contract term, workers must obey the employer and must not boycott.
3. Upon arrival in the Congo, each Chinese laborer would receive 45 francs in monthly pay.
4. The employer would provide room and board for the Chinese workers.
5. The employer would pay the workers' round-trip fares.
6. If a Chinese worker wished to remain in Congo at the end of his contract term, he would receive 400 francs in cash from his employer.

There were a total of 542 people applying, including 536 Chinese males and six male children. In September 28, 1892, boarding the German steamship Walstein, these Chinese workers departed Macau and headed for the Congo. Among the workers, there was a Chinese laborer who brought along his wife. Later on, labor traders in Macau and Hong Kong secretly went to Qiongzhou and Shantou to recruit Chinese laborers for the Congo Free State. The recruits were gathered in Macau or Hong Kong and then shipped to the Congo. There were records on these Chinese labor recruitments in the China Custom Annual Trading and Commerce Records (1892) and the Business Report by the British Consulate in China (1892).

Upon arrival, the Chinese laborers were assigned to build the Congo railway. They worked under the blazing sun and extreme heat, logging trees in the dense forest, and hauling rocks to pave railroads. The working conditions were extremely harsh; workers faced a terrible climate, circulating diseases, a poor diet, and mistreatment by foremen. Some laborers fell ill while others escaped or rebelled. In the end, most of the laborers died in the forest. There were reports on the miseries of these Chinese laborers published in Hong Kong newspapers at the time, which caused a stir in China.

The performance of these Chinese laborers was unsatisfactory, thus the Congo Free State indicated that it would no longer recruit Chinese laborers. However, Leopold II continued to seek Chinese laborers. To reach his aim, the special representative of the Congo Free State became very active in the circle of European diplomats in China. In the end, the China and Congo special chapter was agreed upon in Beijing between the two parties on July 10, 1898. In it, there were two items; the second stated, "It was agreed upon that Chinese citizens can at will move to and live in the Congo Free State. All properties, movable or unmovable, can be purchased or traded. Whether for shipping, business, crafts, or arts, Chinese citizens will receive the same treatment as citizens of the most favorable countries."[53] Based on this passage, it is apparent that the purpose of the agreement was to allow the Congo Free State to recruit labor from China. Afterwards, the Congo Free State successively recruited Chinese laborers four times, in 1901, 1902, 1904, and 1906.[54]

Portuguese West Africa, Spanish West Africa

Portugal occupied São Tomé Island, Príncipe Island, and Portuguese Guinea (present-day Guinea-Bissau) in West Africa. Spain occupied Fernando Po Island. All three colonies had a notorious history of plantation slavery. After the abolition of the slave trade and slavery, the three islands wanted to find other means to recruit plantation laborers, and successively recruited a number of Chinese laborers.[55] In 1908, the

Portuguese colonial administration exiled a Macau resident to Guinea to engage in road construction. Because the majority of the indentured Chinese laborers in Portuguese West Africa and Portuguese East Africa (Mozambique) were imported from Portuguese Macau and the means by which Spanish Fernando Po Island imported Chinese laborers were mostly hidden, there is very little available information. The return of Macau to China would be helpful in the further study of this subject.

Other African Regions

Regarding the Chinese laborers in the Suez Canal region, I have seen references in only two documents. One is an article published in Qiao Wu Ji Kan;[56] the other is Chen Zixian's chart of statistics.[57] Due to lack of data, we must leave the subject mostly unresolved for now. We know only that in British Rhodesia (present-day Zimbabwe), immigration laws were passed in 1901 and 1902, announcing that immigrants from certain countries were allowed to immigrate to Rhodesia; the passing of these laws was mainly to facilitate importing Chinese laborers.[58]

Indentured Chinese Laborers in South Africa, 1904–1910

In 1652, a group of Dutch individuals led by an East India Company clerk landed at Table Bay in the Cape of Good Hope. They quickly established the Cape Colony and started encroaching land of the Africans. After bringing the indigenous San people to the brink of extinction and enslaving the KhoiKhoi people, the Europeans vehemently denied the AmaXhosa's right to their land. In the eighteenth century, the Dutch already reached the Great Fish River region and wanted to advance even farther, but were stopped by the AmaXhosa. In 1778, colonial governor Van Plettenberg wanted to set the Great River as the border and demanded that the AmaXhosa retreat from the Zuurveld region. This unreasonable demand was refused by the AmaXhosa. In 1779, the Europeans expelled the AmaXhosa in the first "Kaffir War."[59] Hereafter, this European occupation and anti-occupation war lasted an entire century.

In 1806, the British started its invasion. It did not take long before conflicts erupted between the British, whose economic model was based on capitalist industry, and the Boers,[60] whose economic model was based on farming, herding, and the enslavement of Africans. When England announced the abolition of slavery in its colonies, the Boers, in an attempt to break away from the British colonial government's rule and to maintain their way of life, started their great migration.[61] In 1867, a 21-carat diamond, which was later named the Eureka Diamond, was discovered on the banks of Orange River. Two years later, the famous Star of South Africa was discovered. Meanwhile, the "gold fever" grew even more crazed than the diamond fever. In 1870, in the Zoutpansberg region, located on the north banks of the Vaal River, a concentration of rich goldmines was discovered; three years later, more concentrations of goldmines were discovered in the Fort Leiden region. In 1884, valuable mines were discovered in the Barberton region; two years after that, in the highland of Witwatersrand (will hereinafter be referred to as the Rand), rich goldmines were discovered. All of a sudden, the gold rushers poured in from all over the world. The "Gold Town" of Johannesburg was built by gold rushers in 1886. Following the development of the mining industry, frictions between the British Cape Colony and the Boers increased by the day. In the end, it had to be resolved by wars.

The British Boer War (1899–1902) ended with a British victory. The Treaty of Vereeniging (May 31, 1902) affirmed British's ruling authority, while the Boers received three million pounds in compensation from the victor.[62] Postwar South Africa needed a full-scale reconstruction. The gold mining industry attracted large amount of capital. In merely one year's time, it "already spent several millions pounds, established 299 new companies, and raised a lot of money to develop mineral resources in the country."[63] Although the number of laborers (including both blacks and whites) already exceeded the prewar number, it was still not sufficient to satisfy the needs arising from the large-scale mining expansion. Under these circumstances, investors of South Africa's mining industry suggested importing Chinese laborers. The suggestion was quickly put into action. From 1904 to 1910, a large number of Chinese laborers worked in goldmines in South Africa and Transvaal, contributing to the gold mining in South Africa.[64]

The British government's original plan was to import 200,000 laborers from China. For various reasons, the British government was forced to abandon recruitment in China in November 1906. There were disagreements on the number of goldmine laborers exported to South Africa from China from 1904 to 1907.

1. From England: Based on the British official statistics, 63,811 Chinese laborers were shipped from China and the number that arrived in the Rand was 62,960.[65]
2. From China: Based on a 1906 report from South Africa consul Liu Yulin, at the time there were 47,212 Chinese laborers mining in South Africa; adding to it the 16,000 worker permits issued to the Chinese laborers who had yet to arrive, the total came to be 63,212.[66]
3. From Chinese scholars: (1) One claim is that the workers numbered 50,000. Li Changfu believed that "Chinese laborers in South Africa originated in 1904; they were indentured laborers recruited by England. The number reached 55,000 at its peak."[67] Based on this claim, Chen Zexian stated, "The British recruited 55,000 Chinese laborers from Yan Tai and Qing Huang Dao, and then shipped them to Transvaal."[68] Ai Zhouchang and Chen Bisheng also believed this claim.[69] Most of the Chinese scholars studying overseas Chinese agreed on this claim as well as Taiwanese scholars.[70] (2) A second claim is that the workers numbered 70,000. Chen Hansheng stated, "From 1904 to 1910, over 70,000 Chinese coolies traveled to South Africa."[71] Peng Jiali also wrote, "There were over 70,000 Chinese laborers abducted to South Africa by the British."[72] (3) A third claim is that the workers numbered 150,000. Xu Yipu stated that "in the past, many scholars merely used the 55,000 'going abroad' statistics collected in Tian Jin and Qing Huang Dao. This apparently was an incomplete count. Based on analysis of currently available data, our estimate is around 150,000." In the same article, he also stated, "The recruitment number exceeded 200,000."[73]
4. From non-Chinese scholars: Peter Richardson, conducting research based on Transvaal government files and mining administrative documents, believed that from the first group in June 1904 to the last group in 1907, there had been thirty-four groups of Chinese laborers exported from various Chinese ports, including three groups from Hong Kong, three groups from Da Gu, and the rest from Qing Huang Dao and Yan Tai. The total number

of Chinese laborers departing China was numbered at 63,938; the total number of Chinese laborers arriving at Port Durban was numbered at 63,695.[74]

Let us analyze the statistics of Chinese laborers based on currently available historical data. In his writings, Xie Zixiu listed the number of Chinese laborers arriving in South Africa in the first five groups.[75] Based on his calculation, the first five groups numbered 9,130. A noteworthy point here is that the five departing ports listed here match the reference data provided by Peter Richardson. And the arrival counts are basically the same.

2.3 *The First Five Batches of Chinese Laborers Arriving at South Africa's Goldmines (per Xie Zixiu)*

Date	Departing Location	Arriving Location	Number
June 6, 1904	Hong King	Durban	1,054
July 27, 1904	Tian Jing	Natal	1,969
August 1, 1904	Tian Jing	No records	1,988
Sept. 1, 1904	Da Gu	No records	2,151
Sept. 26, 1904	Qing Huang Dao	No records	1,968
Total			9,130

2.4 *The First Five Batches of Chinese Laborers Arriving at South Africa's Goldmines (per Richardson)*[76]

Boat Batch No	Departing Location	Arriving Location	Number
1	Hong King	---	1,005*
2	Da Gu	---	1,969
3	Da Gu	---	1,988
4	Da Gu	---	2,148
5	Qing Huang Dao	---	1,966
Total			9,076

By September 1904, the number of Chinese laborers recruited for the goldmines was around 9,100. This can be proven by foreign newspapers archived by the Kai Luan Coal Mine.

> *By September 30 of this year, the number of Chinese laborers employed by the Committee (Transvaal Mining Committee) had reached 9,039. In October, four steamships brought in 4,089 more laborers, which raised the total count to 13,128. We need to subtract from this number the 25 deaths and 135 released workers. The reason for the release was due to beriberi. We believe that these ill workers should be sent back to China. Therefore, the total worker count on October 31 is 12,968... Regarding the total number of Chinese laborers employed: As of October 31, it was 12,968. The following data may also be of interest to you. There are currently three steamships (i.e., Kblal, Sikh, and Inceame) in the ocean heading our way, carrying 6,246 Chinese laborers. By December 31, we should have approximately 24,000 laborers.*[77]

The two words, "our way," implied that the article was from a South African newspaper. By the end of 1904, the number of Chinese laborers arriving in South Africa had reached 24,000.

The statistics from 1905 could be obtained from another local newspaper. Based on January 10, 1906 issue of British Morning Post, at the time, the British had decided to terminate recruitment of Chinese laborers. In his telegram to the British Colonial Secretary, South Africa Governor Lord Selborne mentioned the recruitment of Chinese laborers at the time. By December 20, 1905, 47,241 laborers had arrived, and with another 14,700 laborers yet to be recruited, the total count was 61,941. Lord Selborne also specifically mentioned the number of licenses issued for importing Chinese laborers.[78]

2.5 Number of Licenses the South Africa Governor Issued for Importing Chinese Laborers in 1905

Batch No	Month	Number
1	January	4,225
2	February	5,374
3	April	1,931
4	May	3,477
5	June	2,485

6	July	1,529
7	August	2,221
8	October	2,351
9	November	13,199
10	December	3,000
Total		39,792

Judging from the telegram, Governor Selborne only held on to the 3,000 December licenses and had already issued licenses for 36,792 workers. But note that this was merely the number of Chinese labor recruits permitted by the government, not the actual recruitment counts. If we add to it the previously mentioned 24,000 Chinese laborers who arrived at the end of 1904, the total number of Chinese laborers in South Africa by February 1906 would be numbered around 61,000 to 62,000. A more believable number was the 47,241 Chinese laborers present at the end of 1905, as previously mentioned by Lord Selborne. For the entire year of 1906, Transvaal rushed in over 15,000 Chinese laborers.[79] Hence, South Africa's goldmines imported a total of 63,000 to 64,000 Chinese laborers. This is more in line with the historical facts.

In my opinion, there ought to be three benchmarks in studying this issue. First, the timing must be confirmed. We need to determine if May 1904 should be used as a boundary. In South African official archives, there were records of Chinese laborers in South Africa in the nineteenth century. If we cannot confirm the timing, we would not be able to reach an agreement. Second, the location must be confirmed, whether we are looking at the recruitment counts at a Chinese locale, the departing counts at a Chinese port, the arrival counts at a South African port, or the arrival counts at the Rand gold mine.[80] Third, the research subjects (or the concept of Chinese laborers) must be confirmed. Are the subjects of our research the Chinese laborers in South Africa, the indentured Chinese laborers in South Africa, or the indentured Chinese laborers in South African goldmines? The three concepts are different.

We need to pay attention to yet another fact. In the process of importing Chinese laborers, there always existed two different voices. The South African Boers were vehemently against the practice. Against such backdrop, it was impossible that smuggling Chinese laborers on a large scale would not have caused some kind of public response.

The Number of Indentured Chinese Laborers in Africa, 1700–1910

In summary, importing Chinese laborers by African colonies already took place on a significant scale. French colonies were the first to practice it; the fate of the Chinese laborers introduced in the Congo Free State was tragic. Spain and Portugal were stealthy in their means of importing Chinese laborers. Those laborers in German East Africa mainly served in railway construction. And of all nations involved, British South Africa imported the largest number of Chinese laborers.

So, how many indentured Chinese laborers were imported to the many African colonies? There has not been a proper count thus far. Based on the existing archival data and published research, there has only been one casual reference made by the Chinese minister to England, Zhang Deyi. On October 16, 1903, in his report to the Chinese foreign minister on the need for a treaty governing labor recruitment in South Africa, Zhang mentioned that the British had already dispatched personnel to China to conduct research on labor recruitment in China: "Once the matter is settled, if we do not plan ahead, the welfare of the Chinese laborers will be in seriously jeopardy." He also pointed out three issues regarding the welfare of the Chinese laborers and termed them the "Three Harms": wages too low, control too tight, benefits too poor. "With the 'Three Harms,' if we ignore them now and let the British do whatever they please, not only we will be allowing harm to the over 100,000 Chinese laborers already in Africa, leaving them in a helpless state; we will also be allowing harm to those who are coming. We will likely see the repeat of the labor torture incidents in Peru and Brazil."[81]

The "over 100,000 Chinese laborers already in Africa" was not an invented number. And "Africa" here was also not likely a reference to South Africa alone; it is likely to mean the entire continent. And "Chinese laborers" here should mean "overseas Chinese." Zhang Deyi was a diplomat and thus not likely to give a false account; meanwhile, he spent long periods in London, the so-called European center of politics, and thus must have been well-informed. For instance, in a confidential letter that he sent to the Chinese foreign minister on the same subject in the same year, he wrote, "There are officials and merchants returning to London from Africa nearly every month, thus it is very easy to learn about its state. The other day, the son of the taxation official Jin Denggan returned to England from South Africa and touched on this subject; he said there had already been a large number of Chinese there, but the rights enjoyed by them were far beneath those enjoyed by citizens of other countries."[82]

Chen Zexian's indentured laborer estimation chart includes African regions, but it has four shortcomings. First is its timing; his count started in the nineteenth century, but in certain regions of Africa, the introduction of indentured Chinese laborers started before this time. Second are its locations; his count was incomplete, missing places where indentured laborers were introduced, such as French Madagascar, French West Africa, British West Africa, South Africa, Portuguese São Tomé–Príncipe Islands and Spanish Fernando Po Island during 1876–1900. Third is its scope of the classification, "Chinese indentured laborer"; in his research of Chinese laborers in German Tanganyika, Chen failed to include the historical facts that Germans used Chinese laborers to build railroads. Fourth, Chen's statistics do not list the number of indentured Chinese laborers in Africa, but placed African statistics under other regions in a generalized fashion.[83] Due to lack of data, it is not possible to come up with an accurate count, at least for the moment; however, we can make a rough estimation.

1700–1800

In the eighteenth century, with the exception of Mauritius, there had been overseas Chinese in South Africa, Réunion, and Madagascar. Although the majority of them were free immigrants, we cannot rule out the possibility that some of them were indentured Chinese laborers or ex-indentured Chinese laborers. During this period, Mauritius brought in approximately 5,000 indentured Chinese laborers; among them were the well-documented three groups imported in 1760, 1762, and 1783, as well as other undocumented ones. With the exception of the ones who died on Mauritius Island, these laborers likely relocated to the South Africa region later on.[84] In this century, there were another 1,000 Chinese laborers going to other African regions, thus the total count should be 6,000.

1800–1850

From 1801 to 1850, there were two documented group of imported Chinese laborers: 1829 (400 people) and 1843 (1,000 people). Li Zhuofan counted 3,000 people from the end of 1840 to July 1843, and her chart, "List of Ships that Carried Chinese Laborers (1829–1843)" had a total count of 2,701. The numbers were calculated by the author based on data available in newspapers at the time. Among them were two groups, totaling 398 people. There was only a two-day time lapse between the arrival dates of the two ships, July 27 and July 29, respectively; both ships came from Singapore. Based on the locations, time, and numbers, this was likely the aforementioned group of 400. In 1843, there were six groups counted, with a total laborer number of 670. Based on the span of ship arrival dates (from January to July) and the number of people, these do not appear to be the same groups as the aforementioned ones. If we include the undocumented numbers, Mauritius imported approximately 5,000 Chinese laborers during this period. The most important reference was found in a government file, which listed 8,000–9,000 people from 1840 to 1844. Based on that, Mauritius brought in 12,000 Chinese laborers from 1800 to 1850.

In 1827, the Réunion government decided to import Asian immigrants. In 1829, the government issued a regulation, "On Indian and Chinese Laborers and Other Free Asian Civilians," an indication that there were already Chinese laborers at the time. The documented statistics on Chinese laborer are as follows: in 1843, the governor decided to bring in 1,000 people; in 1844, the Su Fu Lun Hao vessel delivered 54 Chinese laborers from Southeast Asia; on July 7, 1844, Ye Ya Hao shipped 75 Chinese laborers, among which six died on route. In August of the same year, Goddess Paris delivered the third group of Chinese laborers; in October, Xin Hui Gui Hao delivered 178 Chinese laborers from Singapore, which was followed by a fifth group. Most of these Chinese laborers were from Fujian and were more obedient in their demeanor. Réunion's government decided to recruit Chinese laborers directly from Fujian, China.[85] In 1845, there were two more groups from Xia Men. In 1848, there were another 4,200 Asian laborers arriving in Réunion. Upon the arrival of these laborers, to facilitate labor management, employers did not register them by nationality or names, but instead gave each worker a number and assigned tasks based on numbers. Among these laborers, there must have been several Chinese, but the exact number remains unknown.[86]

Based on this information, the total number of Chinese laborers introduced in Réunion during this period was approximately 3,500. Among records of Saint Helena, there were two groups, with a total number of 200 people. In 1816, the governor requested 350 Chinese laborers. For a certain period of time, the number of Chinese laborers on the island stabilized around 400 people.[87] If we include the Chinese brought in later on, the total number would come to 500. There were a total of 1,000 people in North Africa, islands in the Atlantic Ocean (such as Portuguese São Tomé–Príncipe and Spanish Fernando Po, both famous for their plantation economy and slavery), and South Africa. During this period, African colonies brought in a total of 17,000 indentured Chinese laborers.

1851–1900

From 1851 to 1900, in addition to the aforementioned regions, German East Africa, French Madagascar, French West Africa, British West Africa, and the Congo Free State successively brought in Chinese indentured laborers. One of the reasons for the Germans to import laborers from China was to provide labor to plantations, but the real purpose was to build the Tanga–Moshi Railroad and the Dar es Salaam–Kigoma Railroad. For these reasons, the Germans successively recruited laborers from Jiaozhou Bay and Shantou of China, Macau, and Southeast Asia. Although only four groups were documented (twice in 1892, once in 1896, and once in 1898), there had to be more than what was on record. This claim rests on two bases. First, the African colonies occupied by the Germans were still in the appeasement stage and the colonies had their own labor needs; therefore, there was a labor shortage in Africa. Second, Germany was unlike England, which had a populous colony like India and easy access to labor. Hence, from 1892 to 1900, by estimation, Germany imported 4,500 indentured Chinese laborers; among them, 2,500 were recruited from China and 2,000 from Southeast Asia. Madagascar also imported a large number of indentured Chinese laborers during this period. It was not until 1896 that the French completely conquered Madagascar. Prior to that, the French colonialists regularly brought in Chinese laborers from

China and Southeast Asia. According to a local Chinese named Xiao, a group of Chinese came to Diego Suarez in the north towards the end of the 1880s. They were Chinese laborers recruited from Guangzhou Wan. The arrival of this group of Chinese laborers actually took place in 1890. They were 500 of them.[88] This was an irregular or even illegal labor trade. In 1897, the French governor announced the abolishment of slavery in Madagascar; subsequently, the labor supply became an issue. The first officially introduced indentured Chinese laborers numbered 3,300, and arrived in Madagascar in 1896, mainly for the construction of the Tamatave–Antananarivo Road. If we include the undocumented Chinese laborers that were brought in, the total count would be around 5,000.

In the second half of the nineteenth century, the French Réunion colonial government continued entrusting French merchants in China to recruit indentured Chinese laborers. In 1852, Réunion's government brought in 27,100 Asian laborers. However, similar to the Asian laborers introduced in 1848, no data were kept on these laborers' nationalities and names, only assigned numbers. Hence, we do not know how many among these laborers were Chinese. However, because Réunion's government was experienced in recruiting Chinese laborers in the Straits Settlements and China, we can estimate the total Chinese count among this group of laborers to be around 7,000. In 1867, French once again imported indentured Chinese laborers to work in the local sugar plantations.[89] Other than the documented 2,101 Chinese laborer recruitment in 1881 and 812 Chinese laborer recruitment in 1901, the Réunion colonial government resumed recruitments from China during 1885–1901 and imported indentured Chinese laborers several times. By the end of 1901, 3,000 Chinese laborers had been recruited from Fujian. We can estimate the total Réunion imported Chinese laborer count during this period to be 12,500.

French West Africa also introduced indentured Chinese laborers during this period. As previously stated, the main purpose of importing indentured Chinese laborers was for the construction of municipal projects in Dakar—the Dakar–Saint Louis Railroad, and Kankan–Conakry Railroad. Data on the exact number of Chinese laborers involved are lacking. However, at the time, the French successively conducted large-scale recruitments in Guangzhou, Shantou, and Shanghai, and also took the effort to form a Chinese–French trading company; therefore, the number of imported Chinese laborers had to be greater than 5,000. British West Africa did not seem to have imported many Chinese laborers. The Gold Coast imported 16 Chinese laborers and quickly returned them. As for Sierra Leone, due to lack of data, we do not know the exact number. We can only estimate the number of Chinese laborers in this region to be around 500. Starting from 1892, the Congo Free State, through its agents in China, imported indentured Chinese laborers from Macau and Guangzhou. The first group of recruits numbered 542; this was also the only documented statistics during this period. Later, agents of the Congo Free State again recruited indentured Chinese laborers from places such as Guangzhou and Shantou. The Congo Free State imported 1,000 Chinese laborers during this period.

We can only estimate the number of indentured Chinese laborers imported to Portuguese São Tomé–Príncipe Islands and Spanish Fernando Po Island. The Portuguese occupied Macau, thus were able to transport Chinese laborers stealthily. Meanwhile, the plantation industries of São Tomé–Príncipe Islands were well-known. The number of indentured Chinese laborers on these islands was estimated to be 1,500; Spanish Fernando Po Island was estimated to be 500.

Another key location during this period was South Africa. Based on the research of Ye Huifen, from 1849 to the end of the nineteenth century, indentured Chinese laborers had successively surfaced in places such as Cape Town and Natal. For instance, on January 12, 1849, several Chinese carpenters arrived at Port Elizabeth; in 1857, the Cape Colony introduced a group of Chinese laborers. In 1859, a South African sugar cane company brought in a group of Chinese laborers; on August 16, 1875, 75 Chinese laborers, brought in from Mauritius by the Natal colonial government, arrived in South Africa. On November 10, 1881, 20 Chinese laborers arrived in South Africa; two in the group died en route. In 1882, 152 indentured Chinese laborers boarded a ship in Hong Kong; 126 of them arrived in South Africa safely.[90] The number of Chinese laborers introduced during this period was estimated to be around 1,000. After goldmines were discovered in South Africa, many Chinese laborers relocated here from neighboring islands, which we will not include in our count to avoid duplication.

During this period, other regions in Africa also brought in Chinese laborers. In Portuguese East Africa, the Chinese contributed to the construction of the railway between Port Beira of Mozambique and Zimbabwe during 1892–1898, and the construction of the railway between Lourenço Marques (later named Maputo) of Mozambique and South Africa during 1886–1894.[91] Based on data collected by Philip Snow, the Portuguese imported thousands of laborers from Guangdong to Mozambique. At the time, there were frequent riots in the southern region of Mozambique; it was under such difficult circumstances that the Chinese laborers built the first railway in the Portuguese East African colony.[92] Due to the lack of data, it was estimated that Portuguese East Africa imported around 3,000 Chinese laborers during this period. If we also include the imported Chinese laborers in North Africa, the Suez Canal, British East Africa, and Mauritius, there were approximately 5,000 Chinese laborers imported during this period.

1901–1910

During 1901–1910, the largest importer of indentured Chinese laborers was British South Africa. In addition to the aforementioned 63,695 people, statistics of recruited indentured Chinese laborers in South Africa must also include those South African gold miners recruited by the British prior to May 1904 and those recruited to South Africa during this period. By doing so, there should have been 70,000 Chinese indentured laborers in British South Africa during 1901–1910. Xu Yipu asserted that there were more Chinese laborers departing Chinese ports than most scholars' estimation. I believe some of the laborers were sent to the neighboring British Rhodesia and Portuguese Mozambique. Although we do not have direct supporting evidence, in the early twentieth century, British Rhodesia did enact immigration legislation to bring in indentured Chinese laborers, and Mozambique did face an increased Chinese population and the issue of illegal immigration. For example, in Mozambique, Chinese numbered 52 in 1893, 84 in 1900, and 287 in 1903. In 1906, there were indeed several Chinese from Lourenço Marques (Mupato) entering Transvaal illegally.[93] We can estimate that 500 indentured Chinese laborers were imported to each of these two colonies, which brings the total count to 1,000.

In the twentieth century, Madagascar continued bringing in indentured Chinese laborers. Two documented groups were the 764 imported in 1901 and the 3,000-plus successive recruits (shared with Réunion) during 1901–1902. In October 1901, 812 Chinese laborers on a German ship arrived in Réunion.⁹⁴ If we also include the undocumented ones, Madagascar imported approximately 2,500, and Réunion 2,500. With data lacking for French North Africa, the number there is estimated to be 1,000.⁹⁵

After its treaties with China, the Congo Free State recruited Chinese laborers from places such as Macau successively in 1901, 1902, and 1904. In 1906, it recruited approximately 500 from Hong Kong. The total number of laborers it imported from China during this period was around 2,000. The German's two railways were completed in 1911 and 1914, respectively. Building railroads is arduous work; it requires constant labor replenishment. After Jiaozhou Bay became a German concession territory in 1907, the Germans in Jiaozhou Bay directly participated in labor recruitment for their African colonies. The number of Chinese labor recruits was approximately 2,500. Other regions (including Portuguese Guinea) imported approximately 1,000 Chinese. In summary, from mid eighteenth century to 1910, Africa imported a total of 142,000 indentured Chinese laborers from China.

Fei Zhengqing in his analysis of the origins of overseas Chinese pointed out, "Nineteenth century overseas Chinese communities were built upon Western trade, Chinese and local trade (including the foreign 'coolie trade' in the nineteenth century). Similar to opium imports, exporting shiploads of indentured Chinese laborers required unofficial Sino-Western cooperation; and in the end it became co-managed by official governments."⁹⁶ The indentured Chinese laborers were major components of early phase overseas Chinese. Although they are not the ancestors of the modern-day Chinese in Africa, their experiences are tied to the Chinese in Africa.

First of all, the indentured Chinese laborers made significant contributions to the economic development of the regions in which they served. This indirectly affected local overseas Chinese communities. Some Chinese came to Africa accompanying the indentured Chinese laborers. Their main purpose for coming was to provide support to the Chinese laborers. These Chinese became the major component of early phase Chinese in Africa.

2.6 Statistics of Indentured Chinese Laborers in Africa, 1700–1910

Period	Region	Estimated people count	Total
1700–1800	Mauritius	5,000	6,000
	South Africa, Madagascar, Réunion	1,000	
1801–1850	Mauritius	12,000	17,000
	Saint Helena	500	
	Réunion	3,500	
	Other regions (North Africa, islands in Atlantic Ocean, South Africa)	1,000	
1851–1900	Tanganyika	4,500	36,500
	Madagascar	5,000	
	Réunion	12,500	
	French West Africa	5,000	
	British West Africa	500	
	The Congo Free State	1,000	
	São Tomé–Príncipe	1,500	
	Fernando Po	500	
	South Africa	1,000	
	Other regions	5,000	

1901–1910	South Africa	70,000	82,500
	Rhodesia	500	
	Mozambique	500	
	Madagascar	2,500	
	Réunion	2,500	
	French North Africa	1,000	
	The Congo Free State (Belgian Congo after 1908)	2,000	
	German East Africa	2,500	
	Other regions	1,000	
Total			142,000

Second, the arrival of the indentured Chinese laborers allowed African residents to have a preliminary understanding towards China. In some sense, this laid the groundwork for future Chinese incomers to Africa. After a number of Chinese laborers returned to China, the people in China also received a deeper understanding of Africa. The information was helpful to those struggling Chinese farmers and others in various sectors of the society who were looking for better lives in Africa. Third, the arrival of the indentured Chinese laborers also intensified the anti-Sino tendency in certain regions (such as in South Africa) and led to some colonial administrations (such as Madagascar) to increase its control over local Chinese. Although the majority of these Chinese later returned to China, there were a few who remained in Africa and started new lives with local Chinese immigrants.

CHAPTER III

THE ESTABLISHMENT OF OVERSEAS CHINESE COMMUNITIES

We recommend complying with the legislation established for government funding and regulations... in establishing a Chinese charity organization. We suggest that every licensed Chinese merchant pay 5 percent income tax to fund this charity.

—A memo from Mauritius Chinese Merchants to the colonial governor, June 22, 1890

Starting from today, all the Chinese who reside in Tamatave or its vicinity must register as a member of the aforementioned Committee within a month. All Chinese who come ashore in Tamatave are bound by this order.

—An order issued by the Tamatave, Madagascar government, December 1, 1896

Sometimes we have only one shilling. In a Chinese shop, we would be able to purchase things such as three-pence bread, three-pence cheese, three-pence sugar, and three-pence coffee. For us poor people, this is of great help... If we can let the Chinese live among us, we poor people view this as a great concession from the government.

—A plea to the government from South African whites in poverty, February 28, 1898

Lives in Africa for the early overseas Chinese were a history of pain and tears. In their struggle to survive, these Chinese came to the African continent with their fortitude and courage, and opened up a new lifeline. In the process of establishing communities, the early overseas Chinese demonstrated their hard-working nature, as well as their solidarity of spirit. This chapter will describe the pioneering experiences of the Chinese in various parts of Africa, depict their community lives (mainly their economic lives and community organization activities), and through a comprehensive analysis, identify the characteristics of early Chinese communities.

Free Immigrants among Chinese in Africa

In the nearly two centuries prior to 1910, there were 142,000 indentured Chinese laborers who came to the African continent. In both Chinese and foreign academia, there exists the view that ancestors of the present Chinese in Africa were the indentured Chinese laborers.[1] Although at the time, indentured Chinese laborers were in the majority among Chinese in Africa, many of them died on jobs while others returned to China upon contract fulfillment. Thus, the backbone of Chinese communities in Africa was composed of free immigrants. Included among the free immigrants were the prisoners who were exiled from Batavia (now Jakarta) to Cape Town and completed their sentences, Chinese who emigrated directly from Asia, and the few Chinese who remained after fulfilling their indentured contracts.

The earliest Chinese in Africa were likely the prisoners that the Dutch colonial administration shipped from Southeast Asia. In May 1638, the first Dutch governor, C. S. Gooyer, brought with him twenty-five people who were stationed in Mauritius by the Dutch East Indian Company. The population on the island later reached eighty after two ships brought in a number of people, mostly prisoners.[2] Among them, there were likely some Chinese. Van Riebeeck, who in 1652 went ashore at Table Bay in South Africa and established the Cape Colony, had seen Chinese engaging in various trading activity in Asia. In his voyage journal dated April 21, 1652, he talked about "diligent Chinese"; he made several requests to the Dutch East Indian Company to send Chinese laborers to South Africa, but the request was unsuccessful.[3]

In 1593, the Portuguese transported some Chinese to southern Africa; in 1654, Dutch colonialists transported three Chinese from Batavia, Indonesia to Mauritius. These were well-documented early Chinese immigrants arriving in Africa.[4] In 1660, a Chinese prisoner named Wancho was transported to Cape Town from Batavia. He is likely the first Chinese resident in Africa. Hereafter, Chinese in Batavia continued being sent to Cape Town as prisoners. Free immigrants already existed in the early eighteenth century. In 1702, a Chinese named Abraham Deweifu was baptized and became a protestant in Cape Town. In 1722, a group of Cape Town Chinese and free Africans formed a self-defense alliance, similar to a neighborhood militia, for emergency needs.[5] These early free immigrants likely were Chinese prisoners who had completed their sentences.

The Chinese population expanded quickly in South Africa, at least in the eyes of the European immigrants. In 1779, influenced by Adam Smith's *The Wealth of Nations*, and what Benjamin Franklin and others were doing in North America, whites in Cape Town held a secret meeting. They selected four representatives to deliver a petition in Amsterdam. In the petition, they made numerous demands, including a call for strengthening control over Chinese merchants on the grounds that some of the Chinese and Javanese ex-prisoner shop owners accepted stolen goods from slaves. This excuse was insufficient in explaining their other demands. They requested that, with the exception of ex–East Indian Company workers, all foreigners be restricted in housing, purchasing and renting properties, and also be banned from free trade and free movement.[6] One logical explanation for this is that Chinese had gradually become their business rivals and they wished to curb Chinese expansion through legislation by the Dutch administration.

3.1 Statistics on Chinese in South Africa, 1725–1882[7]

Year	Arrival or Resident	Number of People	Identity	Location
1725	Resident	2	Free black	Cape Colony
1743	Resident	38	Paroled prisoners	Cape Colony
1750	Resident	16	Free black	Cape Colony
1760	Resident	14	Free Chinese	Cape Colony

1770	Resident	5		Free Chinese	Cape Colony
1774	Resident	3		Free Chinese	Cape Colony
1775	Resident	3		Free black	Cape Colony
1814	Arrival	23		Laborer (private hiring)	Cape Colony
1815	Arrival	25		Laborer (government hiring)	Cape Colony
Jan.12, 1849	Arrival	Unknown		Laborer	Port Elizabeth
Aug. 6, 1875	Arrival	75		Laborer (government hiring)	Natal Colony
Jan. 1876	Resident	53		Laborer (government hiring)	Pietermaritzburg
Nov. 10, 1881	Arrival	18		Laborer	Port Elizabeth
Dec. 1881	Arrival	Unknown		Laborer	Port Elisabeth
1882	Arrival	126		Laborer	Natal Colony

At the time, the Dutch colonialists at Batavia were concerned about competition from local Chinese, thus they adopted policies and took measures to restrict their Chinese competitors, which of course led to resistance from local Chinese and eventually led to the Red River Affair in 1740. A large number of Chinese involved in the uprising were killed while others were exiled to the Cape Colony.[8] In the eighteenth century, a number of Chinese chose to remain in South Africa after completing their sentences. At first, they were categorized as "free blacks"; later they became "colored."[9] In the beginning of the nineteenth century, to assist with the development of South Africa, the British government asked the British representative in Guangzhou to help with recruiting immigrants from China.

Based on documentation, in 1815, a group of Chinese carpenters and masons boarded a British Royal Navy ship and arrived in South Africa; they assisted with the construction of a Christian church located near the Simonstown Shipyard. In 1849, several Chinese chefs, gardeners, and carpenters arrived in South Africa as laborers on board a British vessel.[10] In 1834, Saint Helena Island became a British Royal colony; a large number of Chinese laborers on the island were sent to the Cape Colony; some of them continued to work as laborers. Chinese continued immigrating to South Africa from China, Southeast Asia, and neighboring islands. Some came as coolies on their own initiative; some were smuggled in by the local European immigrants; others were brought in by the Cape Colony government and the Natal Colony government. According to records at the time, some Chinese immigrant laborers participated in the construction of South African ports. In 1880, several Chinese in South Africa made a special trip to Mauritius to persuade local Chinese there to immigrate to South Africa, but without much success. In the meantime, some of the new immigrants participated in local construction projects. For instance, a number of Chinese immigrants engaged in the construction of Port Durban that started in 1875.

However, Chinese immigration to South Africa did not peak until the second half of the 1880s; this was due to three factors: the discovery of goldmines, a change in Mauritian immigration policy, and the opening of railways in South Africa and Portuguese East Africa.

At the time, South Africans had successively discovered diamond and goldmines, which were very tempting for the struggling Chinese. Some of them were farmers from the Chinese coastal regions who lived in desperation under the rule of the Qing Dynasty. They were laborers available for recruitment. Since Hawaii started restricting Chinese immigrants, they had to look elsewhere. Some of them already had relatives settled in Africa, and through these relatives, they sought a way out. Others were Chinese from neighboring islands or other African regions; they came to follow their "golden dreams."

Second, in 1877, the Mauritius colonial government canceled the requirement that all foreigners must be pre-approved prior to immigration; a large number of Chinese immigrated as a result. In 1871, the Chinese population in Mauritius was 2,284; in 1881, it reached 3,549. Some of those Chinese experienced difficulty finding local jobs and had to relocate to South Africa and join the gold rush.

3.2 Statistics of Chinese in South Africa, 1904[11]

Location	Male	Female	Total
Cape Town	1,366	14	1,380
Natal	161	4	165
Transvaal	907	5	912
Total	2,434	23	2,457

Third, in 1897, railways in Transvaal and Portuguese East Africa connected; Chinese from some of the neighboring regions entered Transvaal via Delogoa Bay. Li Zhuogan believed that during 1888–1898 around 1,800 Chinese immigrated to Transvaal. A large number of them immigrated from Mauritius, Réunion, and Portuguese East Africa. In the two-year period between 1896 and 1898, there were over 1,000 Chinese arriving at Port Elizabeth in South Africa from Mauritius.[12] Of course, not all of them were free immigrants; some of them could have come as indentured laborers. By 1904, there were over 2,000 Chinese in South Africa; by 1911, the number of Chinese decreased. The majority of Chinese in South Africa came from Guangdong Province and could be grouped into those from Guangu and those from Kejia. The former mainly came from villages around Nanhai and Shunde; the latter mainly came from the Mei Xian region.[13]

3.3 Statistics of South Chinese in Africa (1911)[14]

Location	Male	Female	Total
Cape Town	804	19	923
Natal	161	11	172
Transvaal	905	5	910
Total	1,870	35	1,905

The earliest Chinese arrivals in Mauritius did leave behind their footprints. Based on *The Réunion Chinese History*, in 1750, several Chinese names were discovered on a rock in Mauritius. On April 20, 1761, the names of two Macau Chinese were recorded in the Mauritius census registration book. At the end of the eighteenth century, trade between China and Mauritius Island was very active; Mauritius exported ebony to China and imported utensils, porcelains, silk products, and bamboo furniture.[15] A military draughtsman named Milbert who lived in Mauritius during 1801–1804 wrote, "The Chinese that I met on Francis Island were discreet. They were free and did not have much contact with the slaves; they were willing to interact with companies owned by whites. They spent time leisurely, sitting in coffee shops and smoking cigarettes. They were docile and reticent."[16]

The first governor, Farquhar, encouraged immigration. He explained his view on Chinese immigrants: "The Chinese who just arrived on this foreign land feel lost. Thus, the government must give them a certain level of protection during this adjustment period, so that they can return home and convince more people to immigrate here." His previous experience in the Southeast Asian colonies allowed him to fully appreciate the importance of Chinese in the development of colonies. For this reason, he suggested a list of measures to settle Chinese immigrants, especially legislation that was fitting for Chinese immigrants. "In this fashion, we will be able to keep the Chinese, as we are the main beneficiaries of Chinese immigrants."[17]

In 1817, someone passing through Mauritius interestingly mentioned that Port Louis at the time already had "a not too big residential area occupied by yellows and called China Town."[18] Local Chinese leader Lu Caixin settled here and established a few shops. To further expand his business and to help friends and relatives back home earn a living, he decided to travel to China and recruit workers. In 1821, he received special permission from the governor of Mauritius to recruit from China; on December 3, 1826, he returned with five Chinese: Whampoo, Hankee, Nghien, Hakhim, and Ahim. Starting from the 1830s, Chinese immigrants in Mauritius began to increase.[19]

3.4 Statistics of Free Chinese Immigrants in Mauritius, 1833–1846[20]

Year	Number	Year	Number
1833	8	1842	44
1834	5	1843	49
1837	10	1844	64
1838	12	1845	45
1839	28	1846	58
1840	59		
1841	59	Total	411

Based on the above table, in fewer than fifteen years, 441 Chinese immigrated to Mauritius. Data from 1835 and 1836 are missing in these statistics. (Certainly, it is also possible that there were no Chinese immigrants in those two years.) If we also include the Chinese already living there (such as the ones who chose to stay after their labor contracts ended), there should be a total of around 600 people. In 1853, a British encountered many Chinese in the capitol of Mauritius; among them were coolies and cabinet workers.[21] In the few years prior to 1857,

202 Chinese immigrated to Mauritius from Réunion after their contracts ended.[22] In 1859, Chen Tingzhi, a Kejia person from Guangdong (Mei Xian region), and his wife Hong Shi (from Fujian) arrived in Mauritius from Singapore.[23]

3.5 Statistics of Chinese in Mauritius, 1850–1911[24]

Year	Male	Female	Total
1850	586		586
1851	1,086		1,086
1861	1,550	2	1,552 – 2,006
1871	2,284	3	2,287
1881	3,549	9	3,558
1891	3,142	9	3,151
1901	3,457 – 3,459	58	3,509 – 3,517*
1911	3,313	355 – 359	3,662 – 3,668*

Later on, the first peak of Chinese immigration in Mauritius occurred in 1860, triggered by two factors. First, southern China was in a chaotic state following the rise and fall of the Taiping Tianguo movement. A large number of refugees flooded abroad. Second, starting from 1860, overseas immigration became legal. In fact, in 1859, local officials in Guangzhou were issuing public announcements that permitted foreigners to recruit indentured Chinese laborers. Within the one-year period of 1860, the number of Chinese arriving in Mauritius reached 379.[25] In the late Qing Period, overseas Chinese immigration reached its peak. The number of Chinese immigrating to Africa also increased; they often went ashore at Mauritius first, and then relocated to other regions. Based on table 3.5, the Chinese population drastically increased after 1860. A noteworthy point here is that there were more than 400 fewer Chinese in 1891 than in 1881. A logical explanation is that some Chinese, after going ashore in Mauritius, relocated to neighboring islands or to Transvaal in South Africa where goldmines had been discovered.

The first group of Chinese in Réunion arrived on April 13, 1844 as coolies; there were 54 of them. As previously mentioned, shortly after their arrival, they were sold by two human traffickers, Merlot and Shipley, at the price of 450 francs per person. By July 1846, there were

458 Chinese coolies in Réunion. By 1848, the island had 728 Chinese; by 1862, only 415 remained. According to their contemporaries, nearly all the Chinese were merchants. In 1857, a merchant named Chen Zhangman from Fujian opened a shop in Réunion. Another merchant named Li Tianbo arrived in Réunion in 1885; he was the first Kejia person to arrive in Réunion. Afterwards, some of them immigrated to Madagascar and South Africa while other new immigrants arrived.[26]

Among the early Chinese immigrants, Liu Wenbo (whose French name is Maurice Akwon Lawson)[27] was exceptional. He was born in 1872 in Shunde, Guangdong. His father came to Mauritius in the early years. Liu Wenbo arrived in Mauritius in 1887 and quickly learned the local language. His language talent was noticed by a local Chinese leader, Affen Tank Wen, who took him in as a godson. Liu Wenbo was bright and studious. Under Tank Wen's guidance, he ran a very well-managed and successful business. After living in Mauritius for a period of time, he learned that Réunion was rich in natural resources. He suggested to Tank Wen that they should expand their business to that island. Tank Wen was impressed with the idea and provided capital for Liu to open a trading company in Réunion. In 1901, Liu Wenbo arrived in Réunion and established the first trading company built on Chinese capital in Saint Denis; the company was named Guang Liu Xin Hao. Hereafter, he remained in Réunion to manage its business. After four to five years, Guang Liu Xin Hao became established and its business expanded.[28] Afterwards, Chinese continued to come to Réunion from Mauritius.

3.6 Statistics of Chinese and Total Number of Immigrants in Réunion[29]

Year	Number of Chinese Immigrants	Total Number of Immigrants
1858	451	60,800
1862	413	72,377
1877	654	67,048
1880	608	64,411
1881	518	46,822
1892	412	37,469
1901	1,026	23,326
1907	810	12,879

The earliest Chinese in Madagascar should have all come from Mauritius and Réunion.[30] These two islands not only had Chinese residents very early on, but also maintained active trade with China. It was thus logical for people to migrate from these two small islands to the "big island." First of all, these two islands are geographically closer to China; most of the Chinese immigrants came ashore here first (especially Mauritius). Second, Mauritius is bigger, thus a more attractive destination. It appears that the first Chinese surfaced in Madagascar's records in 1862.[31] A British missionary, Ellis, discovered a family-run Chinese grocery store during his visit to Tamatave in May of that year. This piece of information offered support for two claims: at the latest, by the 1850s, there were Chinese in Madagascar; Chinese owned their own properties there. In 1866, there were already six Chinese on Bay Island.[32]

3.7 Statistics of Chinese Immigrants in Réunion, 1848–1911[33]

Year	Number	Year	Number	Year	Number
1848	728	1859	436	1878	637
1849	644	1860	420	1879	620
1850	562	1861	417	1880	618
1851	522	1862	415	1881	532
1852	503	1864	977	1887	537
1853	475	1866	1,123	1892	412
1854	460	1871	1,179	1897	547
1855	448	1872	935	1902	1,378
1856	445	1873	792	1907	810
1857	451	1875	707	1911	884
1858	445	1876	688		

However, the Chinese in Madagascar held their own beliefs. In 1939, Chen Jingbo was dispatched by the Republic of China to inspect overseas Chinese in Africa. During his visit in Madagascar, Chen interviewed an elderly Chinese, Cen Huiru, who had lived in Madagascar for fifty-six years at the time. The interview report was valuable in understanding the history of Chinese on Madagascar. The story circulating among the Madagascar Chinese was that their ancestor was Chen Ao from Shunde, Guangdong, who was a fisherman in

Mauritius. During his fishing trips, Chen Ao learned that Madagascar had vast land and few residents; he then relocated to the island with several others. Accompanying him in the relocation were three or four people from his hometown: Chen Ruxun, Chen Zu, and Chen Neng. The data, however, are no longer traceable.[34]

Ancestors of a wealthy Chinese merchant in Madagascar named Chen Guongming (from Shunde, Guangdong) engaged in trade with Mauritius. Chen migrated to Réunion and established Yuan Fa Long Shang Hao. Subsequently, during a trip to inspect his branch shops in the neighboring islands, Chen's boat was caught in a storm and landed in Madagascar; he then established Guang Li Rong Shang Hao on the island in Tamatave. In 1883, the French colonial military ordered him to supply its troops. This shows that Chen's business was significant in size. After the French occupied Madagascar, due to Chen's contribution in supplying the troops, he was awarded the rank of four-star general. Chen later returned to China in his old age and turned over Guang Li Rong Shang Hao to his cousin Chen Qiu, but he still kept his military rank. In 1886, fifteen Mauritius Chinese merchants arrived in Tamatave, Madagascar. Towards the end of the nineteenth century and early twentieth century, some of the Chinese laborers recruited by the French colonial government also remained here; records were found with names such as Wu De and Deng Xian from Mei Xian, Guangdong.

The earliest arrivals in the Diego region of northern Madagascar were indentured Chinese laborers; subsequently, Wei Shunfa and others from Fujian migrated here. They made their living by growing vegetables. From 1890 to 1892, Deng Jingxiu, Chen Mingjing, Liang Wenrui, and He Zhao from Shunde, Guangdong, moved here to conduct trade; other Chinese engaged in planting and trading coffee and vanilla for a living. Also included among the early Chinese pioneers were: Guo Yafu of Jia Ying and Mai Jing of Fan Yu in the southern city of Fianarantsoa; in Antananarivo, Huo Sen, Cen Shangsheng, Liang Xuan, Li Mo of Shunde; and latecomers Guan Xin, Guan Tang, Huo Chen, Huo Ying, Cen Yiteng, Cen Tang, and Liang Qiu and others. The majority of these people migrated from Mauritius and Réunion after the French completed its occupation in Madagascar. Their number visibly increased.

3.8 Number of Chinese Immigrants in Madagascar, 1862–1910[35]

Year	Number	Year	Number
1862	1	1903	284
1866	6	1904	452
1893	40	1905	460
1896	190 *	1905	463
1897	195 *	1909	512
1899	62	1910	540

In the Portuguese East Africa (i.e., Mozambique), Chinese started migrating towards Lourenço Marques in the late nineteenth century. The majority of early Chinese came from Macau. The reason for their immigration was neither politics (not tolerated by the government) nor economics (given the difficulty making a living); they were exiled here by the Portuguese government. Two Chinese who were still alive in the 1930s made this revelation: While in exile, they were required to perform hard labor, clearing forests and lands. Many of them died from the harsh climate. At the end of their exile, they were set free to survive on their own, with no help from the government. All the exiles had to survive using their own stamina. At the time, the Lourenço Marques region was barren; it was the strength and perseverance of these Chinese that helped to transform this desolate land into a land of prosperity.[36]

Subsequently, a number of craftsmen from Guangdong Province arrived. The first group of immigrants came in the last two or three decades of the nineteenth century. Most of them settled in the Lourenço Marques region; some of them set up trade shops. At the turn of the nineteenth and twentieth century, Chinese living in Mozambique competed with Indians and a small number of Eastern Europeans in selling alcohol products.[37] In 1903, a Chinese pioneer carpenter/architect named Ja Assam donated a piece of land to the Chinese community in Lourenço Marques (Maputo) to build a "China Pavilion." Later on, a Chinese school was established here by a community committee. In 1893, there were 52 Chinese in Lourenço Marques; by 1903, it was increased to 287. In 1900, there were 84 Chinese. In addition to independent carpenters, some worked in Manika and Sofala for sugarcane and mining companies, while others contributed to the construction of two railways, i.e., the railway between Port Beira of Mozambique and Zimbabwe during 1892–1898, and the railway between Lourenço Marques and South Africa during 1886–1894.[38]

There were also a small number of Chinese in other African regions. For instance, among the Chinese in Seychelles, some were from Hong Kong; some were from Guangzhou; many were from West Indian Ocean Islands, especially Mauritius. In 1898, a Chinese named Low Shang filled out his citizenship application this way: "Merchant, seller, plant and process vanilla in the Bo Lou Region, age thirty-three, Chinese ethnicity, born in Guangzhou, spouse: Ya Rujia, Chinese, live in Hong Kong. Low Shang originally worked in the silk industry; he came to Seychelles on December 25, 1893 with plans to engage in trade. Since his arrival, Low has been engaged in trade, and growing and processing of vanilla. Low currently owns no property in Seychelles, but intends to live here for a few years. He hopes to obtain citizenship in Seychelles and purchase real estate properties in Seychelles."[39] In Luodili Island, there were also several Chinese. The earliest settlers were four individuals from Fujian led by Lin Wei; they migrated here from Mauritius in 1850. Lin Wei experimented with opening a shop while others joined the locals in farming and herding. Around 1910, another group of Chinese arrived here; they worked hard, established shops and engaged in minor trade.[40]

3.9 Chinese Growth in Seychelles, 1891–1911[41]

Year	Seychelles Resident Number			Chinese Resident Number		
	Male	Female	Total	Male	Female	Total
1891	8,302	9,138	17,440	44	1	45
1901	9,105	9,432	18,537	108	2	110
1911	11,557	11,134	22,691			81

The earliest Chinese counts of Chinese in Africa surfaced in the April 1907 Issue of *Wai Jiao Bao*. At the time, the number of overseas Chinese around the world was 8,954,889, with 7,000 in Africa.[42] These were estimates.

Economic Activities within the Early Chinese Communities

The activity of early Chinese communities in Africa mainly was composed of two types: economic and organizational. With the exception of new immigrants, regardless of whether he was an indentured Chinese laborer who had completed his contract obligation or a Chinese immigrant from elsewhere, nearly everyone established a small shop with his life savings. This type of small business became a model and was a common practice among early Chinese.

Most of the newly arrived Chinese were penniless. Their only means of making a living was to sell their own labor. At the time, Mauritius had a large-scale sugarcane industry; the abolition of the slave trade and slavery posed a threat to the growth of the sugarcane plantation. After the British took over Mauritius in 1810, the island's first governor, Farquhar, encouraged the importation of foreign laborers. The sugarcane plantation owners were impressed with the hard-working and persevering nature of the Mauritius Chinese immigrants from Southeast Asia and China. They viewed the Chinese as the most hard-working and reliable workforce. After several years of difficult labor work, with their small savings as seed money, the plantation Chinese laborers would start up their own small shops or retail business with the support of hometown friends and relatives.

The earliest Chinese leader, an immigrant from Fujian named Lu Caixin (also called Yaxian), established a company whose size was between that of a large department store and a small shop.[43] In 1826, Lu brought back with him five Chinese from China and hired them as employees of the "Lu Ji Company." After training these new immigrants, he let them manage his branch stores; this led to the fast expansion of his business. In 1831, he sponsored a Chinese named A Wan. From then until 1847, he was the main sponsor of all Chinese arriving in Mauritius. He settled the new immigrants in Malabar where immigrants congregated, and tried to open shops all over the island. He employed new immigrants in his shops and was the indisputable leader among local Chinese. Lu was awarded British citizenship by the local government in 1847.

Affen Tank Wen, who devoted his entire life to serving local Chinese, arrived in Mauritius on October 31, 1851 (1861 according to a different source). Upon arrival, he was employed by the largest trading firm on the island, Asim Company; he later became a shareholder of the company. Because of his integrity and his familiarity with the company operations, he was later promoted to manager.[44] Some Chinese took the lead in introducing farming to the mountainous area to expand their business. In 1850, there were 586 Chinese in Port Louis, the capitol city of Mauritius; of them, thirty-eight took the lead in moving to the rural farms. One of the authors gave this description of the situation at the time:

> In the past, at least in the several years prior to it, there were few Chinese; most of them were mobile vendors or merchants running small shops in remote areas, selling mostly products from China. Nowadays, whether judging by ability or by number, they rival the entire business community, running both retail and also small-scale wholesale businesses. They gradually dominate the best neighborhoods, carrying a wide variety of products. By now, they control the fate of the British, Creole, and French merchants.

These statements may be exaggerated, but the Chinese influence in business was apparent. By the end of the nineteenth century, "Seven hundred Chinese retailers controlled the food business, serving 311,000 residents."[45] By 1901, of the 31,515 Chinese, 2,858 (or 81.3 percent of them) were merchants. Early Chinese stores included Nan Xing Hao, opened in 1836, and the largest Yuan Long Hao, opened in 1880. In 1901, of the eighty-five large trading firms, five of them were Chinese trading firms.[46] To protect Chinese business interests, Mauritius Chinese established the Chinese Business Hall in 1908, which was later renamed to the Mauritius Chinese Business Association.

3.10 Mauritian Imports from China and Hong Kong, 1881–1910[47]

Period	Import Amount from China*	Import Amount From Hong Kong*
1881–1890	164,717	815,208
1891–1900	1,506,834	640,194
1901–1910	1,550,931	59,897

The Chinese business activities in Mauritius also stimulated China–Mauritius trade. Based on statistics in Li Zhuofan's book, in 1892, the Mauritian import amount from China was 1,642 rupees; in 1893, it was

2,472 rupees; and in 1894, it surged to 168,493 rupees. Hereafter and until 1907, trade between Mauritius and China/Hong Kong remained consistent.[48]

Like Chinese in Mauritius, Chinese in Réunion and Madagascar also experienced the transition from coolies to businessmen. In the early years, they either worked on the sugarcane plantations or worked in the shops of hometown friends and relatives. These Chinese frequently worked in their employers' branch store for a period of time, learning the trade while learning some simple local languages before starting their own business. The majority of Chinese adopted the mobile vendor style of trade. They transported daily essentials to rural areas and bartered for various handcrafts and vegetables; these mobile vendors then took the vegetables and handcrafts back to the city downtown and sold them in the streets. After doing so for a period of time, they would accrue savings and open up small shops of their own. To keep a stable customer base, they usually chose shop locations near sugarcane plantations or factories; this also solved the practicability issue for the local farm workers.

In Réunion, the first group of Chinese shops started in 1860; it quickly grew to eleven Chinese shops in the following year. By 1900, there were seventy shops. In 1911, of the 1,160 Chinese in Réunion 957 of them (or 82.5 percent) were in business.[49] In the early years, business activities among Réunion Chinese were close-knit; they were self-organized among hometown friends and relatives. This was so that they could help each other out with capital and also avoided some unnecessary costs. This type of cooperative relationship was the secret of their early success. In December 1876, four Chinese petitioned the government for permission to form a "Mutual Aid Society." In the following year, the first Chinese community organization in Réunion was established.

Chinese in Madagascar had the same business characteristics as those in Réunion: playing the roles of intermediates. The indigenous peoples seemed not to conduct much trade, and the Europeans were unfamiliar with local customs and languages and did not want to trek far for a small profit. "Under the circumstances, small-businessmen from China played an important role; they became the intermediates between the Europeans and locals."[50] In addition, Chinese were also very good in maintaining their client base. Whenever there was a road or railway construction in progress, the Chinese grocery shop would follow the progress of the construction and relocate. A mobile vendor in Fianarantsoa named Mai Jin was a typical example. With luggage on his back, Mai would travel all over southern Madagascar, making and selling sausages to Mauritius and Réunion. Later, he would follow road construction workers and sold to them various products at their construction sites and opened up Mai Jin Company branches in other regions. In southern Madagascar, Mai Jin's "business empire built with luggage on his back" is a favorite tale among Chinese.[51]

By the end of the nineteenth century, Chinese business was growing steadily, which alarmed the French colonial governor. On December 28, 1899, in a letter to the French colonial secretary, he stated that the influence of Chinese and Indian merchants were growing, "The trend indeed exists that the Asians and Africans, through certain means, hoard and monopolize retail business in several key centers in the colony. This puts our citizens, who are not fully protected by current legislations, in a disadvantage." At the time, he just assumed the position of Madagascar's governor and believed in the need to take measures:

> *The situation is clear. At the moment, I believe it is necessary that we take action. In this country, we should not permit the existence of certain Indian or Chinese large trading firms that could take over and control the market at any moment. It is beneficial to the Europeans to have Asians be retail intermediates; please note that the draft of this legislation did not include this point. However, their function should be limited to this. When certain a business situation arises, such as Chan-Soon[52] of Tamatave being the biggest merchant in the city, it would become a threat to us. If we really want to take the annuity portion of our profits from the colony and leave it for our citizens, we must immediately protect ourselves.*[53]

Business had always been the main trade for Chinese in Madagascar; it was that way in the early years and continued to be so later on. On one hand, Chinese in Madagascar imported cheap Asian products and put them on the market to compete with French merchants. Because their target customers were average workers and farmers, and their products were items such as salt, sugar, soap, petroleum, and fabrics, their sales were relatively stable. On the other hand, they actively purchased local products, such as raffia grass, coffee, pepper, cloves, vanilla, and sea turtles, and exported them to Asia. Most Chinese in the cities were retail grocers. In their shops, they carried all sorts of goods, from expensive items to a single cigarette; customers could buy anything they needed. Chinese restaurants were alike: there were high-class ones, serving upper-class customers; there were working-class ones, severing coolies and the like.[54] In 1906, Chinese in Tamatave established Nan Shun Hall. Due to strict control by the French colonial government, it was not until 1909 when this Chinese community organization was successfully registered. It was later renamed to the Chinese Business Association.

The early Chinese in South Africa experienced a more difficult time than Chinese in other regions. Some exiled prisoners remained after completing their sentences. In 1726, a Chinese in Cape Town opened a bakery; he had the help of several enslaved Africans and dispatched workers to peddle products in the street. This approach caused dismay and complaints from other bakery owners. As a result, the government issued an order to ban peddling bread in the street. In 1740, there were about ten Chinese merchants running restaurants and peddling products in the street in Cape Town. A sailor arriving in the Cape in 1772 recalled that even before their ship reached the shore, several Africans and Chinese were already peddling clothes, meat, vegetables and fruits to them in small boats. "All those products were what we sailors desired." However, the success of Chinese merchants did trigger various complaints from the Dutch merchants.

By the nineteenth century, there were more and more free Chinese immigrants engaging in business; some opened ships; some opened restaurants; some peddled goods as mobile vendors; and some worked for employers. Because of the thrifty nature of the Chinese, their business model of a small profit margin with a large market share, and their humble manners, their businesses prospered. Some white immigrant merchants started attacking Chinese from all angles, accusing them of practicing "unfair competition," claiming that Chinese "destroy local business wherever they go" and "take in all they can but give nothing in return," in spite of the irreplaceable community service that Chinese provided to the poor. In 1898, poor whites in a Johannesburg suburb submitted a petition to the government; it included services that they received from Chinese stores:

Sometimes we have only one shilling. In a Chinese shop, we would be able to purchase things such as three-pence bread, three-pence cheese, three-pence sugar, and three-pence coffee. For us poor people, this is of great help... If we can let the Chinese live among us, we poor people view this as a great concession from the government.

If the Chinese do not travel to markets in Johannesburg and Fordsburg to purchase large quantities of wood, potato, and other products and sell to us in retail, these market owners are going to be in trouble. If Chinese were not here, we poor people would have to spend at least six pence each time to purchase products in other shops...[55]

From this petition, we can tell the following. First, the Chinese shops had agile marketing tactics, offering all sorts of products to meet customers' needs based on the principle of a small profit margin and a large market share. Second, they allowed poor whites to purchase with credit in their shops. Third, Chinese businesses already reached remote areas; some white families were very pleased with and nearly dependent on the Chinese stores. Clearly, their petition not only expressed their appreciation to the Chinese shops, but also conveyed that Chinese shops had become an indispensible part of their lives. They were hoping that the government would let the Chinese stay in their community. Towards the end of the nineteenth century, Chinese in Johannesburg submitted two petitions asking for permission to remain; both petitions were signed by local whites. In 1903, whites in Transvaal submitted a petition expressing that Chinese were indispensable to the local community.[56]

Nevertheless, cries from the poor whites would not work in a society like South Africa, where white immigrants were designated the ruling class. Racial discrimination was the foundation for sustaining a white supremacy system; restricting the Chinese was inevitable. In 1909, there were ninety-four Chinese grocery stores in Port Elizabeth, having a market advantage. At the time, fifty-two were British-owned stores; sixteen were Indian-owned stores. Thus, it was not surprising that European merchants requested legislations against Asians to "exterminate these devils." The Chinese business advantage also existed in food and laundry industries.

3.11 Distribution of Chinese in South African Professions, 1905–1906[57]

Profession	Cape Colony	Transvaal
Clerk and helper	729	861
Laundry worker	263	39
Gardener	46	69
Chef	28	42
Craftsmen and laborer	21	20
Others	15	28
Total	1,102	1,059

In reality, Chinese business was trapped in a dilemma: If the business stopped growing, it would not survive; if the business continued to grow, it would attract jealousy from rivals and stir up new trouble. Under the pressure from white immigrant merchants, the Cape Town colonial government issued Legislation No. 37 on September 22, 1904; Item 17 related to various licensing requirements to regulate local Chinese business:

> *Based on this law, licenses for alcohol, mining, merchandise, imports, vending, and others cannot be issued to any Chinaman who does not hold a registration exemption certificate; these Chinamen also are not allowed to show any direct or indirect interest toward the above listed business licenses; any Chinaman without a registration exemption certificate cannot sign work contracts with anyone holding a license in mining, farming, household help, laundry, industry, or any business profession covered under this legislation.*[58]

The intent of this legislation was very clear; it was to restrict the increasing number of Chinese immigrants, especially Chinese merchants. Meanwhile, the government also set strict limits on Chinese immigration applications. Take Natal, for example: according to its statistics, in the first six months of 1897, fifteen Chinese were refused immigration; between 1900 and 1904, the colony accepted fifty-four qualified Chinese but refused 752.[59] After the British government decided to import indentured Chinese laborers for South Africa goldmines in 1904, the various South African colonies further tightened their control over Chinese immigrants. To safeguard interests of the Chinese, Guangfu

Chinese in South Africa formed a society. In 1904, Chinese in Cape Colony formed the China Federation of Trade Unions.

Chinese Organized Community Activities in the Early Years

Another aspect of the Chinese community during this period was its organized community activities. The purpose of these activities was multifaceted. First, being in a foreign land, Chinese needed to unite to overcome obstacles and to fight for their rights to survive and grow. This was their ground for establishing various community organizations. Second, Chinese strongly identified with the culture and traditions of their motherland and wanted to be watched over by their deities; this led to organized religious activities, especially ones centered on the Guandi temples. Third, to safeguard their economic interests and encourage mutual cooperation, various business societies were established on a regional basis. Fourth, following the increase of immigrants, various clan societies also spun off regional organizations.

In the early years of Chinese settlement, some Chinese community leaders stepped up on their own initiative to fight for the rights of Chinese. In 1821, Lu Caixin, a Mauritius Chinese, requested that the government allow him to immigrate to the island on his own expense; this paved the way for him to later become a local Chinese leader. In 1839, he submitted an application to the government on behalf of the Chinese requesting permission to build a Guandi temple in Port Louis; he also donated 1.5 acres of land for the construction of the temple.[60] In March 1829, a Chinese leader in Cape Colony, William Assaw, submitted a petition asking the government to designate a piece of land as a Chinese burial ground. This request was eventually approved eleven years later; on the May 1, 1840 issue of *Cape of Good Hope News*, Assaw and other Chinese leaders made the public announcement that with Chinese funding, the Chinese burial site was established, and all deceased Chinese could be buried there.[61] In April 1838, Assaw twice petitioned the government, pleading for reasonable treatment towards those Chinese laborers who migrated from Saint Helena Island.[62] During the anti–racial discrimination movement between 1907 and 1911, Chinese leaders Liang Zuojun, Ye Yuandong, and Huo Huiduan led Chinese in their indomitable struggle.

Activities centered on clan societies were even more prominent. In 1851, the number of Chinese in Mauritius increased to 1,086. People from Guangdong Nanhai and Shunde also visibly increased. In 1859, Chinese from Nanhai and Shunde established the Nan Shun Society Company, with the aims to unite fellow Chinese from the two regions and to promote close ties among its members. In 1894, the Nan Shun Society raised enough funds to build a meeting hall. On August 3 of that year, Affen Tank Wen renamed Nan Shun Society Company to Nan Shun Society. Tank Wen was named president of the organization, along with vice president Yalian Huojian, second vice president Chen Bao, and directors Chen Jiu, Guan Hou, Liang Shen, and Cen Dui. In the same year, the Nan Shun Society registered with the government. In 1902, the society was expanded to include a Guandi altar and an ancestor altar. All Mauritius Chinese from Nan Hai and Shun De—regardless of sex, age, economic and social status—were accepted as members and received equal treatment. After the establishment of the Nan Shun Society, all Chinese clans that were scattered around the islands were united, including the ones in the remote mountainous area; the organization helped new arrivals look for work and shelter, and offered free room and board to the sick and ill-adapted. This was the first Mauritius Chinese community organization; it facilitated everyday life for the local Chinese.[63]

During the Qing Dynasty's Xian Feng Period, Guangdong those from Kejia successively immigrated to Mauritius and established the Jia Ying Fellow Society. In 1869, the Jia Ying Fellow Society was renamed to Ren He Hall (later renamed again to the Ren He Society, the Ren He Hostel, and the Ren He Company), but it did not have a fixed meeting site.[64] Each year, the organization met and discussed issues at the Guandi temple built by Lu Caixin; a director and assistant directors were elected to manage business within the organization. The three groups, Fujian, Guangfu, and Kejia, gradually formed forces; other than mutual cooperation, inevitably there also existed some conflicts among the groups. In 1874, Lu Caixin died two years after he returned to China. In the same year, after routine worship and discussion in the Guandi temple, fellow Chinese from Jia Ying, including Ren He Society director Wang Yangbing and assistant directors Zhu Tang, Li Gengguang, and Wang Delu suggested the establishment of their own Sheng Di Temple. Ren He members overwhelmingly supported the suggestion and donated to the cause. It did not take long for a site to be selected (in the western part of Port Louis, the current capitol city of Mauritius) and ground broken.

At the time, there were over three thousand Chinese in Mauritius, about half of which were those from Kejia. In 1877, Ren He completed its new hall, which was the site of the later Ren He Society. The new hall was grand in scale; on its front entrance there was a couplet: "Through the Wind of Benevolence We Sail in a Foreign Land; in Politeness We Remember our Motherland." The Nan Shun Society and other local Chinese societies sent congratulatory gifts, including a horizontal inscribed board expressing their goodwill. The Ren He Society did not have its own emblem then and had not registered with the government. Its main goal was to worship Guandi and enhance ties among fellow Chinese.

In 1903, to further advance the organization's agenda, Chen Runsheng from Jia Ying gathered friends to draft the first constitution of the society and hired Yang Chunxun as its full time secretary responsible for all correspondences. On December 19, 1904, the Ren He Society submitted an application to the government and registered to become an official society, with the registration number A2215893. The purpose for the organization at the time was to "sponsor charity events for Chinese; help the needy and poor, and resolve disputes." The society offered to help poor Chinese, assist Chinese overcome daily obstacles, and resolve disputes. Whenever there was a dispute among two Chinese, neither party would want to go through the official court system; both sides would file complaints with the Ren He Society which would then resolve the issue to both sides' satisfaction. Because the Ren He Society was highly regarded by the local Chinese, it enjoyed the reputation of being the "God's Company."

In 1905, Chen Runsheng, Chen Guo, Zhu Tang, Deng Fa and others purchased a house on the New Xiao Shang Street (nowadays Josephville Street) from a Westerner; it served as short-term lodging for members and associates of the Ren He Society. On October 10 of the same year, it was registered as the Ren He Hostel, with Zhu Tang as its manager, Chen Guo as its treasurer, and Deng Fa as its associate. Its official registration number was B-95-5504. The Ren He Hostel included a market area and a Cai Shen Ye altar; it reestablished a constitution, actively recruited members, and elected a board of directors. After registering with the government, the Ren He Hostel was designated to manage properties of the Ren He Society. In this manner, the Ren He Society and the Ren He Hostel became one.⁶⁵ By the beginning of the twentieth century, although the total number of Chinese in Mauritius did not increase much, the "number of those from Kejia grew rapidly." To ensure that future Chinese generations do not forget the culture of their motherland, members with foresight on the Ren He Hostel's Board of Directors raised funds, rented a house from a local Westerner, hired a scholar from China, and established a Chinese school. This was the beginning of organized Chinese education in Africa.⁶⁶

*3.12 Early Réunion Chinese Societies*⁶⁷

Name	Founding Date	Aim	Person in Charge	Notes
Chinese Mutual Help Society	June 1877	Encourage mutual help among Chinese		Located on Joseph Street in Saint Pierre
Fujian Society	End of the nineteenth century	Encourage networking and friendship among those from Fujian		Society building foreclosed by the government due to long overdue property tax
Guangdong Society	Around 1896	Encourage networking and friendship among those from Guangdong		
Shi Chang Tang	1896	Encourage networking and friendship among fellow Chen clans from Guangdong Nanhai and Shunde	Chen Shaoguang	Located on Saint Annie Street in Saint Dennis

Li She Tang	1897	Encourage networking and friendship among fellow Zhou, Liu, Tang clans from Guangdong Shunde and Tengchong	Zhou Huanduo	Located on Saint Annie Street in Saint Dennis
Mei Xian Company	1897	Encourage networking and friendship among fellow Guangdong and those from Kejia	Chen Longchang	Located in Saint Pierre

In June 1877, Chinese in Saint Pierre, Réunion established its first "Chinese Mutual Society," located at 88 Saint Joseph Street. Its aim was to provide urgent help and offer information to fellow Chinese. Members met two to three times every month to exchange news and information. Each member paid a certain monthly due that was kept by a treasurer. When a member died, the society paid for his funeral and purchased a burial site for him. This was how organizers of the society explained their mission in a letter to the governor of Réunion:

> *The aim of the society is to establish a self-help chest with donated funds to help fellow Chinese when they encounter afflictions or hostile attacks. For the sick, disabled, poor, and elderly unable to work, the society pays for their medical expenses and burial costs. The society is governed by a council that includes a chair, a vice chair, a secretary, and a treasurer. The treasurer safeguards funding and keeps a book. All the council positions are unpaid. If a need arises, the council would check the self-help chest. The society has a registration book; in it, all members are listed. The book also includes records on members who faltered in their business or private lives. Other than charities, members of the society also organize networking gatherings via business meals, family meals, or meetings at the society. The society frequently meets to plan events at special and well-known places, in hope of setting a positive example through lawful and healthy entertainment activities. In summary, the*

goal for the members of the society is to help each other in the foundation of an honest and diligent Chinese body and protective government legislation.[68]

The Chinese in Madagascar had already formed their own organizations by the end of the nineteenth century. Here, the Chinese were more concentrated; with the exception of the few Chinese in the north, the majority of them came from Guangdong, Nanhai, and Shunde. In 1896, Tamatave Chinese formed a Chinese Association. In 1906, Tamatave Chinese established the Nan Shun Society.

Chinese in South Africa also established various clan societies. A South African society organized by those from Guangdong is worthy of special mentioning. The English name of the society was the Cantonese Club; it was the first Chinese organization in Johannesburg, established in 1898. A noteworthy point is that on its membership card, it stated, "This society was established in 1908 to resist harsh government legislation"; the year very likely was especially chosen to note its split from the Lian Wei Society in 1908. The society opened and offered services to all those from Guangdong. In 1903, the president of the society, Lai Mun James, explained the aim of his organization was to provide education and information to members, to loan books and magazines to members, and to offer a meeting or entertainment gathering location. "We have similar views as the Europeans; we are law abiding people, just like the Europeans."[69]

During his time as a lawyer in South Africa, Gandhi, the distinguished leader of the Indian independence movement, organized a nonviolent resistance movement to fight against the government's racial discrimination policy, and had forged a profound friendship with local Chinese. Gandhi visited the Chinese society and was very impressed by it.

Because Chinese do not own their own residences, they established the Cantonese Club (i.e., the Society). The place serves as a gathering location, a lodge, and a library. They signed a long-term lease for a piece of land and built a first-rate bungalow on the land. In the bungalow, everyone takes good care of the place and keeps it tidy and clean. From the inside out, the entire club looks like a pleasant European club. The club is divided into many single rooms with different signs posted, such as a painting room, dining hall, conference room, office, and library, etc.

> *Every room has its designated use which is rarely altered. The adjacent rooms were rented out to individual boarders. The entire club is clean and comfortable; any visiting Chinese gentleman can make overnight stays here. Initial membership fee is five pounds per person; annual dues vary depending on individual member's profession. The club has around 150 members who gather on Sundays to play games for entertainment. Members can also use various club facilities any time in the week.*[70]

Based on its English name, the society seemed to have been set up solely to serve those from Guangfu; in reality it was not so. Before its split, the organization served all Chinese (those from Kejia included) from Guangdong; and hence it strengthened ties among Chinese in Transvaal. Funding for these societies came mainly from donations, membership fees, and "Pumps."[71]

3.13 Chinese in South African Societies in the Late Nineteenth to Early Twentieth Centuries[72]

Name of Organization	Founding Date	Early Address	Society Leader
Cape Town Chinese Association	Prior to 1902	168 Loop St.	Tin Fat (1922) *
South Africa Gauteng Chinese Association	1903	No permanent address	Ye Yuandong, Martin Eastern
East London Chinese Association	Prior to 1905	No permanent address	Tan Pak Fah **
Port Elizabeth Chinese Association	Around 1905	No record	W. Singson
Cape Colony Chinese Association	1905	No record	Tsai Guanglou
Kimberley Chinese Association	Prior to 1908	Malay Camp	No record
Wei Yi Society	1898	Fox & Alexander Strs., Ferrierastown	Li Wenzhang, Lai Mun James

Liang Wei Society	1909	Wolhuter & Commissioner Strs., Ferrierastown	He Ling
Natal Chinese Association	1909	500 West St. Durban	L. Mundon
Uitenhage Chinese Association	Prior to 1911	No record	No record
Jia Ying Society	1895	Malay Camp	No record
Mei Xian Chinese Business Society	Beginning of the twentieth century	162 Queen St.	No record
Zhi Gong Tang	End of the nineteenth century	Secret society, no record	No record. Some believe this is the same organization as the Xing Zhong Society branch, founded after Yang Quyun arrived in South Africa in 1896.

During this period, Chinese associations were founded in South African cities such as Cape Town, Transvaal, East London, Port Elizabeth, Kimberley, Natal, and Uitenhage.

Religious events were an indispensible part of the social activities the Chinese in Africa. Like the Chinese in other regions around the world, Chinese in Africa were respectful of Guan Yu. Most Chinese communities included a Guandi temple, which was a special feature. Another noteworthy point is that all Chinese religious temples were multi-functional; they were the community gathering places, altars for venerating ancestors, and sites for family and clan activities.

In 1818, in order to have a place to worship and pray to ancestors to watch over the safety of later generations, Chinese leader Lu Caixin decided to lead the Chinese in building a Guandi temple in Lassaline, "a community center, an employment agency, a lodge, and a temple."[73] In 1839, an application was submitted to the government; those from Fujian, Kejia, and Guangfu co-financed for the project, and the Guandi temple quickly broke ground. The first Chinese temple in Mauritius and also the first temple for Chinese in Africa was inaugurated on

January 29, 1842. At the time, there were 113 Chinese in Mauritius; Lu Caixin sent out this written announcement: "I urge you, gentlemen, employers of Chinese, to allow your Chinese employees who had requested to participate in the temple's naming ceremony, because this is the first Chinese-built temple."[74] The Guandi temple still keeps a painting of Lu Caixin.

This Guandi temple is situated in an excellent location, with its back against a mountain and its front facing the ocean; its view is a wonder. Inside the temple, there was a large bell and a copper imprint, both were especially made in Guangdong and shipped to Mauritius during the construction of the temple. This temple was renovated three times, in 1869, 1890, and 1968; Chinese on the island came here regularly each year to venerate Guandi and their ancestors. Worshipers would present food (such as fruits and meat), light candles and incense, and pray for Guandi's protection. Meanwhile, there were no memorial tablets for the ancestors; the Chinese would find different means (such as burning paper money) to venerate their ancestors. Dinners were usually held after the ceremonies; there was no vending, gambling, or entertainment. It was a way to strengthen ties among fellow clan members and unite the Chinese. There were few Chinese at the time; they had limited financial resources and got along with each other well. The temple was jointly led and managed by representatives from Fujian, Kejia, and Guangfu clans. Although Kejia Chinese, Guangfu Chinese and other Chinese groups later successively built their separate Guandi temples and centered their lives on their temples and clans, this Guandi temple continued to be the most popular one and also came to symbolize the local Chinese.

In Réunion, at the end of the nineteenth century and the beginning of the twentieth century, there were already four sites for venerating Guandi and ancestors, including Shi Chang Tang and Li She Tang.[75] There were two Guandi temples in Madagascar. Chinese in northern Diego-Suarez built a Guandi temple in 1902; it was said that another Guandi temple in Tamatave had an even earlier construction date. These two temples also served as the sites of Chinese associations.[76] In 1892, a Chinese leader in South Africa, Li Shenghe, wrote a letter to the government on the subject of building a Chinese temple, asking the government to allocate a piece of land; the request was denied.[77] Because there were other community sites that could hold religious ceremonies, South Africa did not have many Guandi temples. Near the end of the nineteenth century or the beginning of the twentieth century, Chinese in Kimberley built a Guandi temple.[78]

Interior arrangements and functions among Chinese temples in Africa were similar. The altar of the residing god or goddess (such as Guandi, Tian Hou, or Cai Shen) was situated in the center of the temple, and altars of the founders and deceased situated on the two sides. The memorial tablets on the two sides were inscribed with names of the deceased to permanently commemorate those who contributed to the community. Every temple had a managing committee; members of the committee were elected to serve the community as volunteers. Other than being a place for religious ceremonies, a temple also held charitable events, group congregations, and other community activities.

In the meantime, there were also Chinese who converted to Christianity. In 1702, a Chinese named Abraham De Weifu were baptized and accepted into the Protestant Church in Cape Town. The local religious committee at the time claimed that there were two more Chinese ready to be baptized.[79] Some of the indentured Chinese laborers in South African goldmines also were converted to Christianity. Meanwhile, a few churches were permitted to distribute bibles and allowed to hold activities during Christmas, Easter, and Sundays at the mining sites. A newspaper in Johannesburg once reported that ten Chinese miners were baptized in December 1905. In December 1906, there were also Chinese laborers being baptized.[80]

3.14 Deities Worshiped by Chinese in Africa by Date

God/Goddess	Veneration Date (Based on the Chinese Lunar Calendar)
Tian Gong	January 9
Tiang Hou Sheng Mu	March 23
Guan Sheng Di Jun	May 13
Guan Shi Yin	June 19
Tu Di Shen (Da Buo Gong)	June 29

Towards the end of the nineteenth century, a converted Chinese woman in Mauritius became a local influential Chinese Christian.[81] The famous Mauritius Chinese leader Affen Tank Wen also was baptized on his wedding date, June 12, 1872, and renamed Luis. After becoming a Christian, Affen Tank Wen devoted his life to religious and charity work. He helped churches convince Chinese to convert to Christianity; to show his gratitude for the Virgin Mary's love for the Chinese, he built a Chinese religious memorial hall. In 1899, Port Louis had a plague epidemic; Effen Tank Wen built an epidemic hospital to treat sick Chinese.

We must not ignore the fact that all early overseas Chinese were singles who went abroad to earn a living. Due to the monotonous lives outside of their busy jobs, some of them became addicted to vices such as gambling, opium, and prostitution. Mahjong gambling had always existed among Chinese in Africa; it was not until after the end of World War II and the forming of new community organizations that the situation improved. Opium smoking among indentured Chinese and free immigrants was a grave issue; it was brought to the attention of the Qing Dynasty's South African Consul Liu Yi. In his letter to the Chinese Ministry of Foreign Affairs in 1908, Liu described the Chinese opium smoking situation in Transvaal and Cape Town as such: "Every province has over one thousand people; thirty to forty percent of them are smokers." To ban Chinese from smoking, he even contacted the Cape Town colonial government and Transvaal government to discuss countermeasures.[82]

At the time, in Johannesburg and its adjacent suburbs, many young women were forced into prostitution; the majority of them were Europeans. South African historian Wenslin made a systematic study of this phenomenon; he believed that this was the inevitable outcome accompanying the poor white laborers working in the gold mining industry. According to police archives at the time, these young prostitutes often sold their bodies to the Chinese merchants in the Johannesburg suburbs. This phenomenon was termed "Yellow Peril" by the English newspapers at the time. In 1911, a young prostitute in Vrededorp named Susan Broderick was "sold" to a Chinese named Ho King as his wife. Prior to it, she was sold to Afrikaans (descendents of the Dutch) several times, thus it triggered the sensational case of "Mrs. Ho King."[83]

Features of Early Chinese Community Activities

In comparison with other ethnicities, business ventures among Chinese in Africa were very successful. Besides the Chinese characteristics of being diligent, thrifty, and humble, there were several other factors involved. First, Chinese business ventures were pervasive. With a humble beginning and a diligent, hard-working nature, they went to places where the European merchants refused to go; they did work that others did not want to touch (such as long-distance trade and mobile vending). Chinese merchants trekked through sugarcane plantations in Mauritius and Réunion, mountains in Madagascar, remote regions in South Africa, all the farmland, and the immigrant region in Malabar.

Furthermore, they were very agile in their business dealings. When they first arrived, not knowing the local language, they would leave a cane on the counter for customers to point out needed items and they would use coins to negotiate prices.[84] To attract customers, Chinese would give out free candies to encourage visits from children.[85] One of the most prominent features of Chinese in Africa business was barter.

Moreover, Chinese stores frequently supported the purchasing-on-credit system, which was convenient for the poor. For instance, the Chinese in South Africa offered it to poor white families; Mauritius and Réunion Chinese offered it to sugarcane factory workers; Madagascar and Seychelles Chinese merchants all implemented the purchase-on-credit system. On one hand, it helped customers, especially the poor; on the other hand, it helped the merchants themselves in maintaining a stable customer base. The system was also referred to as the "turnover" system. Customers would visit the same store every day to purchase goods, and pay down a portion of their debt at the end of each week or at the end of each month. In the following weeks or months, customers would pay down more of the old debt while accumulating more new debt. Thus, the owners and customers became codependent; if either party failed to fulfill its end of the agreement, both parties would lose. Whenever an unexpected economic crisis or a major migration took place, those Chinese offering purchase-on-credit would suffer a financial catastrophe.

Lastly, businesses abided by the practice, "low profit margin and high market share, because friendliness brings fortune." Chinese grocery products at times seemed very insignificant, selling a single cigarette or a single cup of coffee. In reality, not only did these stores reach their goal of selling goods, but also made a good impression on its customers, which was important in maintaining a stable customer base.

In summary, the economic life of the Chinese communities during this period had the following characteristics.

The majority of Chinese experienced the difficult process of progressing from a coolie or mobile vendor to a businessman.

Early Chinese showed solidarity in their ventures, which was the basic insurance for their business success.

To protect their own interests, Chinese had their own organizations, especially business organizations.

Chinese were very agile in their business dealings, which was the reason for their success, although this often led to jealousy and unfounded accusations from white immigrants.

For early Chinese, community events revolved around religious activities. Religious activities everywhere centered on Guandi and ancestors. Why were all the early temples Guandi temples? The answer has ties to traditional Chinese culture. Guandi is also called "Guan Gong," "Guan Sheng Jun," "Guang Sheng Di Jin," or "Guan Lao Ye." Chinese needed this Guan Yu image for several reasons. First, they needed Guandi as their "guardian angel." Chinese traveled across oceans to make a living in a foreign land; they were alone and helpless; their worst fear was to die in the foreign land. Once they settled, they then wished for a safe and peaceful life and a successful career. In this foreign land, without caring relatives, material assurance, or the emotional support of living in a mainstream culture, Guandi, the "God of Merchants," "God of Fairness," and "God of Justice" became their spiritual support for overcoming obstacles.

Second, making a living in a foreign country, facing various pressures, prejudice, and fierce competition, the Chinese required solidarity and mutual support. In such an unusual environment, sincerity became a crucial element in relationships; the words "loyalty" and "honesty" had very significant meaning, too. In addition to being a "Bear Tiger General" and "God of Justice," General Guan Yu was a man who exemplified "loyalty and honesty." Guan Yu's concept of loyalty in reality was three-tiered: towards the country, towards masters, and towards friends. Being alone in a foreign land to earn a living, overseas Chinese not only missed their motherland and hometown, but they also needed the financial and emotional support of friends and relatives. The latter part was dependent upon loyalty and honesty, and Guan Yu exemplified this emotional requirement.

Third, Guan Yu by nature treated evil as a deadly foe, and showed no mercy to anything evil. Guandi had always been regarded as the god that defeated demons. Living in a foreign land and facing uncertainty, overseas Chinese prayed for good outcomes. Therefore, before major events or decisions, they visited a Guandi temple to pray for good fortune; when uncertainly hung in the air, they prayed for a happy outcome. On ordinary days, facing everyday worries and concerns, Chinese came to the temple to light incense, *kowtow* (respectful act of kneeling and bowing), and pray for Guandi's protection against mishaps.

The Chinese's persistence towards their national religion attracted the attention of some sympathetic European colonialists. Mauritian governor Pope Hennessey, in the colonial government legislators' debate session on July 20, 1886, expressed his view on Chinese. He first pointed out that based on the population ratio, Chinese paid the most tax to the treasury, had the lowest crime rate, and spent the least amount of the national budget on medical care and on collecting welfare. He then responded to the accusation that the Chinese had no religious belief.

> *You must know, they do have their own religion. For people who understand them, this is a known fact: They are a nation of people who hold great respect for their ancestors and the deceased, believing that the deceased have the same faith as they do. This is the foundation of the overseas Chinese's belief. Walking into any Chinese grocery, what will you see? You see a lit oil lamp in a corner at night. You only notice it at night; but it is actually there the entire time, right in front of the altar. This is their religion. We cannot criticize their religion because we believe our own religion is more perfect. To sum up, without a doubt, they are people with religious belief. They are one of the most religious people in the world.*

In reality, this type of persistent pursuit of religion was a way to preserve Chinese culture; it was also a means to influence fate in unpredictable surroundings.

We also noticed that the early Chinese in Africa organizations (such as societies and temples) were multifunctional organizations. First, leaders (heads, boards, and committees) were elected by members and were usually respected individuals who had financial resources, were enthusiastic towards public service, served as leaders for both religious and regular affairs in their communities, and bridged between the Chinese community and local government. Hence, through these organizations, the community found trustworthy and reliable support. For members, the organizations' functions were unlimited and far-reaching. They also gave members a sense of belonging.

Second, these organizations served their purpose of leading and managing local Chinese. Because the leaders were elected, members would ask them to resolve disputes and help them seek justice without going through the court system. Due to discrimination policies, the court system was not only ineffective, but it often brought more trouble from the government. This type of self-management and self-regulation saved members unnecessary troubles.

Third, members could get together to worship. In the early phase of immigration, Chinese were situated in a social environment entirely different from their home culture, and they were often lost in the differences. More importantly, they were uncertain about the future, manipulated by others, and lacking confidence. In this new context, praying for protection from their deities and ancestors became an important social event. Through worship, solidarity was formed.

Fourth, on Chinese New Year, Fall Festival, and other various holidays, members would gather to celebrate. On one hand, they could fully enjoy the entertainment and forget everyday worries and loneliness; on the other hand, members had the opportunity to interact with and enjoy the warmth of family and friends.

Finally, these Chinese organizations offered various services and assistance to members, such as translating official documents, providing proof of identity, and even arranging for marriages and funerals; they also assisted members with job searches, lodging, and hardship financial aid. More importantly, being in a foreign land and encountering various discriminating and unjust treatment, only through solidarity were Chinese able to prevail, overcome difficulties, and face a harsh environment. This was the main reason behind the many thriving societies among early overseas Chinese.

CHAPTER IV

OPPRESSION, DISCRIMINATION, AND PROTEST

After this legislation is issued, all Chinese who come to live in Cape Colony are deemed illegal, except for the ones with signed licenses from the governor.

—Chinese Exclusion Law, 1904

In Krugersdorp Prison, I recall that one morning there were 72 prisoners being whipped before breakfast. The reasons was that the labor department promised them five pounds per month pay, but the employer only paid two pounds; so, they refused to work.

—*The Times News*, November 4, 1904

Overseas Chinese know, actively resisting this legislation can only bring about material destruction and possibly expulsion for all Chinese. Over nine hundred overseas Chinese signed this solemn declaration to reject the shameful legislation.

—Petition to Chinese Minister to England from the Chair of Transvaal Chinese Association, Liang Zuojun, October 4, 1907

Early Chinese in Africa faced a series of difficulties and obstacles. The indentured Chinese laborer system was, in reality, modern-day slavery. Chinese laborers faced a harsh environment, strict control, and cruel penalties. By various means, they resisted oppression and searched for justice. Other overseas Chinese struggled, too. The many colonial governments established racially discriminatory policies against Chinese in Africa, so that they could take advantage of the cheap Chinese labor, but also avert the threat of Chinese competition. The Chinese community had its own special way of resisting while adapting. It is a long held view by academia that the Qing government only persecuted, not protected, overseas Chinese. This chapter, based on the historical record, does not deny the corruption of the Qing Dynasty government; meanwhile, it analyzes the actions taken by the Chinese diplomatic agencies in South Africa to protect overseas Chinese laborers and citizens. This chapter is divided into four parts: (a) treatment received by indentured Chinese laborers and their resistance; (b) discrimination policies towards overseas Chinese; (c) nonviolent resistance by the early overseas Chinese; and (d) the Qing government's policy towards Chinese in Africa.

Inhumane Treatment of Indentured Chinese Laborers

The earliest indentured Chinese laborers in Africa were employed in either railway construction or plantation labor. They received very inhumane treatment. Some employers did not fulfill their contractual responsibilities; some abused Chinese laborers; some were apathetic to their suffering and illness; and some even persecuted their families. Chinese laborers in South Africa, Madagascar, Réunion, and Mauritius often complained about and resisted the ill treatment that they received.

In 1829, the British Mauritius colonial government imported the first group of indentured laborers, including four hundred Chinese laborers and five hundred Indian laborers.[1] It subsequently imported indentured Chinese laborers a few more times. The treatment that they received was horrifying, and beyond tolerable in the view of some compassionate plantation owners. A small plantation owner named De Plavitz witnessed the torture received by some laborers. He then drafted a petition and received 9,610 signatures before submitting it to the governor. Because of it, England dispatched two investigative teams.[2] In the report published by the Royal Investigation team in 1875, there was a passage on how a plantation owner persecuted indentured Chinese laborers.

> *A Chinese named Wei Lun died suddenly; the police went to 'Meng Shu Waqi' to conduct investigation. Gu Ben (a Chinese laborer) was questioned; Gu Ben answered that Wei died from lack of medical treatment and that since the beginning of the year, no one in the plantation had seen a doctor. According to Gu Ben, on the day Mr. Berlin (the plantation owner) beat him, Mr. Berlin called him over from home and asked him why the police came to the plantation and what he said to the police. He replied that they asked him if doctors had been to the plantation this year and he told them no. Therefore, the defendant (Berlin) hit him on the body and on the head several times, and pushed him towards a bucket of boiling water. He jumped over the bucket and avoided falling into the bucket. The defendant then ran up to him, held down his hair and cut off the hair. The next day, he went to local officials to file a lawsuit, but did not have enough money to pay for a lawsuit. He had no choice but to return home.*

Afterwards, Gu Ben refused to return to work. The plantation owner then dispatched thugs to beat his wife, who was pregnant at the time. Several days later, Gu Ben's frightened wife gave birth to a dead fetus; the wife herself also died. The ruthless plantation owner was jailed for only three weeks (with additional crimes that he had committed) before being released.[3]

Indentured Chinese laborers in South African goldmines faced an even more tragic fate. They were the product of modern-day slavery. The Boers believed that importing Chinese laborers would complicate the already prominent racial tensions, while the British laborers viewed Chinese laborers as their potential rivals.[4] Because indentured labor contracts had expiration dates, owners of goldmines would do their best to extract profits from these Chinese laborers. They assigned Chinese laborers the most labor-intensive work in the most dangerous work zones. Meanwhile, they cut worker benefits as much as possible; and in security, they closely guarded the Chinese laborers. They went to the extreme to control their investments on all counts.

Lives and Treatment of Chinese Laborers in South Africa

All labor contracts of Chinese laborers in South Africa addressed worker treatment. They included employment duration, clothing, food, lodging, transportation, medical coverage, etc. In general, they had the following provisions:

1. The Chinese laborer agreed to work in a Transvaal goldmine for a three-year term.
2. The Chinese laborer would mainly engage in unskilled labor work in South Africa goldmines.
3. During the contract period, employers would provide free room and board and medical care.
4. Monthly pay was twenty-five shillings. Daily work hours could not exceed ten hours. The holiday calendar followed Chinese customs.
5. Hospital treatment for sick mine laborers was free of charge.
6. If the laborer was injured or disabled on the job, employer would provide fifty shillings (two and a half pounds) in compensation. If the laborer died from injury, employer would provide five pounds in compensation.[5]

Following their arrival in South Africa, Chinese laborers would go through physical exams and then be sent to mining sites. The condition of their dormitories varied from site to site, but seemed acceptable in general. Xie Zixiu from the Qing Dynasty once was hired as a consultant by the East Transvaal Company. In his South Africa travel journal, there were descriptions of the laborer dormitories in a mine belonging to the company. Some were specially built for the imported Chinese; these were constructed with new bricks and relatively spacious. "In the dormitory, on two sides of each room there were enough bunk beds to accommodate thirty-two to thirty-six people; the rooms had good air circulation." There were also old buildings previously housing the local African laborers. "The old buildings for the blacks now house the Chinese are lower in structure; their air circulation was not as good as in newly constructed buildings; each room accommodated sixteen people. The roof was made of white metal; on a hot sunny day, sitting in the middle was like sitting in a steaming pot."

Meals for the Chinese laborers were poor. When the Chinese laborers first arrived, meals served were rather good; Xie Zixiu also noticed it. The following is an excerpt from the British author Lionel Phillips' book, published in 1905.

> *Within the mining compound of Glen Deep Limited, there was a dining hall with a capacity of 1,500 seats. The dining hall was without a doubt tidy and clean. The kitchen was adjacent to the dining hall; inside it, there were several large containers. Among them, several contained steaming rice and several contained soup with meat and vegetables with appetizing smell. I saw one coolie, a representative of a ten-person table in the dining hall, walk towards the table that distributed food. He was handed two containers, one with rice, the other with cooked meat and vegetables; he brought the two containers back to his table; the ten people at the table then proceeded to help themselves. For the food and tea needed by the coolies, there was no quantity limit; allocation of meat was also adequate. I have overheard a conversation between two coolies; one of them said, 'We live really well here. We get to eat white rice every day.*[6]

The reason was that those mine owners wanted the Chinese laborers to say a few kind words about the place in their letters to family back home, so that other Chinese would want to come to South Africa to work. As time progressed, the food became worse and worse. Xie Zixiu wrote: "Since my arrival, meals for the laborers became worse and worse. Unable to remain silent, I pleaded with the mine owner to not cut back on laborers' food. The owner's reply caught me by surprise: 'The mining business is not picking up and the workers are all very lazy. To save costs, I have to scale back on the food. Why do you even make such remarks?'" According to regulations, the laborers were entitled to three meals a day. But because it was inconvenient for the laborers to return to the dining hall for lunch, each laborer was given a piece of bread to take to the mine to eat as lunch. The bread was made from the roughest chestnuts, and the laborers found it difficult to swallow. Although the laborers were also given some meat and vegetables, the quality and quantity were limited. The laborers had to use their own money to buy supplemental food.[7]

Based on the contract, for a ten-hour workday, the compensation was one shilling (approximately the equivalent of fifty cents in Chinese currency at the time); this was very low even for the standard at the time. Chinese minister to England Zhang Yi noted that before the signing of Labor Protection Charter, he believed the compensation for Chinese laborers was even lower than the compensation for the African laborers.[8] What was even more outrageous was that after Chinese laborers arrived at the mines, the mine owners unilaterally altered the contract stipulating that each Chinese laborer must drill a two-foot hole in a rock every day; otherwise, they would not get paid. Some mine owners found ways to discount the amount of work completed by the Chinese laborers so that they could cut their pay and increase their own profits.

4.1 Transvaal Goldmine Employee Salary Chart, 1901–1910[9]

	Average Employee Numbers				Average Employee Monthly Pay					
	White	African	Chinese	Total	White	African		Chinese	
					s.	s.	d.	s.	p.
1901–1902	4,090	18,887		22,977	409	26	8		
1902–1903	10,285	48,653		58,938	444	38	6		
1903–1904	12,665	74,139	1,004	87,808	491	48	10	33	6
1904–1905	15,371	89,846	22,890	128,107	485	52	0	39	9
1905–1906	18,089	95,599	47,639	161,327	505	51	11	41	6
1906–1907	17,513	102,420	53,062	172,995	515	52	3	44	3
1907–1908	17,655	131,931	36,044	185,630	469	49	1	47	3
1908–1909	19,891	166,845	12,206	198,942	465	46	4	55	2
1909–1910	23,341	180,283	2,245	205,869	456	48	7		

From Table 4.1, we can see that up until early 1908, Chinese laborers' pay was indeed lower than that of the African laborers. Also, the laborers had to pay for their daily essentials and the price of goods in South Africa was several times higher than in China; everything cost at least three pence, which was the equivalent of thirteen cents in Chinese currency. What was worse was that the Chinese laborers' living quarters were fenced in, thus Chinese laborers could only purchase essentials within the mining compound. One Chinese laborer in South Africa exposed this in his letter: "Regardless of quality, the price of goods sold within the mining compound was ten times that of what they were sold for in stores; therefore, the monthly income of one pound five shillings was never sufficient to meet the expenses for the month. After the end of a three-year contract, a Chinese laborer would still be penniless, thus he would have no choice but to continue slaving away; some died without ever saving a single penny."[10]

The majority of Chinese laborers worked underground in the mines. Based on the 1904–1905 statistics, the percentage of Chinese laborers working in the mines was 79.18 percent, indigenous Africans 67.18 percent, and whites 42.15 percent.[11] Clearly, Chinese laborers had the highest rate of laborers working in Transvaal's mines at the time. The depth of the mines varied, with some 100–200 feet deep and some 500–600 feet deep; mechanical equipment was used to move workers up and down, but any mishaps would cost lives. Mining tasks were arduous. Chinese laborers drilled into rocks with metal sticks and blasted rocks with explosive; sometimes the rocky wall would collapse or loose rocks would fall off. Stories of Chinese miners killed by falling rocks were common. Miners also needed to be very cautious with explosives; there were times when the explosives set up by the previous team did not detonate, and if the following team was not careful, the resulting explosion could cause many casualties.

Based on Richardson's research, during 1904–1910, there were 3,192 Chinese laborers who died in Transvaal, of which 986 were caused by working conditions, i.e., on-the-job injuries.[12] This statistic was not complete. Many deaths of Chinese laborers were indirectly caused by terrible working conditions, too. Due to working underground for long periods of time, many Chinese laborers were infected with different types of diseases. The most common ones were gastrointestinal diseases, respiratory diseases, and arthritis.[13] Based on Chinese scholar Chen Zexian's calculation, during the period between May 1, 1904 and

December 31, 1906, the number of Chinese laborer deaths was 2,485; the number of disabled (i.e., those who permanently lost their ability to labor) was as high as 3,787.¹⁴

Management and Control of Chinese Laborers

Mine owners kept tight control of their Chinese laborers. To manage them, each mine had one general manager, one general supervisor, and one onsite foreman. The general supervisor was in charge of Chinese labor affairs. Most supervisors were hired from China; because they had lived in China for a long time and were familiar with Chinese customs, they would make their own decisions, change regulations, and make life difficult for the Chinese laborers. Those mine foremen, due to their unfamiliarity with Chinese language, often became emotional, punished the Chinese laborers at will, and left the Chinese uncertain of how to behave to avoid punishment.¹⁵ Douglas Blackburn once wrote a letter to the *Times* of London on the abuse of Chinese laborers in South African goldmines. In the letter he mentioned this incident:

> *I once went with a mine foreman to inspect the Chinese laborers' identification documents. After he had finished the inspection and we were about to leave, all of a sudden, two Chinese laborers ran after us while saying something aloud; they held the foreman by his arm and made hand gestures. I could tell that the foremen did not understand what they were saying because he was screaming back at the two and appeared to panic. At the end, he punched the two to the ground and called over the guards to lock them up. He subsequently beat the two men up for lack of discipline. The next day he told me in private that he made a mistake. He accidentally put the identification documents of those two in his pocket during inspection. When the two men came to ask him for their papers back, he thought they were threatening him.*¹⁶

At the recruitment site in Qing Huang Dao, the living quarters for Chinese laborers were fenced in with eighteen-foot iron bars; once a Chinese entered, he was not allowed to leave.¹⁷ After the Chinese laborers arrived in the South African goldmines, mine owners did not permit them to leave the work site or visit each other; Chinese laborers were not allowed to let their relatives stay with them, either. Anyone who kept or hid others would suffer serious consequences, with fines as high as five hundred dollars and a prison term of several years of hard labor. Mine owners paid the laborers in iron coins; other than within the fenced-in compound, no one would exchange goods for them. It was not until a laborer completed his contract term when the mine owner would exchange iron coins for gold coins based on the exchange rate. Other than the possibility of embezzlement (such as when a Chinese laborer died), the aim of this system was mainly to control the Chinese laborers' movements. Because these iron coins had absolutely no value outside the mine site, Chinese laborers without money were immobile. In this manner, Chinese laborers were "tied up like cows and horses."[18]

Sick Chinese laborers were also closely monitored as a measurement to guard against feigning illness. Worse yet, some mines built jailhouses adjacent to the onsite hospitals for jailing Chinese laborers when they were deemed by doctors to be feigning sickness. For the jailed Chinese laborers, no food but rough chestnut paste was provided. If a fellow Chinese laborer was kind enough to deliver food to the jailed man, he would also be locked up; at times, there were over thirty people in a single jail room. Doctors' diagnoses often erred. Xie Zixiu once witnessed two immobile jailed Chinese laborers; the mine owner had to order other laborers to carry them out of the hospital on wooden boards. This was sufficient evidence to prove doctor's misdiagnosis.[19]

The most important means in controlling Chinese laborers was punishment, which included lynching, lashing of the back and buttocks, expelling, ankle-cuffing, handcuffing, hanging by the arms and the braid, as well as locking the prisoner up in a pitch-dark room or depriving him of food. Very rarely were the workers sent to the judicial system. The following explores these punishments in more detail

Whipping

In the July 1904 amendment promulgated by the Transvaal government, it was stated that when a Chinese violated mining rules, he could be whipped. In the early history of Chinese labor in Africa, the main punishment used by mine owners was lashing with whips made of rhino skin.

For instance, in Norse Mine, the rules for punishing Chinese laborers were very cruel. Every worker in each shift was required to dig a thirty-six-inch hole; otherwise, he would be lashed unless there was a doctor's note proving that he was indeed ill. The torture instrument was a rhino whip, and the punishment was carried out by a Chinese foreman. The rule was to whip the buttocks until the dictated number of lashes was reached; the executioner was not allowed to stop even when the laborer was bleeding. Subsequently, the mine replaced rhino whips with rubber whips because rubber whips inflicted more pain but left little trace behind. Sometimes, short bamboo sticks would replace whips.

Handcuffing

Later on, the British government banned whipping Chinese laborers; the mine owners had to use other torture means to replace whips. Handcuffs were one of them.

This was a very painful punishment. The Chinese laborer's hands would be cuffed to a horizontal beam; the distance between the beam and the ground was arranged so that the Chinese laborer could neither stand nor sit. He had to lower his back in a half-squat position. After staying in this position for a sustained period time, a man would no longer be able to stand.

Hanging by Wrist or Braid

This punishment was conducted with a thin rope, one end tied to the left wrist of the Chinese laborer, the other end to an iron ring attached to a horizontal beam about nine feet above ground. When the rope was tightened, the left arm of the Chinese laborer rose to a position perpendicular to the ground in order for him to touch the floor with the tips of his toes. He would be hung like this for several hours. If he didn't want to be hung entirely in the air, he would have to try very hard to touch the ground with the tips of his toes.

Hanging men by their hair braids was even crueler. After being stripped of all clothing, the braid of the Chinese laborer being punished would be nailed to a wooden stake in the center of an area. The mine owner would order other Chinese laborers to circle around and watch the poor man suffer.[20]

Sometimes, a mine owner would punish Chinese laborers in person. A witness named McCarthy once saw Bridges, a goldmine owner, torture a Chinese laborer. Bridges soaked the unfortunate Chinese laborer in cold water before soaking him in hot water; afterward, the laborer was stripped of all clothing, his feet bound together, his wrists tied together with a rope, and his braid tied to his hands and hung in the air by a large nail on the doorframe. What was even crueler was that Bridges brought appetizing food and placed it right in front of the Chinese laborer for him to smell and see, but not eat. This Chinese laborer was hung like this from 7 p.m. until 11 a.m. the next morning. He was later sent to the hospital.[21]

A noteworthy point here is that the beating of Chinese laborers was supported by the British government. According to the *Times* of London, Littleton, a British colonial minister, in his Lower House response to inquiries on treatment of Chinese laborers, said that the South African legislation on regulating Chinese laborers dictated that "whipping is not used in ordinary circumstances; if a crime is committed, only stick beating is used and it cannot exceed twenty-four strikes. Furthermore, the punishment must take place in the presence of an overseeing committee member, a doctor, or a prison supervisor, and there must be a doctor's note stating that the criminal was physically fit to take the punishment; local officials were not allowed to carry out punishment without the approval of the Judiciary."[22] The outcome of a twenty-four-strike beating of a malnourished, sleep-deprived, chronically anxious miner is not difficult to imagine.

The Resistance of Chinese Laborers: Strategies and Forms

Confronting the despondent living environment and abuses by the mine owners, the Chinese laborers refused to yield. They took up different forms of resistance, which could be grouped into two categories: passive resistance and active resistance. Active resistance included two forms, nonviolent and violent. Of these, violent resistance included rioting, taking revenge on a foreman, and harassing whites (including local residents); nonviolent resistance took on forms such as strikes, refusal to pay penalties, establishing organizations, and destructive activity. Passive resistance took on forms such as passive sabotage, playing deaf, feigning illness, spreading rumors, escaping the goldmines, or committing suicide.

In 1760, French navy general Valery Giscard d'Estaing, by holding hostages, kidnapped a group of Chinese laborers to Mauritius, intending to utilize them as farm laborers. These Chinese laborers were kidnapped at gunpoint in Bencoolen (Bancoul). After arriving in Mauritius, they were under strict restrictions. The person in charge tried to coerce them to work. He gave the laborers spending money, clothes, vegetables, bacon, and alcohol; he "treated them with kindness and worked hard to win them over" so that the Chinese would help him grow crops. In a letter to his company, he wrote,

> *I gave them the castle garden, the entertainment garden of my company housing, and the company garden owned by the Count to let them grow crops; I promised to let them keep and sell the harvested vegetables on the market freely. But they showed no interest and claimed that they were merchants, not farmers. I once planned on giving them a piece of land on the island to let them establish an organization, which they again refused. In the end, I proposed that they scatter around to serve families that needed help and gain significant benefits; they still refused.*[23]

Confronting the coercion from the French colonialists, the Chinese were unmoved and united. Under the insistence of the Chinese, the French had no choice but to send these Chinese back to where they came from.

Mauritius, Réunion, and Madagascar were all famed sugarcane colonies. The Chinese laborers working on the sugarcane plantation used various means to resist meager wages and inhumane treatment, including strikes, passive sabotage, escape, and theft. Sometimes, the colonial government had to send them back home. To dodge the extremely harsh working conditions, some indentured Chinese laborers escaped into the mountains.[24] For instance, Huo Wo of Fujian, ancestor of the Chinese in Mananjary, southern Madagascar, was an indentured Chinese laborer who escaped into the mountains.[25] In other African colonies, indentured Chinese laborers in railway construction also resisted, often by escaping.

In Réunion, indentured Chinese laborers carried out resistance in various forms. Based on records from October 27, 1847 to January 26,

1848, within three short months, there were thirty-eight Chinese laborers involved in arson, theft, and assassination. Condemnations from all sides forced the colonial governor to conduct an investigation of the employers of the indentured Chinese. On one hand, the employers were displeased with the performance of the Chinese laborers; on the other hand, "nearly all the Chinese complained that the employers did not fulfill their contractual responsibility and that they received poor treatment." Apparently, seeing no way out, they had to resort to violent means to resist the unjust treatment that they received. Meanwhile, one of the undercover police involved in the investigation pointed out, "These foreigners did so in hopes of being sent back home; because of it, they acted impulsively."[26] So, why did the Chinese laborers wish to be sent back home? The explanation is simple: They could not tolerate it any longer.

Chinese laborers' resistance in South Africa was even more intense. News of riots often showed up on newspapers. Although Transvaal goldmines tightly controlled information to prevent leaks, the information still eventually got out. The British media were especially interested in such news. Starting in July 1904, the Chinese staged successive violent resistance activities.[27] A young South African policeman wrote in his letter to his parents in England,

> *The Chinamen in the mine site often caused trouble. Last week, five thousand people participated in a riot. We dispatched one hundred foot soldiers and two hundred South African security police to put it down; this was our usual task. When we charged towards them, they tossed broken bottles and rocks at us; some of us were injured. Chinamen had homemade ammunition; when they threw the bombs at us, in order to stop them we had no choice but to open fire on them. We aimed our shots low and injured many Chinamen. These people were difficult to deal with under normal circumstances; among a big crowd, they were very aggressive.*[28]

Revenge against mine foremen happened frequently as well. Due to the language barrier, Chinese laborers could not understand orders from their white supervisors or foremen, thus they often received punches, kicks, and curses from the white foremen. To counter this type of irrational punishment, Chinese laborers often returned the treatment with "rocks and wood." In Blancfirst Spirit goldmine, a white man was killed with a knife by a Chinese laborer. His body was stabbed 50 times. The reason behind the revenge was very simple: He made Chinese laborers endure hunger for long periods of time. The outcome was predictable: Four Chinese laborers were sentenced to death in a Pretoria prison.[29] It was not surprising that the author of *John Chinaman on the Rand* wrote, "Those mine owners had pictured the Chinamen to be docile and easy to manipulate; but in reality, once they reached the mine, they did whatever they wanted to do and it will continue to be this way." Although the sentiment was exaggerated, it reflected the spirit of the indentured Chinese laborers in controlling their own destiny.

To rid themselves of their slave destiny, some Chinese laborers escaped from the mine site. During the day, they would endure hunger in the wilderness and at night they would come out to seek food. The Boers hated them. Hence, it was inevitable that conflicts occurred between the escaped Chinese laborers and the Boers. On August 17, 1905, a Boer was killed by an escaped Chinese laborer, which led to extreme panic locally. On September 22, 1905, the tenth item in the "Import Labor Amendment" legislation was passed; it stated that anyone was allowed to capture Chinese laborers found outside of Transvaal without an arrest warrant. This further intensified conflict between the escaped Chinese laborers and local white residents. Between 1905 and 1906, among the Chinese laborer criminal cases, 210 involved illegal entrance of private residences.[30]

Among nonviolent resistance means, strikes were frequently used by the Chinese laborers.[31] In July 1904, Chinese laborers in the New Comet goldmine refused to work night shifts and vandalized glass windows. In October 1904, 1,400 Chinese laborers drove away administrators in a French-managed Transvaal goldmine and occupied the goldmine.

On October 24, 1904, the mine owner of the John Poore goldmine locked up two Chinese laborers due to violation of mine regulations, which led to a strike by the entire Chinese labor force. The mine owner tried various tactics in vain to coerce the Chinese laborers to return to work. In the end, the mine owner had to seek help from the local government in charge of Chinese labor affairs; forty Chinese leaders were arrested. On April 1, 1905, in the Brenda Fontaine goldmine, there was a serious Chinese laborer strike. The strike was due to a miscalculation of six-month wages by the Chinese laborers. On January 6–7,

1908, 40,000 Transvaal Chinese laborers, in support of South African Asians (Indians and Chinese) in their anti-racial and discrimination legislative fight, successively carried out strikes in various mines.

Chinese laborers also established their own secret societies, such as Hong Men. These organizations had strict codes; all members vowed to solidarity in health and in sickness. At times, the organization would decide to take revenge against a certain white foreman; the person chosen for the job would be prepared to die for the crime. In return, the secret organization would make arrangements on his behalf, including taking care of his family, so that he could carry out his duty without hesitation.[32]

The most common form of passive resistance was passive sabotage and escape from the goldmine. When a Chinese laborer got tired or hungry at the mine site, he would stop his work and squat to eat the lunch bread that he brought with him. While eating, he would ignore things that the white foreman said or did, such as punching, kicking, cursing, and persuading. After the meal, he would sometimes light up a cigarette without care. He knew full well that if productivity was low, it would not be his fault alone; the white foreman would also be held responsible. So, he often gave the reasonable reply, "I only make one shilling and I have already done enough."[33]

There were many escaped Chinese laborers from the goldmines. Between June 1904 and July 1905, 580 coolies were sentenced for lacking permission to leave their compound; 1,165 coolies receive harsh sentences for escaping, with 250 of them still at large. Between June 1904 and July 1905, there were a total of 21,205 cases of Chinese laborers violating mine regulations. From 1905 to 1906, the number of intentional escape cases among Chinese laborers increased further and reached 1,700.[34] Worse yet, some used death to rid themselves of torment and torture at the hands of mine owners. Xie Zixiu recorded such an incident. Chen Ziqing from Guangdong, who once served as a Wuping high official in the Chinese government, was lured by recruiters to South Africa to work as a miner. On October 20, 1904, he thought about his honorable past and decided not to be humiliated in South Africa; he chose to commit suicide by taking poison. Before death, he wrote the following:

After growing up and spending forty-three years of my life in China, by misfortune I arrived in this foreign land. Any hero would find himself helpless here. It is nearly impossible to return to China. Today I leave the world behind, but others continue to live in great anguish here. After completing your three-year terms, my fellow countrymen, kindly return your brother's soul back to our motherland.

There was another Chinese laborer named Chen Yingcai from Ninyi. Unable to bear the harsh labor, he attempted suicide in the dormitory lavatory; fortunately someone else spotted the attempt and rescued him. Afterwards, due to the concern that he might attempt to commit suicide again, the mine owner did not want him to work in the mine; instead, he was reassigned to work as a handyman.[35] There were different reasons behind the suicides. Some did not want to live their lives as slaves; most of these men were kidnapped and lured to South Africa without their knowledge and consent. Others could not bear the hard labor and punishment. For them, death would free them from the suffering. Regardless of the reasons, these were all acts of resistance against modern-day slavery in the goldmines. Based on Chen Da's calculation, up until June 30, 1906, forty-nine Chinese laborers committed suicide.[36]

Although the Chinese lived in a hostile environment, they adapted. They continued to survive in the harsh surroundings. Those who sang Chinese opera organized their own clubs, bought props, assigned performance roles, rehearsed, and performed on holidays on temporary stages. Some Chinese built stilts and walked among the crowd at gatherings. Some Chinese planted wildflowers around their dormitories; some raised and trained birds to follow instructions. These activities undoubtedly alleviated their homesickness and reduced the psychological pressure from oppression and abuses. Sometimes, they would hold different types of competition games with the African minors. Of course, due to loneliness, some Chinese were addicted to vices such as opium smoking and gambling.[37]

In summary, Chinese laborers found various channels to express their dissatisfaction and to resist oppression. We noticed that between late 1904 and early 1905, Chinese laborers' resistance visibly intensified. It was triggered by two factors. First, the first group of Chinese laborers who arrived in South Africa knew nothing about South Africa; all they heard was the rosy propaganda given by their recruiters. Once they arrived at the mines, their experiences and the stories they heard were totally unlike what they had pictured. Therefore, they were furious about being tricked and being abused. Second, at the time, the Chinese consul to South Africa had not yet arrived. Liu Yulin did not arrive in Johannesburg, South Africa until May 1905. It was one year between the arrival of the first group of Chinese laborers and the arrival of Liu Yulin in South Africa. During this period, Chinese had nowhere to turn, and thus they found their own ways to correct circumstances or to take revenge on mine owners.

The author of *A Chinaman on the Rand* was clearly a typical racist; he made all sorts of attacks against Chinese. However, one of his lines reveals the fundamental truth, "Without saying, the direct cause behind the Chinese committing the above listed crimes was the abuse that they received."[38]

Overseas Chinese in Context: Discrimination Policies, Infighting, and Competition with Other Ethnic Groups

For the European colonialists, there was a single purpose for importing Chinese: labor supply. When they needed labor, they encouraged Chinese to immigrate, although they still restricted immigration through guaranteed deposits, living area limitations, and a tax policy. Once they determined that the Chinese were a threat to their economic interests, they would stir up public opinion and draft laws to corral the Chinese.

In Mauritius, even during the early nineteenth century when immigration was encouraged, to receive an immigration permit, a Chinese person had to find a guarantor to provide guarantee deposits, the equivalent of $1,500. There were also restrictions on where immigrants could live. Newly arrived immigrants were not allowed to live inside the city; they had to find housing in Malabar. In 1842, Mauritian colonial government promulgated the nullification of foreigner's right to own or inherit land and real estate. When the Chinese submitted an application in 1851 requesting a piece of land for building a temple, the inspector general denied the request based on the 1842 legislation. "The only way for Chinese to build a temple was by acquiring citizenship."[39] In the second half of the nineteenth century, there were three waves of anti-Chinese movements in Mauritian politics.

Due to the abolishment of slavery, starting from the middle of the nineteenth century, Réunion, with sugarcane production as the backbone of its economy, worked hard to recruit Asian immigrants. In order to control immigration, the contracts of indentured Chinese laborers dictated that they return home after fulfilling their contracts. There were free immigrants who arrived following the indentured laborers; the government did not set any special policies regulating them. But following the growing number of Asian immigrants, the government established new policies. Those Chinese who arrived after 1897 were required to apply for residence permit as soon as they came ashore; the permit was good for three months. If a Chinese wished to remain, he must pay a "residence tax." The tax amount was based on the immigrant's salary. For those with income over 350 francs, they had to pay 150 francs in tax annually; for those with income under 350 francs, they only needed to pay half of that amount.[40]

Madagascar's immigration policy had two features. First, it grouped Chinese under "Asians" in its policy and legislation; very rarely, it established laws specifically for the Chinese. Second, the colonial government copied its "association system" from its Indochina colonies. The so-called association system was in reality an indirect ruling system. On November 3, 1896, the colonial government promulgated the 84th Legislation on Asian Immigration Matters, which included laws governing registration, fees, and tax classifications. Its major content includes the following:

1. All Asians who wish to remain in Madagascar must report to the local government within three days upon coming ashore to apply for a residence permit.
2. An applicant must provide his/her identity, profession, and intended destination; the residence permit must be renewed on January 1 of each year.
3. A male Asian immigrant age 18 or over must pay a fee of 25 francs. For those engaging in certain trades and professions, the following sales surtax must be paid: type I, II business permit holders pay 50 francs; type III, IV business permit holders pay 25 francs.

After the promulgation of the 84th Legislation, in view of the population clusters of local Chinese, the Madagascar administrator decided to organize Chinese into "associations," based on the French experience in its Indochina colonies. Each association had a designated president to facilitate member management. Starting from December

12, he ordered all Chinese in the area to register. The order promulgated on December 1, 1896 stated, "Starting from today, all Chinese living in Tamatave or its adjacent area must register as a member of the above organization within a month. All Chinese who come ashore in Tamatave must abide by this law."[41] Gallieni, the colonial governor, conducted an island-wide inspection. He noticed that the Indians and the Chinese were fast growing in the northwest and in the east, and thus decided to tighten the restriction. On July 26, 1987, the government promulgated its 829th legislation to raise the surtax for special and type I business permits to 1,000 francs, ten times the original amount; the surtax for type II and III businesses were raised to 400 francs, eight times (for type II) and six times the original amount; type IV was raised to 100 francs, four times the original amount. The intent of the legislation was to systematize the association system. Its main contents includes the following:

1. Asian immigrants (mainly Indians and Chinese) must establish associations.
2. Presidents and vice presidents were appointed by officials based on member requests and local officials' recommendations. The president of an association was in charge of association affairs and was protected by police.
3. The main responsibility of the association chair was to assist the French colonial government in managing its members, including verifying members' tax and penalty amounts. The association had the right to refuse an application; in which case, the police would directly monitor the person and specify where he was allowed to live.[42]

In December 1898, the government once again rectified the scope of the business surtax imposed on Asians. The legislation dictated that type I, II, III permit holders pay 1,000 francs; type IV and V holders pay 400 francs; type VI holders pay 200 francs; and retailers who purchased from French wholesalers pay 100 francs.

In 1902, to further restrict Asian merchants and to facilitate colonial government inspections, the Madagascar government dictated that all business books must be recorded in a local or European language. The legislation promulgated in 1904 expanded association presidents' scope of responsibility.

1. On the first of each month, the association president must report to local officials with information regarding newly joined members and departed members in the previous month, based on the membership roster.
2. The association president must truthfully report all changes that took place within the association to the local officials (such as address changes for members, deaths, departures, escapes, etc.)
3. The association president must work with the administrator to oversee its members. When necessary, he can request for help from the administrator to maintain public order.[43]
4. South Africa has its unique features. European immigrants here always held a discriminatory or even hostile mentality towards outsiders. Starting from the end of the eighteenth century, various racial discrimination legislations successively surfaced. In the 1790s, although free Africans and Chinese enjoyed various rights, they were not on equal grounds with the white immigrants. For instance, while out of town, they had to carry passes while free citizens were not bound by this regulation.[44] In the nineteenth century, the four South African colonies respectively passed many discrimination laws targeting the Chinese (or Asians).[45]

These laws were far reaching; they restricted Asians in immigration, business permits, business territories, land rights, etc. Take the example of the "Coolies, Arabs, and other Asians Legislation" (i.e., the 8th Legislation) promulgated in 1885 by the Transvaal government. This legislation nullified Asians' real estate and business rights. The legislation dictated the following:

1. Asians must pay a three-pound fee to settle or conduct business in Transvaal;
2. Asians cannot enjoy the rights of a citizen;
3. Asians cannot own fixed assets registered under his/her name;
4. Asians can only live on specified streets in specified areas.[46]

From the end of the nineteenth century until the beginning of the twentieth century, there were several openly discriminatory laws promulgated by various South Africa locations.

4.2 Discriminatory Laws Promulgated by South Africa (late 1800s to early 1900s)[47]

Promulgation Location	Legislation Name	Promulgation Year	Amendment Year(s)
Transvaal	Coolies, Arabs, and other Asians Legislation	1885	1907
Transvaal	On Labor, Asians and Chinese Regulations	1893	
Natal	Immigration Restriction Legislation	1897	1900, 1903, 1906
Natal	Merchant Wholesale Retail Permit Legislation	1897	1923, 1935, 1942
	Gold Legislation	1898	
Transvaal	On Labor Region Regulations	1898	
Transvaal	Governing Bulletin	1899	
Cape Town	Immigration Legislation	1902	1906
Transvaal	Government Bulletin	1903	
Natal	Immigration Restriction Legislation	1903	
Cape Town	Chinese Exclusion Act	1904	1906*
Transvaal	City Government Amendments	1905	1936
Transvaal	Acting Governor Bulletin	1905	
Transvaal	Nonprofit Governor Local Legislation	1906	1907
Natal	Immigration Restriction Legislation	1906	

Transvaal	Asian Legislation Amendments	1906	
Transvaal	Immigration Restriction Legislation	1907	1908
Transvaal	Precious and Lower-valued Metal Legislation **	1908	

The laws shown in Table 4.2 are representative rather than comprehensive. For instance, the 1901 law promulgated by Orange Free State prohibited Arabs, "Chinamen," coolies, and other colored Asians from living there; Asians passing through the state on their way to somewhere else were allowed to stay for seventy-two hours.[48] This legislation was not rectified until 1986 when Chinese were finally permitted to reside in the state. All the discriminatory policies brought significant economic and social inconveniences to the local Chinese. In addition to the colonial governments' discriminatory policies, Chinese communities also had to deal with natural and manmade disasters. For instance, in 1865, Port Louis and the coastal area of Mauritius had a malaria epidemic. A large number of people died; following it, there was a large-scale migration towards the central plateau region which inflicted a major financial loss for the Chinese stores that were dependent on the purchase-on-credit system.

Infighting was also an obstacle for Chinese development. In 1900, Affen Tank Wen, the Chinese leader in Mauritius, passed away. At the time, the Chinese community already had over 35,000 people, with significant numbers of those from Guangfu, Kejia, and Fujian. Lacking a well-respected leader like Lu Caixin or Affen Tank Wen, each clan rivaled the other; the three clans fought over the leadership position of Guandi Temple. After five years of futile fights, the leaders of the clans turned over the dispute to the high court for a ruling. On June 21, 1906, a Mauritian high court judge made the following ruling:

1. Leadership of the Guandi Temple was to be evenly divided among the three clans; the Guandi Temple leadership role must be rotated each year.

2. A fifteen-member governing committee was to be formed, with five representatives from each clan.[49]

This was a temporary solution. Li Zhuofan believed that the passive nature of the ruling prolonged the fight among the three Chinese clans. More importantly, due to the decentralization of power, the traditional communication between the Chinese community and the government broke down. In reality, this reflected an even more serious issue confronting the Chinese. That is, the traditional authoritative organization could not adapt to meet the needs of new developments. "At this historical juncture, Chinese once again gained a new inspiration from the structures of their home country. Based on the model of Shanghai Chamber of Commerce, established in 1902 to consolidate national resources for commercial growth, they formed a Chamber of Commerce."[50] The Mauritius Chamber of Commerce was established in 1908 (not approved by the government until 1909), the year following the high court ruling. This was an indication that the Mauritius Chinese were very keen on the ability to react to new situations.

The Chinese in South Africa also had a significant and consequential internal split during the 1907–1911 nonviolent resistance movement. At the time, Chinese held different views on whether to continue resisting. The "compromising camp" challenged the representation of Leung Quinn (also known as Leung Cuixuan), the Transvaal Chinese Association president, and broke away to establish "Lian Wei Hui." The "resistance camp" still held "Wei Yi She" as the core of their leadership. The split among the Chinese further intensified conflicts between those from Guangfu and those from Kejia because the majority of the "Wei Yi She" members were from Kejia.[51] This split significantly weakened the Chinese communities in South Africa.

Racial discrimination was a hurdle to Chinese development. Racial discrimination by the European or white immigrants was flagrant, but other immigrants also discriminated against Chinese. For instance, in the second half of the nineteenth century, the price of sugar fell in the European market. Mauritius was forced to find new markets for its cane sugar. At the time, India was the main supplier of rice in Mauritius; it quickly became a key buyer of Mauritius's cane sugar. Thus, the economy of Mauritius grew to be dependent on India. In 1877, to balance its budget, Mauritius had to adopt Indian rupees as its currency.

Although both colonies belonged to the British Empire, from the perspective of the regional economy, this measure had a significant impact on the local Chinese economy. The influence of Indian and Muslim merchants was significantly strengthened; it gradually controlled trade of rice, grains, and fabrics in Mauritius. At the time, there were fewer than three thousand Chinese on the island. Mauritius's imports from China and Hong Kong were close to zero,[52] and the supplies of the Chinese stores were controlled by Indian and Muslim merchants. To avoid interruption of product supplies, the Chinese had to give in to their demands. When a Chinese bought rice from Muslim merchants, he had to pay extra (in the local currency) for surtax per bag for the construction of mosques.[53]

REACTION AND COUNTERMEASURES OF CHINESE IN AFRICA

Nearly every colonial government had a discriminatory policy against the Chinese (or Asians). Hence, the political activities of early Chinese laborers were limited to one aspect: resistance to protect their own interests and to counter unjust immigration policy. Confronting the many discriminatory policies and developmental obstacles, the reactions and countermeasures of the Chinese included the following: self-organization, self-restraint, self-monitoring, fighting for legal rights by submitting petitions, and expressing personal viewpoints in local newspapers. And when all options were exhausted, the overseas Chinese would take the last-ditch measure of moving away.

First of all, all communities had their own societies and their own regulations and rules, as discussed in the previous chapter. The early Chinese community leaders also negotiated with the government through various means to obtain rights for the Chinese. Most of the time, while introducing or bringing in new immigrants, they preferred people from their own families, clans, or villages. As we explain this phenomenon, we should not emphasize this simply as a reflection of the rooted concept of family and clans among these Chinese's. This is only one perspective on the issue.

Looking from the angle of social control, we discover a more important factor. That is, only by introducing a familiar and a trustworthy person, such as relatives, clansmen, or friends, the character of a potential immigrant could be fully guaranteed and thus would not stir up trouble for a stable community. Under certain circumstances, community leaders would investigate the person who wished to immigrate to Africa through their Southeast Asian connections. By judiciously welcoming or rejecting potential new community members, the organizations demonstrated to the local government that the Chinese community was law abiding.

In addition, through petitions, the Chinese conveyed the unjust treatment they received and made reasonable pleas to the government (in China or to the local government). On November 7, 1844, three Chinese laborers in Réunion co-wrote a letter to local administrative officials, pleading for the permission to remain in Réunion to conduct business.[54] In 1885, a law of the South Africa Republic (Zuid Afrikaansche Republiek [ZAR]) dictated that Asians not be permitted to own real estate. This law was amended in 1886 to allow Asians to own real estates, but only within government-specified areas.[55] Chinese in Johannesburg challenged the legislation and requested that they be allowed to live in the area where they had already established their businesses. In 1902, the South Africa Republic became the British Transvaal colony. Once again Chinese petitioned the British government and the Chinese minister in England, protesting the legislation that forbade them from owning real estates. In the petition, they stated they were "peaceful, law-abiding, and diligent people, an essential part of the community; the local community also needed Chinese." These two petitions were co-signed by Transvaal whites. In 1903, local whites submitted a petition, stating that the Chinese were an essential part of their local community.[56]

On September 14, 1904, ninety-seven Durban Chinese co-petitioned the Natal colonial government, pleading to change the discriminatory legislation that required the Chinese to carry passes with their fingerprints at all times. They protested that the fingerprints were an insult to the Chinese; as in China, only criminals had to be fingerprinted for identification. After the promulgation of the Chinese Exclusion Act, Chinese in East London immediately submitted a petition to the British colonial minister; and through various means, they conveyed the fury of the Chinese community.[57] Another example was the Chinese leaders' petitions to local governments regarding the construction of temples. This demonstrated how the Chinese community fought for their religious rights.

Whenever possible, they would utilize local newspapers to dispute racially discriminatory speeches against Chinese. South African whites often held discriminatory attitudes and attacked Chinese for gambling, opium smoking, and immorality. On April 4, 1890, three Chinese co-wrote and submitted a letter to *Kimberley Diamond Mine Advertisement News*, disputing the misconceptions and attacks made by the whites.

> *'We gamble.' Indeed, we frequently enjoy taking a little risk among ourselves. Once you ban slot machines and the stock market, and expel all card players in your clubs, we shall immediately follow your admirable example. 'We smoke opium.' For now, we disregard whether this type of strictly controlled behavior is harmful in itself. Instead, we want to ask: Where did we receive the opium? If our smoking opium were evil, then you who sell us the opium would be a thousand times more evil. And in reality, you, who make laws, encourage the selling of opium. 'We are immoral.' Here, you are asking us to prove a negative viewpoint. Using your lawyers' words, the accusation is 'vague and embarrassing.' We refuse to engage in this debate; perhaps we could say that Chinese marriages are much more sacred than the European marriages that we know of.*[58]

When discriminatory policies or hostility became flagrant, Chinese would move elsewhere. Although such situation was infrequent, it occurred in Mauritius, Réunion, and Madagascar.

The biggest impact to the Chinese in South Africa were the various laws passed in the early 1900s, such as the "Labor Import Legislation" (mainly targeting indentured Chinese laborers) passed by the Transvaal government in 1904, the "Chinese Exclusion Act" passed by the Cape Colony government on September 22, 1904, and the "Asian Legislation Amendment" passed by the Transvaal government in 1907.

On September 22, 1904, the Cape Colony government promulgated the "Chinese Exclusion Act." In addition to mandating all Chinese residing in Cape Colony to register and receive exemption certificates, this legislation also regulated the granting and canceling of the certificates. For instance, article 4 permitted exemption certificates to be issued by colonial officials at will. Article 5 gave the governor the right to cancel exception certificates at will. In addition, article 12 stated, "Police officers, policemen, and administrative officials in their jurisdiction can at will ask any Chinese age eighteen and over to see his/her certificate; if unable to present a certificate, the Chinese is to be taken to local county officials for further investigation. If a violation is determined, the Chinese can be detained and sentenced based on articles in this legislation." According to article 17, "Alcoholic, mining, merchant, importer, vendor, and all other permits cannot be granted to any Chinaman without a registered exemption certificate; these Chinamen are not permitted to show any direct or indirect interest towards the above listed business permits; any Chinaman without a registered exemption certificate is not permitted to enter a contract in becoming a minor, farmer, any other profession, family helper, and laundry worker, or to work for any holder of a permit covered under this legislation." Moreover, police could search a Chinese residence at any hour.[59] Chinese in Cape Colony reacted swiftly: 1,380 Chinese in Cape Colony formed a "Chinese Society," headed by Cai Guanglou, to resist this racially discriminatory legislation.

In August 1906, the Transvaal government promulgated an "Asian Legislation Amendment" (i.e., "Asian Registration Legislation"), with a total of twenty-two articles. Its main content includes the following:

1. All Asians must re-register by a given date. All children age eight and under must be registered by his/her parents or guardians; otherwise, they would be fined or sentenced to a three-month jail term, or extradited.
2. Business licenses were granted based on registration records; no permit would be issued without registration.
3. If a policeman or a registration inspector requested to see the registration paper, the paper must be presented immediately. Registration must include fingerprints and detail all body markings and scars for permanent identification.[60]

Chinese immediately dispatched a representative, Lai Mun James, who was accompanied by Liu Yulin, the Chinese consul in South Africa, to London to submit a petition to the Chinese minister in England, asking the Chinese government to negotiate through diplomatic channels.[61] Subsequently, due to factors such as Transvaal government elections, the execution of this legislation was terminated. On January 1 of the following year, England permitted Transvaal to form a "responsible government," a notion rooted in the Westminster system of British parliamentary governance. An election was held on February 20 and a Transvaal Parliament was formed in March. In the first parliamentary meeting, the issue of the Asian Legislation Amendment came up; within twenty-four hours, it was passed after three readings and passed as the second law of 1907. This legislation was quickly approved by the British government and took effect on July 1, 1907. The Chinese community vowed that they would rather go to jail than register, and proceeded to carry out their resistance in three ways.[62]

First, Leung Quinn, the chair of the Transvaal Chinese Association, petitioned to the Chinese minister in England on October 4, 1907. Its main content included the following:

1. The legislation unreasonably grouped Chinese and Indians together. India was a British territory while China and England were allies, and the British enjoyed the most favored national treatment in China.
2. The legislation dictated that Chinese register with fingerprints. "Only slaves, no free men, would accept the legislation." Although they faced many potential consequences, the Chinese chose to boycott this legislation.
3. To assist the local government in managing immigrants, the Chinese Association already recommended that Chinese voluntarily re-register to demonstrate the sincerity of Chinese immigrants.
4. If the recommendation was refused, the Chinese Association deemed it necessary to voice strong protests to the British government.[63]

Second, in the struggle to resist the Asian Legislation Amendment and to garner fellow Chinese's support, Chinese in South Africa actively communicated with news media in China, looking for assistance. At the time, several Chinese newspapers and magazines carried news of South Africa's harsh laws against Chinese. On July 31, 1910, *Eastern Magazine* carried the bulletin by the Chinese group Wei Yi She on resisting the harsh law, which came after the fourth arrest of Liang Zuojun:

> *Liang Cuixuan, the resistance movement representative of this province* [i.e., *Transvaal*], *after being jailed and sentenced to hard labor*

three times, was arrested again on the fifteenth of this month and extradited. In the past half month, there were about twenty people sentenced to be extradited; the extradition news comes daily. Its intent was to expel all Chinese. It has been four years since this harsh legislation was promulgated by the Transvaal government. We East Asians refuse to recognize it; nearly every day there were people arrested and sentenced to hard labor; no one was immune from it. Some were jailed three or five times; some were jailed eight or nine times; some died during their prison sentences; some were bankrupted during their prison sentences; it is impossible to enumerate the suffering. The Transvaal government used tricks and persuasive tactics to lure us Asians, and followed with high-handed measures to pressure us. In the end, with barbarous means, it oppressed us and ignored treaties between China and England. Even with the many voices from righteous individuals, it proceeded to ignore them, did whatever it wanted, and carried out its cruel policies. This year, this organization reached to the following consensus:

1. This organization is devoted to resisting the harsh laws of the Transvaal government. Regardless who is arrested or extradited, stopping the Transvaal government from continuing with the harsh legislation remained our goal.

2. Leung Cuixuan, chair of this organization, has been extradited; Ye Qiyou, our English secretary, was arrested recently and is fighting extradition. One could be a chair within our organization, but to the outsiders, he is a representative of our organization. Henceforth, anyone arrested can express his own intent to resist the legislation, regardless of representation. Our independence as individuals is the foundation of our final victory.

3. With the promulgation of the Transvaal's harsh legislation, pain is felt by everyone. Henceforth, regardless of membership, this organization welcomes everyone who proclaims his unmovable position against the harsh legislation upon arrest.[64]

While the news media were sympathetic to the Chinese in South Africa and condemned the immoral behavior of the Transvaal government, they also called for the Qing Dynasty government to take measures to assist the Chinese in South Africa.

On November 10, a Chinese named Chow Kwai For inadvertently signed a registration form due to advice from his employer. After learning the truth, he was so anguished that he committed suicide. In the suicide note, he expressed his regret: "It was not merely my personal shame, I shamed my entire country. Tragically, I was momentarily blind; my deepest regrets could not undo the act. I could not face my countrymen again. I would like my countrymen to use me as a valuable lesson." This incident caused an upheaval among Chinese.[65] Liang Zuojun spoke at a major Chinese meeting to condemn the Transvaal government and held it responsible for Chow's death.

> *I despise and condemn the rumor that threats and pressure were placed on the deceased by a certain Society. But what is the lesson learned here? For us, it was indeed a big tragedy. It is not time for politeness; I furiously condemn the Transvaal government for murdering an innocent individual. The reason for the murder was none other than that he was an Asian.*[66]

Gandhi attended the meeting representing the Indians. Liang Zuojun and Gandhi, respectively representing the Chinese and Indians, concluded a friendly and mutual assistance treaty.

November 30, 1907 was the deadline for Asian registration in Transvaal. "When the Transvaal government first heard about the Chinese's resistance plan, it was furious and threatened to expel everyone who refused to register by the deadline. In reality, it had no right for expulsion. After receiving only three hundred or so registrations from Indians and three or four registrations from Chinese, it had to extend the deadline by a month. When the new deadline was reached, Asians still refused to register; thus it started arresting and jailing high-standing Chinese and Indians. But the resistance continued, regardless."[67]

On December 28, the Transvaal government arrested leaders of the Asian resistance movement, including Chinese leaders Liang Zuojun, Ye Yuandong (Easton), and Huo Huiduan (Fortoen), and others. In the Johannesburg trial, Chinese leaders presented their reasons for resisting the harsh law. Ye Yuandong claimed that as a follower of the Dao religion, "Giving fingerprints was a violation of his religious belief." Lian Zuojun stated that "the registration legislation was an insult to him as an individual and to his country." Huo Huiduan stated that "registration violated the dignity of him and his country."[68] Afterwards, Liang Zuojun and Gandhi and others wrote to the British colonial minister from their jail cells, requesting that the British government abolish this legislation, so that "we shall assert our influence and have our fellow countrymen register."[69] The government immediately dispatched representatives to meet and negotiate with Liang Zuojun and Gandhi in the jail. Both leaders made the following requests.

1. Stop all new laws.
2. Offer a three-month period for the Asians to register on their own initiative.
3. Exempt scholars, property-owners, and high-standing Asians from the fingerprint requirement and allow their signatures to substitute for fingerprints.
4. Asians who did not want all ten fingers to be fingerprinted for religious reasons are allowed to be fingerprinted on a single finger.[70]

After the negotiation, the Transvaal government and the Asian resistance movement reached an agreement on January 30; subsequently, the government broke its promises and the Asian community resumed its resistance movement. On August 23, conflicts took place in a major Chinese meeting between the "resistance camp" represented by Liang Zuojun and the "negotiation camp"; the two sides had a legal dispute on budget allocation of the Transvaal Chinese Association. On April 18, 1909, fights broke out between the two camps in Johannesburg, which led to four Chinese injured and twenty-nine people arrested.[71] This incident not only seriously weakened the Chinese resistance movement against the harsh laws, but also led to a prolonged split within the Chinese community.

Gandhi's resistance tactic was to neither petition nor appeal; Liang Zuojun, on the other hand, used various means to fight. In April 1901, Liang Zuojun once again petitioned to Chinese minister in England, asking the Qing government to urge the British government to abolish the Asian Legislation Amendment. In May, he and twenty-five other Chinese were extradited to India. In the end of December, Liang Zuojun returned to Transvaal and was arrested immediately for entering Transvaal without registration. In February 1911, the South African federal government proposed a new immigration law. Ye Yuandong, representing the Chinese, wrote a letter to the internal secretary requesting all racial segregation laws and discriminatory measures be abolished. In March, Liu Yi, the Chinese consul in South Africa, offended the South African government by his repetitive requests to abolish the harsh laws, and was called back to China.

Gandhi and General Smuts, the government's representative, reached the following agreement in May 1911: the Asian Legislation Amendment would be abolished, all passive resisters would be given the right to register, and the current rights of the Asian immigrants would be preserved. The Chinese supported this resolution. Owning to the tireless effort by Gandhi, Liang Zuojun, and others, not only did Chinese immigrants receive equal treatment, but those arrested for participating in passive resistance were also released successively. The passive resistance movement thus came to an end.[72]

The Qing Dynasty Government's Policy on Overseas Chinese

Life was difficult for the early overseas Chinese in Africa. Most definitely, they wanted their motherland to support them. Disappointingly, a weak Qing Dynasty government was powerless. Overall, the Qing Dynasty government's policy on overseas Chinese could be broken into three phases. The first phase was prior to 1860, when its overseas Chinese policy was based on hostility and watchfulness. The second phase was between 1860 and 1876, when its policy was rooted in passivity and vagueness. The third phase was after 1876, when the main feature of its policy was powerlessness.[73] Chinese in Africa originated in the Qing Dynasty; the earliest overseas Chinese were the indentured Chinese laborers abducted to Africa. Hence, the Qing Dynasty government's policy on Chinese in Africa actually originated with the intent to protect Chinese laborers' interests.

Prior to 1860, the Qing Dynasty's overseas Chinese policy was premised on watchfulness, to guard against dissidents. This was a continuation of the Ming Dynasty's policy that viewed all overseas Chinese as troublesome, low-class members of society and rebels. Therefore, beheading sentences were carried out for individuals who went abroad to conduct trade or to live. Under the Qing Dynasty laws, it was clearly stated that any official, soldier, or citizen who went overseas to engage in private trade or relocated to an island to farm would be deemed a traitor and sentenced to death. Those who knew but did not report would also receive death sentences. In 1717, the Emperor Kang Xi ordered all overseas immigrants to return and guaranteed them immunity.

After losing the Opium War, China's domestic and foreign policies reached a dead end. Under pressure from the Western powers, China was forced to open its door. In 1860, the Qing Dynasty government signed treaties with the British and the French governments, respectively, and was forced to legalize Chinese labor recruitment by the two countries. In article 5 of the China–British treaty, it was stated:

After the exchanged treaties in the Wu Wu Year, the Emperor of the Qing Dynasty sent down orders to all provincial officials, permitting all willing Chinese citizens (singles or families), who wish to go overseas to work at a British territory or any other foreign locales, to enter contracts with British citizens; they are permitted to go to any ports and are not bound by any restrictions once they disembarked the British ships. The provincial officials should also form treaties with the British royal representatives based on local situations, to safeguard the aforementioned Chinese laborers' interests.[74]

The ninth article in the China–France treaty signed in the same year contained the same content.[75]

For the citizens of the Qing Dynasty, the treaties legalized making a living overseas and settling in a foreign land, which provided alternative means for the struggling Chinese. However, for the British and the French, this undoubtedly facilitated their kidnapping of the Chinese to serve as coolies. Because of this treaty, in 1879, Shi Keqin, the French consul in Guangzhou, asked the Qing Dynasty government for permission to allow French merchants to recruit Chinese laborers on behalf of the French colonies in Africa. Judging from the above law, the Qing Dynasty government seemed to have accepted the legality of Chinese going abroad; but oddly, once a Chinese set foot abroad, he was viewed as a foreigner and not permitted to return by the government.[76] This type of self-contradictory behavior reflected the vagueness of Qing government's policy on overseas Chinese; it remained discriminatory.

In 1866, the Qing Dynasty government signed a labor recruitment treaty with the British and the French Ambassadors to China. The treaty contained twenty-two articles, providing detailed rules on

Chinese labor recruitment by the British and French citizens and their representatives. The treaty defined responsibilities of the British and French consulate officials, gave certain rights to local Chinese port officials, and dictated details such as recruitment terms, work hours, and health benefits in the recruitment contracts. In addition, the treaty also made certain explicit restrictions. For instance, article 11 stated: "In order for a Chinese citizen under the age of twenty to work overseas, there must be a written consent from his parents, stamped with the seal of the local government"; and article 22 stated: "Once a Chinese laborer couple arrives at their destination, they must not be sent to two separate work locations; children younger than fifteen must remain with their parents."[77] The signing of this treaty was an effort by the Qing Dynasty government to safeguard the interests of the Chinese laborers going abroad.

However, because this treaty to a certain degree prohibited the arbitrary way that the British and the French recruited labor in China, the two governments collaborated and used the excuse that they could not agree to article 9 of the treaty and declined to approve the treaty. Article 9 stated the following: "A contract term cannot exceed five years; upon contract completion, if the worker wishes to return to China, the employer must provide the return trip fare in full and make ship arrangements for the worker to return home." The French government thought the term too short and wanted it extended to eight years, while the British government did not want to be responsible for the Chinese laborers' return trip fare. Because the Qing Dynasty government already promulgated the treaty, the rejection by the British and the French governments allowed the British and French merchants to abuse the rights conferred in the 1866 treaty, but not bound by the responsibilities it dictated.[78] There was nothing the Qing Dynasty government could do about it.

In 1876, the Qing Dynasty government dispatched Guo Songtao to Singapore to investigate the overseas Chinese situation. In the following year, it appointed Hu Xuanze, a local Chinese leader, as its Singapore consul. This was indeed an improvement from its previous policy.[79] Unfortunately, the Qing government by this point was already riddled with gaping wounds and unable to defend itself, thus the protection that it offered to overseas Chinese was merely a formality.

As previously stated, prior to 1904, when indentured Chinese laborers were introduced in South Africa, indentured Chinese laborers were already imported into other European powers' African colonies. Even in South Africa, there were already a significant number of laborers and free immigrants. After the Boer War, mining capitalists encouraged public conversations on importing Chinese laborers, which led to the Boers' growing hostility towards the local Chinese. Because of it, the Chinese in South Africa submitted a petition to Zhang Deyi, the Chinese minister in London. In it, the Chinese in South Africa voiced their two concerns: Laws targeting the South African Asians would intensify and pose a potential threat to the Chinese in South Africa. They pleaded with the Qing Dynasty government to establish a consulate in South Africa and appoint a consul. Zhang Deyi forwarded the petition to the Chinese minister of foreign affairs. Because China and England at the time were negotiating on exporting Chinese laborers to South Africa, no immediate action was taken on the appointment of a consul. However, the significance of the petition was that it brought the existence of the Chinese in South Africa to the attention of the Qing Dynasty government.[80]

In 1904, China and England signed a labor protection treaty. Prior to the signing, the South African government already submitted to the British government the legislations and contract treaties passed by the South African parliament. After Zhang Deyi was handed the documents, he repeatedly negotiated with the British between February and May to modify some of the articles. Zhang Deyi asked to add terms such as, "Owners are not permitted to hit laborers or to trade or loan laborers as property," but was refused by the British. Zhang Deyi strived to have the Chinese government dispatch a consul to inspect the lives of the indentured Chinese laborers and to conduct negotiations as a labor representative. Although the Transvaal government was against the idea, the British government was forced to give its consent. In addition, Zhang Deyi also requested that torture be banned, and regardless of where a laborer came from, he must be returned to the same port that he originally departed from, and only British ships be permitted to transport laborers.[81] Both sides signed the treaty on May 15, 1904. But this treaty was a further infringement on Chinese sovereignty. Article one in the treaty stated the following:

> *Henceforth, whenever a British territory or an area under British protection has a need for contracted Chinese laborers, the British royal minister in Beijing will provide to the Chinese government the name of*

the British territory or British protected area, Chinese port cities where recruitments will take place and laborers will be exported from, recruitment terms, and compensation amount. The Chinese government does not need to be specially notified and will immediately notify its local officials in the port cities and request for their assistance in expediting the recruitment effort.[82]

Based on this treaty, whenever labor was needed at a British territory or a British protected area, the British government needed only to notify the Chinese government. Choices of ports, recruitment terms, and labor compensation were dictated by the British government and conveyed to the Qing Dynasty government through the British ambassador to China. The Qing Dynasty government not only had no right to voice its opinion, it also had no right to inspect the contents of the recruitment contracts. All that China had to do was to tell its local officials in the port cities to do their best in assisting the British with their recruitment effort expeditiously.

Article 13 in the labor protection treaty dictated the following:

Fees based on the number of recruits must be paid to the Chinese government for all Chinese laborers recruited under this treaty; they are to cover the recruitment-related expenses… The above fees must be paid to the custom before the ship carrying the laborers receives its red paper, and calculated as the following: for fewer than 10,000 recruits, $3 per person, and for more than 10,000 recruits, $2 per person…[83]

Judging from it, the Qing Dynasty received only a small profit in return. As Zhang Zhiliang pointed out, this was nothing but inspection exemption bribery.[84]

Objectively speaking, the Qing Dynasty government also wanted to assume the role of a powerful nation in its interaction with other nations and to protect China's sovereign right in managing overseas Chinese affairs. Establishing the South Africa consulate was a reflection of this intent. Article 6 in the labor protection treaty dictated the following:

The Emperor of the Da Qing Nation can dispatch consuls or vice consuls to a British territory or a British protected area where Chinese laborers inhabit, to oversee and protect the interests and comfort of the local

Chinese citizens and laborers; the consuls and vice consuls shall enjoy the same rights as consuls of other nations.

Prior to 1904, the British South Africa Transvaal Mining Company already started its recruitment preparation in China. After the signing of the labor protection treaty, the recruitment effort intensified, which led some Chinese officials to recognize the need to dispatch a consul to South Africa for the protection of Chinese laborers. "At the moment, a large number of Chinese laborers have been recruited and successively exported to their work sites; they are in need of protection from abuses by foreigners. Under the sixth article, a consulate and vice consulate can be dispatched[85] to oversee affairs. We should dispatch them as soon as possible to protect the interests of those laborers already exported."[86] Due to requests from the Chinese in South Africa and the need to protect Chinese laborers, the Chinese ministry of foreign affairs decided to establish a South Africa consulate and appointed Liu Yulin (Lew Yuklin) as its consul. Liu Yulin at the time was an official who had studied in the United States, and was able, insightful, and familiar with the overseas situation. His duty was well-defined: to "protect" the Chinese in British South Africa and to "oversee under one jurisdiction" the recruited Chinese laborers, and to "suppress and audit" the Chinese laborers.[87] Liu Yulin arrived at his post on April 11, 1905 (Guangxu 31). On safeguarding the interests of the Chinese laborers and local Chinese in South Africa, Liu Yulin and his successor Liu Yi (Liu Ngai) did the following three things at the minimum.

1. Reported the state of sick Chinese laborers to the Chinese ministry of foreign affairs, negotiated with South Africa and had it pay for sick Chinese laborers to return to China.[88]
2. Fought with South Africa for compensation on behalf of deceased Chinese laborers.
3. Negotiated with Transvaal government on the promulgation of the Asian Legislation Amendment and other overseas Chinese affairs.[89]

In 1906, Transvaal government passed the Asian Legislation Amendment. Leading a group of Chinese leaders in South Africa, Liu Yulin arrived in London in October 1906 to petition Wang Daxie, the Chinese minister in England, expressing the displeasure of South Chinese in Africa and asking for protection from the Qing government. After receiving the petition, Wang Daxie protested to Sir Edward Gray, the British minister of foreign affairs. A noteworthy point was that Wang only protested the registration procedures, i.e., the fingerprinting requirement, not the registration itself. His successor, Li Jingfang, went a step further and asked the British government for a resolution plan in his protest letter. Meanwhile, the Qing minister of foreign affairs met with the British ambassador to China in Beijing to strongly protest to the British government on this issue. He pointed out that based on the treaty signed by China and England in 1904, it was the British government's responsibility to protect Chinese immigrants in Transvaal, and that asking Chinese immigrants to register was a violation of the treaty.

In early June, 1907, Liu Yulin visited Lewis Botha, the Transvaal prime minister, detailing the Chinese objection. He stated that Chinese were prepared to accept harsh penalties imposed by the legislation while they also were willing to conduct their own voluntary registration. Prime Minister Botha expressed his regrets, but said that ignoring the laws would only toughen the government's stance.[90] Liu Yulin's appointment was very short. He was perfunctory with some of the local Chinese requests; but he also did his best in negotiating with the South African government on Chinese labor issues. In addition to negotiating with the local government on the Asian Legislation Amendment, he also joined the local Chinese on some of their petitions, such as asking Governor Selborne (then the highest-ranking British representative in South Africa and the governor of Transvaal and Orange Free State) to give the Chinese the right to own alcohol, which was refused.[91] Liu Yulin left his post on August 12, 1907.

The Chinese consul general in South Africa continued to negotiate with the Transvaal government. He twice sent protest letters to Transvaal governor Selborne to point out that according to Chinese laws, a registration form using fingerprinting was for criminals sentenced to death or expulsion.[92] Meanwhile, Liu Yi also wrote repeatedly to Lord Gladstone, the South Africa governor, requesting the abolition of the Asian Legislation Amendment. In his letter to General Smits, Lord Gladstone stated that Liu Yi's many demands "seemed to have exceeded the scope of responsibility as a consul." At the same time, Liu Yi also twice wrote to General Smits with the same request. Smits too felt that this Chinese consul already went beyond his scope of responsibility and refused to meet with Liu Yi. Four months later, Liu Yi was called back to China; this likely was a result of pressure from the British.[93]

The Qing Dynasty government had forcefully protested the 1906 Asian Legislation Amendment, but with its weak status as a nation and without the backing of power, the British did not respond to the protest. During his term as the South African consul, Liu Yi decided to address the opium smoking phenomenon among the local Chinese. He learned that among the Transvaal and Cape Town Chinese, "approximately thirty to forty percent" were opium smokers, and thought "admonishment alone would not work." He wrote to the Cape Town and Transvaal governments and suggested cooperation with the local government on the matter. He drafted nine measures to address the issue.

1. Chinese smokers needed to have smoking tickets that were handed out by local health officials.
2. Smokers must be examined by doctors in the health department; the smoking dosage allowed for each individual was set at the lowest possible quantity that would not harm the smoker.
3. The smoking dosage was to be reduced by one quarter every three month. Thus, within a year, smoking cessation could be reached.
4. Opium could only be sold in pharmacies.
5. Pharmacies must ask the buyers for smoke tickets and record the quantity sold.
6. Banned smoke equipment from imports.
7. All stores could sell anti-smoking pills.
8. Banned all smoking shops in the province.
9. For long-time smokers, special permission tickets were available to allow for more gradual cessation.

Although his recommendations were appropriate, the two provinces reacted differently. Cape Town had no mining Chinese laborers, and thus agreed with Liu Yi's measures. The Transvaal government, in order to manage its labor force, "had its own opium legislation to control opium supplies to the Chinese laborers," and thus were noncommittal.[94]

During the late Qing Period, Portuguese East Africa already had a large number of Chinese. Local Chinese affairs were managed by the Chinese consul to South Africa. Subsequently, local Chinese asked the Qing Dynasty government for protection by establishing a local consulate. Consul General Liu Yulin went to inspect the area and thought the place was a "major entry and exit passage" for the Chinese in South Africa and "had been in commerce for many years." Therefore, a consulate should be set up to protect the interests of local Chinese. However, due to the tight fiscal budget of the Qing Dynasty government, a German merchant was nominated by local Chinese and appointed to the unpaid position of the vice consul. The consulate affairs were managed by the consulate general in South Africa.[95]

Based on the aforementioned facts, the Qing government did take actions to implement its Chinese in Africa policy; this was demonstrated in two ways. First, the Chinese minister to England conveyed Chinese government's view through diplomatic channels. Second, the Chinese consulate general in South Africa reflected local Chinese's wishes, protested to the local government on its discriminatory policy, and worked hard to negotiate. Nevertheless, the diplomacy of a nation has to be backed by real power. In the late Qing period when the nation was weakening by the day, the policy to protect overseas Chinese remained only on official papers and served little purpose.

From the eighteenth century until 1911, Chinese in Africa faced many difficulties in their pioneering work. They had to confront environmental challenges, cultural prejudice, and racial discrimination. Chinese in Africa fully utilized their Chinese historical wisdom; with various means, they fought hard for their survival right as a minority group. In their negotiation with local administrative governments, they had a profound realization that their helplessness came from being the citizens of a weak nation; in order to fight for their rightful place in a foreign land, their motherland must be strengthened first. Their physical presence in a foreign land gave them a better sense of the world and provided them with a deep understanding of how outdated and corrupted the Qing Dynasty government was, which led to their realization of the pressing significance of changes to come. These factors were the psychological foundation for the overseas Chinese being the "mother of revolution," a revolution in 1911 that saw the successful overthrow of the Qing government and the emergence of the modern state of China.

NOTES

Foreword

1 Originally titled "New Thoughts on the Use of Chinese Documents in the Reconstruction of Early Swahili History," this essay by John Shen, published in *History in Africa* Vol. 22, pp. 349-358, is reprinted with permission from the African Studies Association. The title and first paragraph has been slightly modified to fit the scope of Li Anshan's study. Please note that while Shen's essay, including its footnotes, uses the Wade-Giles system for transcribing the Mandarin Chinese language, Li's text uses the pinyin system, which is used in mainland China and has almost entirely replaced the Wade-Giles system.

2 Ibid., 26.

3 Friedrich Hirth and W.W. Rockhill, *Chau Ju-Kua: His Work on the Chinese and Arab Trade in the twelfth and thirteenth Centuries, Entitled Chu-fan chi* (St. Petersburg, 1911; Taipei, 1967), 128.

4 Duyvendak, *China's Discovery of Africa*, 13.

5 G. S. P. Freeman-Grenville, *The East African Coast* (Oxford, 1962), 8.

6 According to *Contemporary Authors*, Freeman-Grenville had no formal training in Chinese. See Ann Evory, *Contemporary Authors* (Detroit, 1981), 212-13. Freeman-Grenville, *The East African Coast*, 8.

7 David Henige, "Putting the Horse Back Before the Cart: Recent Encouraging Signs," *History in Africa* 13 (1986), 183.

8 Ibid., 182.

9 Justin Willis, review of "Swahili Origins: Swahili Culture and the Shungwaya Phenomenon," *African Affairs* 93 (1994), 148.

10 Gervase Mathew, "The East African Coast until the Coming of the Portuguese," in Roland Oliver and Gervase Mathew, eds., *History of East Africa* (Oxford, 1963), 107.

11 Ibid.

12 Wheatley, "Analecta Sino-Africana Recensa," *East Africa and the Orient*, 95-96.

13 Chang Hsing-lang, *Chung-Hsi chiao-t'ung shih-liao hui-p'ien*, 57.

14 Ibid.

15　Ibid.

Introduction

1　*Foreign News* 79 (June 8, 1904).
2　*Foreign News* 82 (July 8, 1904).
3　*Foreign News* 97 (December 1, 1904).
4　*Foreign News* 25 (October 6, 1902). The original article was published in *The Guardian* on September 1, 1902.
5　This newspaper was republished as *Foreign News Hui Lun* by *Shanghai Foreign News*. It includes 28 volumes, with translated newspaper articles in volumes 3–4, translations on China–Africa relations in volumes 3 and 4, which concentrated on the theme of Chinese indentured labor treatment in South Africa. The twenty-second volume contains negotiation records. Sec. 22 titled, "Chinese Official Documents Collection."
6　Chen Hansheng, "China Official Document Collection" in *A Compilation of Historical Documents on Chinese Indentured Laborers Abroad*, sec. 8 (Zhonghua Book Press, 1985), pp. 1643–1792.
7　Ibid., pp. 1785.
8　Chen Hansheng, "A Comprehensive Book of Chinese Indentured Labors Going Abroad" in *A Compilation of Historical Documents on Chinese Indentured Laborers Abroad*, sec. 4 (Zhonghua Press, 1981), pp. 68–87.
9　Ibid., pp. 407–460.
10　Chen Hansheng, "Chinese Indentured Labors in Africa" in *A Compilation of Historical Documents on Chinese Indentured Laborers Abroad*, sec. 9 (Zhonghua Press, 1984), pp. 75–289.
11　Ibid., "1904–1910 Collection of Historical Documents on the Recruitment of Chinese Gold Miners in Transvaal, British South Africa," "Report on Recruitment of Chinese Indentured Laborers in the British, French, Belgium, Portuguese, Spanish, and German Colonies in Africa," pp. 178–253, 254–277.
12　Ibid., p. 278
13　Labor recruitment in Northern China by Transvaal was contracted by four foreign merchants in Tian Jing and Yan Tai. These were William Forbes & Co. and Chinese Engineering and Mining Co. in Tian Jing, Cornalie Echford & Co. and Silas Schwabe & Co. in Yan Tai. Also involved in this deal were Tai Gu Shipping Company, Mei Fu Co., Ltd., and Chen Qingkai Company.
14　The Editorial Board of Mining History, Kai Ping Coal Mine Committee of Communist China, "Information on the Selling of Chinese Indentured Laborers at Former Kai Luan Mine by the British and Belgium Imperialists," *Bei Guo Chun Qiu* 2 (1960): pp. 76–85.
15　Ai Zhouchang, *Collections of Historical Sino-African Relations, 1500–1918* (Shanghai: Huadong Press, 1989), pp. 209–279.

16 Shao Ting, "The negotiations on the law governing Asians renting properties in Transvaal, South Africa," *Overseas Chinese Weekly News* 14: 9–15.
17 Zi Yu, "A glimpse of Lourenço Marques Chinese in East Africa," *Overseas Chinese Monthly News* (November–December, 1936).
18 Overseas Chinese Revolution History Committee, *History of Overseas Chinese Revolution*, 2 volumes (Taipei: Zhong Zheng Press, 1981).
19 Ye Xun, "Memoir on the Overseas Chinese's State in South Africa," in *A Collection of Historical Documents*, sec. 87 (Beijing: Wen Shi Zi Liao Press, 1983), pp. 61–95
20 Liu Xinlin, "My Personal Witness in Mauritius," *Guangdong Historical Data*, sec. 47 (1986), pp. 43–60. Also see Liu Xinlin, "Conversation on Mauritius Chinese Education," *Overseas Chinese Education*, sec. 1 (April, 1983), pp. 188–191; "Random Notes on Three Trips to Mauritius," *China Today* (August 1995): 56–57.
21 Feng Ziyou, *Informal History of the Revolution*, sec. 4 (Zhonghua Press, 1981), pp. 16–17.
22 Lian Cikuag, "Party Affairs Live in South Africa" (original article in the collection kept by China Kuomintang Central Party Historical Document Compilation Committee), cited in *The Historical Documents of Overseas Chinese's Role in Nation Founding Revolution* (Taipei: Zhong Zheng Press, 1977), pp. 434–435.
23 "Journal on Post British South Africa: New Law Prohibiting Chinese Indentured Labor Entrance," *Eastern Magazine*, 1:10 (December 1904): 161–164.
24 Guang Zhongfang, "Research on the New Mauritius Chinese arrivals," *South Sea Intelligence*, 1: 3 (December 1932): 89–90.
25 Zheng Ming, *Overseas Chinese Historical Documents Directory* (Beijing: China Zhang Wang Press, 1984), pp. 254–255. Notes on information provided by the book: (1) The founding date of *China Times*, 1946, was incorrect; it should be December 10, 1953; (2) The listed merging date between *Overseas Business* and *China Times*, 1953, is incorrect; it should be September 16, 1955.
26 Ji Nan University Overseas Chinese Research Center has a *Jing Bao* collection of more than a decade.
27 This magazine was founded by students of Madagascar Xing Wen School. The publication ended on July 15, 1956 for financial reasons. Publication resumed on August 1, 1957. In 1960, it was revised to include richer content. See "Mauritius," *Citizen Daily News* (January 26, 1962). *Ming Feng* magazine terminated publication in 1975.
28 Edith Wong-Hee-Kam, *La Diaspora Chinoise aux Mascareignes: Le Cas de Réunion* (Paris: L'Harmatian, 1996), p. 333.
29 "Various Overseas Chinese History and Current State," *Sheng Bao* (August 28, 1931).
30 Zhang Fang, "Overseas Chinese in Africa," *Qiao Wu Bao* 1 (1964). *Overseas Chinese News*, an internal publication commenced by Central People's Government overseas Chinese Committee on August 10, 1950, initially a weekly magazine, later changed to semiweekly, then renamed to *Overseas Chinese Reference Data*, also had news related to overseas

Chinese in Africa.

31 Regarding file categorization situation in these two countries' archives, readers can see Li Anshan, "Impression of British Public Records," *World History Research Trend* 12 (1990); Li Anshan, "Introduction of Ghana National Archives," *World History Research Trend* 3 (1993).

32 Peter Richardson, *Chinese Mine Labour in the Transvaal* (London: Macmillan, 1982), pp. 104–165.

33 CO 96/269. Memorandum. "Coolie Immigration, Gold Coast," 28 Mar. 1985; CO 96/300. Dispatch No. 495, Hodgson to Chamberlain, 23 Dec. 1897.

34 Archives Nationales d'Outre-Mer: Fonds Madagascar, MCE 308/778: Immigration—Réglementation de l'Immigration Asiatique et Africaine.

35 C 432/d4517: Arrete du 10 november 1843 sur l'iotroduction de Chinois; C 432/d4600; Immigration chinoise (1845). ANOM is the abbreviation of Archives Nationales d'Outre-Mer.

36 Serie Cabinet Civil, No. 358, Immigration Chinoise, 1912–1930: No. 372, Activities Chinoises a Madagascar, 1932–1953; No. 362, Kuomintang, 1932–52; No. 372, Activities Chinoises a Madagascar, 1932–1953.

37 H. Ly-Tio-Fane Pineo, *La Diaspora Chinoise dans l'Ocean Indien Occidental* (Aix-en-Provence: Presse du GIS Mediterranee, 1981); Melanie Yap and Dianne Leong Man, *Colour, Confusion and Concession: The History of the Chinese in South Africa* (Hong Kong: Hong Kong University Press, 1996); Edith Wong Hee-Kam, *La Diaspora Chinoise aux Mascareignes: La Cas de Réunion*.

38 Report of the Special Committee Appointed to Inquire into the Present Conditions in Regard to the Control of Chinese Indentured Labourers in the Witwatersrand District (Johannesburg: Argus, 1906); Legislative Assembly, Correspondence between Colonial Secretary's Office and Leaders of the Asiatic and Chinese Communities, 28–30 January 1908 (Pretoria: Government Printer, 1908).

39 Chen Zexian, "Report on Recruitment of Chinese Indentured Labors in the British, French, Belgium, Portuguese, Spanish, and German Colonies in Africa"; Chen Hansheng, *A Compilation of Historical Documents on Chinese Indentured Laborers Abroad*, sec. 9, "Chinese Indentured Laborers in Africa," pp. 254–277.

40 *Gold Coast Independent*, August 14, 1897; *Gold Coast Chronicle*, August 14, 1897; *Gold Coast Express*, October 20, 1897.

41 A. Beatson, *Tracts Relative to the Island of Saint Helena* (London: Bulmer, 1816), pp. 186–187. Reproduced from Melanie Yap and Dianne Leong Man, *Colour, Confusion and Concessions*, p. 14.

42 An English Eyewitness, *John Chinaman on the Rand* (London: R. A. Everett & Son, 1905), pp. 47, 95.

Chapter I

1 Xu Yongzhang, "Investigating Several Ancient Sino-African Relation Issues," *West Asia Africa* 5 (1993). Also, on the state of Sino-African historical research, see Zhu Fan, "Review and Outlook of the Sino-African Relations Research," *World History Research Trend* 5 (1987).
2 Zhang Xiang, "Four Climaxes of Ancient Sino-African Interaction," *Nan Kai Historiography* 2 (1987); idem, "On Several Ancient Sino-African Relation Research Issues," *West Asia Africa* 5 (1993).
3 Sheng Fuwei, *China and Africa—Two Thousand Years of Sino-African Relations* (Beijing: Zhonghua Press, 1990), pp. 11–12.
4 Ibid., pp. 70–72.
5 Zhang Xingliang, *A Historical Compilation of East and West Traffic*, sec. 2 (Beijing: Zhonghua Press, 1977), pp. 7–8
6 Yang Renbian, *African General History Compendium* (Beijing: Ren Ming Press, 1984), p. 112.
7 Cheng Gongyuan, *Ancient Sino-African Friendly Contacts* (Beijing: Shang Wu Press, 1985), p. 1.
8 Zhang Junyan, *Ancient China's Contact with Central Asia and Africa by Sea* (Beijing: Hai Yang Press, 1986), p. 11.
9 Sun Yutang, "China and Egypt during the Han Dynasty," *Chinese History Study* 2 (1979): 142.
10 Ai Zhouchang and Mu Tao, *History of Sino-African Relations* (Shanghai: Hua Dong Normal University Press, 1996), p. 1.
11 Fang Hao, *History of East and West Traffic* (1953; reprint Taipei: China Cultural University Press, 1983), p. 150.
12 Xu Zhou Museum, "On Han stone painting in Xu Zhou," *Wen Wu* 2 (1980): 550.
13 "Egyptians Already Used Chinese Silk Products 3,000 Years Ago," *Ren Ming Daily News*, April 2, 1993.
14 Regarding the scale of the shipping factory's archeological site and the shipping technology in Han Dynasty, see Junyan's work in previous references, pp. 11–14
15 Bo Xihe, "The Assertion that Li Xuan is Alexandria," *Tong Bao* (1915); Feng Chengjun, *Translation of Seven Series on Western Zone and South Sea Historical Research* (Beijing: Zhong Hua Press, 1957), pp. 34–35; Ma Wenkuan and Meng Fanren, *Development of Chinese Porcelain in Africa* (Beijing: Zijing Chen Press, 1987), p. 77; Ai Zhouchang and Mu Tao, *History of Sino-African Relations*, pp. 5–8.
16 Sheng Weifu, *China and Africa*, 80 n1.
17 Zhang Xingliang, *A Historical Compilation of East and West Traffic*, sec. 6, p. 20.
18 Xia De, *A Complete Record of the Da Qing Kingdom*, trans. Zhu Jieqing (Beijing: Shang Wu Press, 1964), p. 4.

19   Ibid., pp. 68, 78. See also Xu Yongzhang, "Records Regarding Africa in Ancient Chinese Documents," *World History* 6 (1980).

20   *Ha Shu Yi Wen Zhi* contains 21 families and 445 volumes of astrology. Among them, sea astrology has 6 families and 136 volumes, taking up as much as 30 percent of the book. See also Zhang Junyan, *Contact with Central Asia*, pp. 14–15.

21   Ibid., 23.

22   See Chen Xingxiong, *Sino-African Relations during the Tang Dynasty—Indirect but Powerful Sea Trades*; Wu Jianxiong, *Collection of Essays on History of Chinese Development in Sea*, Vol. 4 (Taipei: Central Research Institute, 1991) pp. 127–129.

23   Zhang Xingliang, *East and West Traffic*, sec. 2, pp. 8–24.

24   Sheng Fuwei, *Sino-African Relations*, ch. 6, pp. 188–240.

25   Chen Xingxiong, *Powerful Sea Trades*, pp. 125–159.

26   Zhang Yichun, *Jing Xing Ji Qian Zhu* (Beijing: Zhonghua Press, 1963).

27   Brian Schneider, *Ancient Chinese's Knowledge about Arabs*, cited in Ai Zhouchang and Mu Tao, *Sino-African Relations*, p. 43.

28   Ding Qian, *Tang Du Huan Yi Xing Ji Geographical Research*, cited in Chen Xingxiong, *Powerful Sea Trades*, p. 131.

29   Zhang Xingliang, *East and West Traffic*, sec. 2, p. 9. Some equate the Morocco assertion to the Maghreb assertion: They "agree to the assertion that Mo Ling is the Maghreb (Morocco)." See Ai Zhouchang, "Examining Du Huan's African Trip," *West Asia and Africa* 3 (1995).

30   Xia De, *Da Qing Kingdom*, p. 81.

31   Berthoid Laufer, *China and Iran*, trans. Du Zhengsheng (Taipei: Zhonghua Press, 1975), p. 238; Dai Wenda, *Chinese Discovering Africa*, trans. Hu Guoqiang, Yi Jingxian (Beijing: Shang Wu Press, 1983), p. 15.

32   China College of Sociology West Africa Research Center, *Africa Overview* (Beijing: World Knowledge Press, 1981), p. 324.

33   This is the view of P. Whitley, See Roland Oliver, ed., *The Cambridge History of Africa*, vol. 3 (London: Cambridge University Press, 1977) p. 193

34   Sheng Fuwei, *Sino-African Relations*, p. 227.

35   Zhang Xingliang, *East and West Traffic*, p. 25.

36   G. S. P. Freeman-Grenville, *The Medieval History of the Coast of Tanganyika* (London: Oxford University Press, 1962), pp. 36–37. See also Chen Xingxiong, "Sino-African Relations during the Tang Dynasty," p. 133.

37   H. Field, *Contributions to the Faiyum, Sinai, Sudan, Kenyan Anthropology* (University of California Press, 1952), p. 2, in cited in Sheng Fuwei, *Sino-African Relations*, p. 233. Sheng Fuwei thought the Bobali Kingdom in *You Yang Za Su* was a country built by the Galla people in northern Somalia.

38   See El France, *General History of Africa*, vol. 3 (Beijing: China Foreign Translation Press,

UN Education Literature Organization Press, 1993), p. 498.
39 Zhang Xingliang, *East and West Traffic*, sec. 2, pp. 11–12.
40 Ibid., p. 159
41 Qing Zhongmian, "Chinese Voyage Route, from the Mouth of Persian Gulf to the Center of East Africa," *Eastern Magazine*, 41:18 (September 1935).
42 Chen Gongyuan, "Sino-African Relations based on Jia Dang's *Tong Hai Yi Dao*," *Central Asia and Africa* 3 (1983).
43 Sheng Fuwei, *Sino-African Relations*, pp. 208–213.
44 Xu Yongzhang, "Research on San Lang Kingdom," *Central Asia and Africa* 1 (1992).
45 Ai Zhouchang and Mu Tao, "Overseas Chinese in South Africa," pp. 29–33; Chen Xingxiong, *Powerful Sea Trades*, pp. 133–136.
46 See Julie Wilensky, "The Magical Kunlun and 'Devil Slaves': Chinese Perceptions of Dark-skinned People and Africa Before 1500," *Sino-Platonic Papers* 122 (2002).
47 Xia Ding, "Porcelain: Evidence of Ancient Sino-African Traffic Relations," *Wen Wu* 1 (1963).
48 Ma Wenkuan and Meng Fangren, *Development of Chinese Porcelain*, p. 4. This book described the discovery of Ancient Chinese porcelain at various African locations from seven different angles, relations between Islamic civilization and Sino-African maritime traffic. See also San Shang Cinan, *Road of Pottery* (Tian Jing People's Press, 1983).
49 Ma Wenkuan and Meng Fangren, *Development of Chinese Porcelain*, pp. 37–55; Chen Xingxiong, *Powerful Sea Trades*, pp. 141–147; R. Coupland, *East Africa and Its Invaders: From the Earliest Times to the Death of Seyyid Said in 1856* (London: Oxford University Press), p. 19.
50 Zhang Tiesheng, *The Initial Research into the History of Sino-African Traffic* (Beijing: San Lian Press, 1972), p. 49n5.
51 Chen Xingxiong, *Powerful Sea Trades*, pp. 147–148.
52 Lin Baoren, "A Conversation Begun with Xi An's Black Clay Figures," *Wen Wu* 6 (1979); Shen Baichang, "Historical Witness of Sino-African Exchange," *Bai Ke Zhi Shi* 3 (1983).
53 Chen Xingxiong, *Powerful Sea Trades*, p. 149.
54 Zhang Junyan, *Contact with Central Asia*, p. 92.
55 I would like to specially point out that this understanding was inspired by an assistant researcher at China's Social Science History Research Center, Wu Yugui. Wu and the author were classmates in history classes at China's Social Science History Research Center. He had been publishing and translating books on the history of the Tang Dynasty and is especially accomplished in the research of Tang culture.
56 Some scholars believe that certain East Africans who lived in Malacca were involved in these indirect trades. See Zhang Tiesheng, *Initial Research*, p. 54.
57 Chang Xingliang, *Powerful Sea Trades*, vol. 2, p. 35.
58 Feng Chengjun, *Zhu Fang Zhi Jiao Zhu* (Beijing: Zhonghua Press, 1956), p. 76.
59 Cheng Jun, *Translation of Seven Series*, p. 67.

60 Today's Maghreb.
61 Zhang Xingliang, *East and West Traffic*, vol. 2, p. 31.
62 Ibid., p. 30.
63 "Without a doubt, this island is today's Madagascar. This Kunlun Zengji Kingdom includes this island and its adjacent African coast," Fei Liang, *Research on Kun Lun and Ancient South Sea Maritime Routes*, trans. Feng Chengjun (Beijing: Zhonghua Press, 1957).
64 Ibid., p. 5.
65 Ibid., p. 49.
66 Ibid., pp. 53–54.
67 Zhang Tiesheng, *Initial Research*, pp. 19–20.
68 Feng Chengjun, *Research on Kun Lun*, vol. 2, pp. 26–28.
69 Su Jiqing, *Dao Yi Zhi ue Jiao Shi* (Beijing: Zhonghua Press, 1981), p. 10
70 There are various opinions on the location of Galita and Tefangli. Some said they were Morocco and Damietta of Egypt. Others said they were Aden and a location in India. This is questionable. See Su Jiqing, *Dao Yi Zhi ue Jiao Shi*, pp. 250–253, 349–352.
71 Wang Dahai, *Hai Dao Yi Zhi*, pp. 346–348.
72 Ibid., pp. 358–360.
73 Ibid., pp. 297–300.
74 Ma Wenkuan, cited in Meng Fanren, *Development of Chinese Porcelain*, pp. 3–6, 8–14, 18–23, 26–29, 31–32, 35. See also R. Oliver, ed., *The Cambridge History of Africa*, pp. 203, 206, 215–216, 225.
75 Ma Jingpeng, trans., *Journey of Ibn Battuta* (Yin Chuan: Ning Xia People's Press, 1985), p. 546. The book was translated from the Arabic edition published by the Egyptian Department of Education in 1934.
76 Cited in Zhang Xingliang, *East and West Traffic*, Vol. 2, pp. 27, 29.
77 Zhang Tiesheng, *Initial Research*, pp. 49–50n5.
78 Ma Wenkuan, cited in Meng Fanren, *Development of Chinese Porcelain*, p. 25.
79 Ai Zhouchang and Mu Tao, *History of Sino-African Relations*, pp. 53–54.
80 See Ma Jingpeng's translation of *The Journey by Ibn Battuta*, "Chinese Porcelains," "Depictions of the Chinese," "Money in Circulation during Travel," "Chinese's Fine Craft," "Boat Docking Registration Laws," etc. pp. 545–549.
81 Sheng Fuwei, *Sino-African Relations*, pp. 385–387.
82 Joseph Needham, *China's Ancient Civilization*, vol. 3 (London: Cambridge University Press), pp. 552–555.
83 Sheng Fuwei, *Sino-African Relations*, pp. 252–258
84 Zhang Junyan, *Contact with Central Asia*, p. 118. Zhang Junyan chronicled occurrences of the Dashi Kingdom dispatching envoys to China during the Song Dynasty, totaling fifty-four. See pp. 111–117.
85 Sheng Fuwei, *Sino-African Relations*, pp. 374–378.

86 R. Coupland, *East Africa and Its Invaders*, book 3, ch. 26 (London: Clarendon Press, 1938), p. 26. Some scholars think the "Madagascar" referred to by Marco Polo was actually Mogadishu. See Sheng Fuwei, *Sino-African Relations*, pp. 380–381.

87 Zhang Junyan, *Contact with Central Asia*, pp. 182–184.

88 In *Ming Cheng Zu Shi Lu*, vol. 103, "December, Yong Le 14, Envoys from Countries Gu Li, Java, Mang La Jia, Zhang Cheng, Xi Lang Shang, Gu Di Su, Liu Shang, Nan Bou Li, Bu La Wa, A Dan, Sumatra, Ma Lin, La Sa, Hu Lu Mo Si, Ke Zhi, Nan Wu Li, Sha Li Wan Ni, Peng Heng, etc. returned home. They were gifted silk fabrics by the Imperial Court." The country names listed coincide with names listed in *Ming Shi Lu*, vol. 182.

89 Zhang Tiesheng, *Initial Research*, pp. 96–97.

90 Ai Zhouchang and Mu Tao, *History of Sino-African Relations*, p. 75.

91 Sheng Fuwei, *Sino-African Relations*, p. 462.

92 "From Xiao Ge Lang, if sailing in the wind's direction, it takes twenty days and nights to arrive." See Feng Chengjun, *Xing Cha Sheng Lan Jiao Zhu*, vol. 2 (Beijing: Zhonghua Press, 1954), p. 21.

93 "From Xi Lang Shang Bie Luo going south, it takes twenty-one days and nights to arrive." See Feng Chengyun, *Xing Cua Sheng Lan Jiao Zhu*, vol. 2, p. 24.

94 Xiang Da, comp., *Zheng He Heng Hai Tu* (1961; reprint Beijing: Zhonghua Press, 1982), p. 57.

95 This passage in *Ji Lu Hui Pian Ban* is more detailed than others. See Feng Cheng-Jun, *Xing Cha Sheng Lan Jiao Zhu*, vol. 2, p. 20.

96 Based on Feng Chengyun's research, "Mi Xi" is the same as "Mi Xi Er" (Misr) in *Ming Zhi*, vol. 332, today's Egypt. See Feng Chengjun, *Ying Yia Sheng Lan Jiao Zhu* (Changsha: Shang Wu Press, 1938), p. 2.

97 Zhang Zhuan, *China's Ancient Maritime Traffic*, corrected edition (Beijing: Shang Wu Press, 1986); Feng Chengjun, *Zhu Fang Zhi Jiao Zhu* (Beijing: Zhonghua Press, 1956); Su Jiqing, *Yi Dao Zhi Lue Jiao Zhi* (Beijing: Zhonghua Press, 1981); Xian Da, *Zheng He Voyage Map* (1961; reprint Beijing: Zhonghua Press, 1982).

98 Ma Wenkuan and Meng Fanren, *Development of Chinese Porcelain*, p. 50.

99 Other than publications of Ma Wenkuan and Meng Fanren, see R. Oliver, ed., *The Cambridge History of Africa*, vol. 3, pp. 574–574, 579–580.

100 Both came from *Ji Lu Hui Bian Ben*, cited in Feng Chengjun, *Xing Cha Sheng Lan Jiao Zhu*, vol. 2, pp. 20, 23, 25.

101 I have been to Ghana and lived in the homes of African friends. They usually view the Chinese as a "white," not "yellow," race.

102 Philip Snow, *The Star Raft*, p. 35.

103 *Report on Shanga Excavation* (Mark Horton of Cambridge University, 1980), cited in Philip Snow, *The Star Raft*, p. 33.

104 A few examples of important books: Matteo Ricci, *The Matteo Ricci World Map*; Giulio

Aleni, *Zhi Fang Wai Ji*; Ferdinand Verbiest, *Kunyu Quantu World Map*. See Chen Yu-Long, "Explanations for Mr. Xiang Da's work before his death: From early Ming Dynasty to pre-liberation (ca. 1405–1948), explanations on selected Sino-African traffic historical documents." See Yan Wenru and Chen Yulong, comp., *A Collection of Mr. Xiang Da's Essays* (Urumqi: Xing Jiang People's Press, 1986), pp. 22–45.

105   Philip Snow, *The Star Raft*, pp. 39–40.

106   See Ai Zhouchang, *A Collection of Articles on Sino-African Relation History (1500–1918)*, part II, pp. 21–25, 29, 38–42, 50–113.

107   Fan Shouyi, noted by Yan Zonglin and Sheng Jianlu, *Shang Xi Shi Yuan Xue Bao* 2 (1959), cited in Ai Zhouchang, and Mu Tao, *History of Sino-African Relations*, pp. 125, 161. For the complete copy of *Shen Jian Lu*, see Fang Hao, *History of East and West Traffic*, pp. 855–862.

108   Sheng Fuwei, *Sino-African Relations*, p. 497.

109   Xie Qinggao, *Hai Lu*, cited in Ai Zhouchang and Mu Tao, *Sino-African Relations*, p. 125.

110   Wang Dahai, *Hai Dao Yi Zhi*, cited in Ai Zhouchang, *Sino-African Relations*, p. 25.

111   Ding Kang, *San Zhou You Ji*, cited in Ai Zhouchang, *Sino-African Relations*, pp. 50–111.

112   Richard Gray, ed., *The Cambridge History of Africa*, vol. 4, p. 465.

113   He Jingzhi, *Réunion Chinese Journal*, p. 12.

114   Xiao Ciying, *Chinese in Africa Economy*, p. 3. For illustrations of the *Qi Ying Hao*, see Melanie Yap and Dianne Leong Man, *Colour, Confusion, and Concessions: The History of the Chinese in South Africa*, p. 11.

115   Yan Yuanren, "Contribution of Overseas Chinese towards World Civilization," *Qiao Wu Ji Kan* 4 (March 15, 1941).

116   Ma Wenkuan and Meng Fanren, *Sino-African Relations*, pp. 51–53, 66–67.

Chapter II

1   At the time, in order to cut off financial support of the overseas anti-Qing groups, the Qing government implemented harsh local policies that made it impossible for locals to make a living. For the origins of Chinese in South Africa, see Melanie Yap and Dianne Leong Man, *Colour, Confusion and Concessions: The History of the Chinese in South Africa*, pp. 32–35. For the origins of Chinese in Mauritius, Réunion, and Madagascar, see Li Zhuofan, *History of Chinese in the West Indies*. See also Fang Zhiken, *A Collection of Overseas Chinese History in Africa*, pp. 144–148, 181–182, 215.

2   Chen Zexian, "The Popular Indentured Chinese Laborer System in the Nineteenth Century," *History Research* 1 (1963): 176–178.

3   Li Anshan, "Foreign Research on the Slave Trade and Slavery (1968–1988)," *World History Research Trends* 2 (1989).

4   UNESCO, *African Slave Trade in the Fifteenth to the Nineteenth Centuries: Expert reports*

and documents in symposiums held by UNESCO (Beijing: China Dui Wai Fan Yi Press, 1984) p. 248.

5 Joseph. E. Inikori, "Slave Trades and Economies of Atlantic Coastal Countries, 1451–1870," in UNESCO, "African Slave Trade in the Fifteenth to the Nineteenth Centuries," pp. 58–84. See also Joseph E. Inikori, "Slavery and the Revolution in Cotton Textile Production in England," in Joseph E. Inikori and Stanley L. Engerman, eds., *The Atlantic Slave Trade: Effects on Economies, Societies, and Peoples in Africa, the Americas, and Europe* (Durham: Duke University Press, 1992), pp. 145–181.

6 For the classic on this issue, see Eric William, *Capitalism and Slavery* (Beijing: Beijing Normal University Press, 1982). For research by Chinese scholars, see Ai Zhouchang and Zheng Jiaxing, *African General History: Recent Times Volume* (Shanghai: Hua Dong Normal University Press, 1996), pp. 25–65, 299–329. Regarding research on this issue by Western historians, see Li Anshan, "Comments on Capitalism and Slavery—50 Years of Disputes among Western Historians," *World History* 3 (1996).

7 British Foreign and Commonwealth Office, FO 97/434; C. W. Newbury, *British Policy towards West Africa: Selected Documents 1786–1874* (London: Oxford University Press, 1965), p. 123.

8 Li Anshan, "On the Nineteenth Century European Business Capital Activities in Africa and Their Influences on Dividing Up the Continent," *Shi Xue Monthly* 1 (1986).

9 Paul E. Lovejoy, *Transformations of Slavery: A History of Slavery in Africa* (Cambridge: Cambridge University Press, 1983).

10 Siyou Abolamowa, *Africa—Four Hundred Years of Slave Trade* (Beijing: Shang Wu Press, 1983), pp. 159–226. This is a significant work.

11 Paul E. Lovejoy, *Transformations of Slavery: A History of Slavery in Africa* (Cambridge: Cambridge University Press, 1983), pp. 146–147.

12 Chen Zexian, "Report on Recruitment," pp. 176–178.

13 Chen Zexian, "The Popular Indentured Chinese Laborer System in the Nineteenth Century"; Peng Jiali, "Chinese Laborers Who Developed Western Colonies in the Nineteenth Century," *World History* 1 (1980); idem, "The Abduction of Chinese Laborers by Western Aggressors in the Nineteenth Century," in Chen Hansheng, *A Compilation of Historical Documents on Chinese Indentured Laborers Abroad*, vol. 4, pp. 174–229.

14 Larry W. Bowman, *Mauritius: Democracy and Development in the Indian Ocean* (Colorado: Westview Press, 1991), p. 8.

15 Philip Snow, *The Star Raft*, p. 55.

16 Zeng Fanxing, trans. Deng Kangsheng, "Searching for Roots, Chinese in Mauritius," *Ming Bao Monthly* 1 (1980): 40–42. "General History of Chinese in Mauritius," trans. Liu Xinglin from an editorial in the *Weekend News of Mauritius*, April 1981, cited in Fang Zhigen, *History of Chinese Africa Selected Articles*, p. 44. Regarding treatment received by these Chinese, see Li Zhuofan, *History of Chinese in the West Indian Ocean*, Appendix 2, "A Letter from

Defuerre to His Company, July 20, 1762," cited in Fang Zhigen, *History of Chinese Africa*, pp. 307–309.

17 Chen Gongyuan, *Friendly Sino-African Contacts in Ancient Times*, p. 49.

18 Li Zuofan, *History of Chinese in the West Indian Ocean*, cited in Fang Zhigen, *History of Chinese Africa*, p. 122.

19 Ibid., pp. 117–118.

20 Zen Fanxing, "Searching for Roots," p. 40; Slawecki, *French Policy towards the Chinese in Madagascar*, p. 42.

21 Persia Crawford Campbell, *Chinese Coolie Emigration to Countries within the British Empire*, p. 338.

22 Li Zhuofan, *History of Chinese the West Indian Ocean*, cited in Fang Zhigen, *History of Chinese Africa*, pp. 273–274, chart 18, pp. 299–301.

23 *General History of Chinese in Mauritius*, cited in Fang Zhigen, *History of Chinese Africa*, pp. 45–46.

24 Edith Wong-Hee-Kam, *La Diaspora Chinoise aux Mascareignes: Le Cas de Réunion*, p. 8. The first group of Chinese coolies brought in to Réunion in 1844, referred to by Slawecki, is likely this group. See Slawecki, *French Policy towards the Chinese in Madagascar*, p. 42.

25 Chen Zexian, "History of Chinese Labor Recruitment in Africa by British, French, Belgium, Portuguese, Spanish, and German Colonies," in Chen Hansheng, *A Compilation of Historical Documents*, vol. 9, p. 263; Dominic Dillon and Ron Hunton, *History of Chinese in Réunion*, cited in Fang Zhigen, *History of Chinese Africa*, pp. 456, 462–463.

26 He Jingzhi, *History of Chinese Réunion*, p. 16.

27 *International Immigration*, vol. 1, pp. 59–60, cited in Chen Hansheng, *A Compilation of Historical Documents*, vol. 9, p. 264.

28 Edith Wong-Hee-Kam, *La Diaspora Chinoise aux Mascareignes: Le Cas de Réunion*, p. 9. Based on Li Zhuofan's book, there were 802 indentured Chinese laborers in this group. See Li Zhuofan, *History of West Indian Oversea Chinese*, cited in Fan Zhigen, *History of Chinese Africa*, p. 175.

29 He Jingzhi, *History of Chinese Réunion*, p. 17.

30 Chen Zexian, "History of Chinese Labor Recruitment in Africa by British, French, Belgian, Portuguese, Spanish, and German Colonies," in Chen Hansheng, *A Compilation of Historical Documents*, vol. 9, pp. 254–258.

31 A. Bearson, *Tracts Relative to the Island of St. Helena* (London: Bulmer, 1816), pp. 186–187, cited in Melanie Yap and Dianne Leong Man, *Colour, Confusion and Concessions: The History of the Chinese in South Africa*, p. 13.

32 Hosee Ballou Morse, *The Chronicles of the East India Company Trading to China, 1635–1834*, vol. 3 (Oxford: Clarendon Press, 1926), pp. 254–255.

33 Chen Zexian, "History of Chinese Labor Recruitment in Africa by British, French, Belgian, Portuguese, Spanish, and German Colonies," in Chen Hansheng, *A Compilation of*

NOTES — CHAPTER II

Historical Documents, vol. 9, p. 275.

34 Slawecki, *French Policy towards the Chinese in Madagascar*, p. 85.

35 Ibid., p. 90.

36 Ibid., p. 96.

37 "Upon discussion among the French consul, the undertaking French merchant Vichi, and the Fu Zhou officials, a petition was made to the governor of Min Zhe Region. The petition was then approved to enhance friendship." Regarding the conditions of this recruitment, see "Madagascar Recruitment Contract (1901, Fu Zhou)," in Chen Hansheng, *A Compilation of Historical Documents*, vol. 9, pp. 174–177.

38 Ibid., p. 98.

39 Chen Zexian, "History of Chinese Labor recruitment in Africa by British, French, Belgian, Portuguese, Spanish, and German Colonies," in Chen Hansheng, *A Compilation of Historical Documents*, pp. 272–273.

40 Chinese worked here for as long as fourteen years. Once the railroad was completed, there were only about six hundred Chinese left. Twenty workers were kept and the remaining workers were sent back. See Qu Zhengmin, "Chinese Built Railroads in East Africa," *Min Bao Monthly* 191 (November 1981), pp. 69–75.

41 Su Wuding, *French Colonial Policy in West Africa, 1800–1900*, trans. Fang Lin (Beijing: Shi Jie Zhi Shi Press, 1960), p. 68.

42 R. L. Buell, *The Native Problem in Africa*, vol. 2 (New York: Macmillan, 1928), p. 26; Su Wuding, *French Colonial Policy*, p. 69. See also Chen Zexian, "History of Chinese Labor Recruitment in Africa by British, French, Belgian, Portuguese, Spanish, and German Colonies," in Chen Hansheng, *A Compilation of Historical Documents*, Vol. 9, p. 265. Chen Zexian believed that the French recruited Chinese laborers in the late nineteenth century mainly for the construction of a railway in the French Congo, but the railway construction did not start until 1909.

43 Ghana government administrative file, CEM 1/1/41. Dispatches from Secretary of State to Governor, 1876, March 24, 1876, Pt. 2, No. 256; Ghana government administrative file, CEM 14.1.5. Minutes of Legislative Council Meeting, April 6, 1889; Ghana government administrative file, CEM 11/1/107. Extract from S.N.A., Case No. 27/1909.

44 *Gold Coast Independent*, August 22, 1896.

45 *Gold Coast Independent*, August 14, 1897; *Gold Coast Chronicle*, August 14, 1897; *Gold Coast Express*, October 20, 1897.

46 Richard Burton and Verney Cameron, *To the Gold Coast for Gold* (London: Chatto & Windus, 1883), pp. 327–328, 336–337.

47 A. B. Ellis, *The Land of Fetish* (London: Chapman and Hill, 1883), p. 273.

48 Ghana government administrative file, CEM 1/496. Proposal to Import Chinese Gold Prospectus, January 7, 1897.

49 *Gold Coast Independent*, August 14, 1897.

50 *Gold Coast Express*, August 21, 1897.

51 *Gold Coast Independent*, August 14, 1897; *Gold Coast Express*, October 16, 1897.

52 Persia Crawford Campbell, *Chinese Coolie Emigration*, p. 170

53 Wang Tieya, *A Compilation of Old Foreign Treaties*, vol. 1 (1957; reprint Beijing: San Lian Press, 1982), p. 785.

54 Chen Zexian, "The Popular Indentured Chinese Laborer System in the Nineteenth Century" and "History of Chinese Labor Recruitment in Africa by British, French, Belgian, Portuguese, Spanish, and German Colonies," in Chen Hansheng, *A Compilation of Historical Documents*, vol. 9, pp. 266–269; Ai Zhouchang, "1898 China–Congo (Zaire) Treaty and Chinese Laborers," *Social Science Frontline* 3 (1983).

55 Chen Xianzi, "History of Chinese Labor Recruitment in Africa by British, French, Belgian, Portuguese, Spanish, and German Colonies," in Chen Hansheng, *A Compilation of Historical Documents*, vol. 9, pp. 270–272.

56 Yan Yuanren, "Contribution of Overseas Chinese towards the World Civilization," *Qiao Wu Ji Kan* 4 (March 15, 1941).

57 Chen Zexian, "The Popular Indentured Chinese Laborer System in the Nineteenth Century," p. 177.

58 Campbell, *Chinese Coolie Emigration*, p. 170.

59 *Kaffir*: This word came from Arabic, meaning "pagan." It was first used by the Portuguese in reference to Africans living along the coast of Southeast Africa; later it was used in reference to the AmaXhosa in South Africa.

60 *Boer* means "farmer" in Dutch. It refers to descendants of Dutch immigrants in South Africa.

61 Li Anshan, "A Brief Analysis of the Economic Factors in the Great Migration of South Africa," *Xi Ya Fei Zhou* 1 (1988).

62 T. R. H. Davenport, *South Africa: A Modern History* (Toronto: University of Toronto, 1991), pp. 201–202.

63 Campbell, *Chinese Coolie Emigration*, p. 167.

64 Regarding the research on this issue, see P. Richardson, *Chinese Mine Labour in the Transvaal*; Song Xi, *Chinese Laborers' Contribution to Gold Mining in Transvaal, South Africa during the Late Qing Period* (Taipei: Hua Gang Press, 1974).

65 This is based on statistics in the British Parliament Files. See Peng Jiali, "History on British Recruiting Chinese Laborers for South Africa Gold Mines during the Late Qing Period," p. 186.

66 "Report to Chinese Foreign Ministry by Liu Yulin, Consul Stationed in South Africa, on the Handling of the Fifth Batch of Chinese Laborers (Guangxu 32, January 8)," in Chen Hansheng, *A Compilation of Historical Documents*, vol. 1, p. 171; Peng Jiali, "History on British Recruiting Chinese Laborers for South Africa Gold Mines during the Late Qing Period," p. 186.

67 Li Chang-Fu, *Chinese Colonial History* (1936; reprint Taiwan: Shang Wu Press, 1983), pp. 227, 350.
68 Chen Zexian, "The Popular Indentured Chinese Laborer System in the Nineteenth Century," *History Research* 1 (1963): 175.
69 Ai Zhouchang, "Overseas Chinese in South Africa in Recent Times," *History Research* 6 (1981): 178; Chen Bisheng, *A Century of History on Overseas Chinese* (Xia Men: Xia Men University Press, 1991), p. 331.
70 Overseas Chinese Historical Committee, *The General History of Overseas Chinese* (Taipei: Overseas Press, 1956), p. 194.
71 Chen Hansheng, "'Piglets' Go Abroad—How Seven Million Chinese Laborers Were Abducted and Sent Abroad," *Bai Ke Zhi Shi* 5 (1979).
72 Peng Jiali, "History on British Recruiting Chinese Laborer for South Africa Gold Mines during the Late Qing Period," p. 187.
73 Xu Yipu, "Initial Analysis of British South Africa Recruitment Case during the Late Qing Period" *Wen Xian* 22 (1984): 72, 79 n1.
74 P. Richardson, *Chinese Mine Labour in the Transvaal*, pp. 192–197, 204.
75 Xie Zixiu, "South Africa Travel Journal," in Chen Hansheng, *A Compilation of Historical Documents*, vol. 9, pp. 278–279.
76 TCE/FLD122-124, fs. 16/1-16/34; TCE/FLD343-53, Contracts of Service, 1904–1907; P. Richardson, *Chinese Mine Labour in the Transvaal*, p. 192. The asterisk (*) indicates the number of Chinese laborers arriving at Durban, South Africa.
77 The People's Republic of China Kai Qi Mining History Committee, "Information on Trading of Laborers by the British and Belgian Imperialists in the Former Kai Qi Mine," *Bei Guo Chun Qio* 2 (1960): 80.
78 "On Chinese Laborer Recruitment in South Africa," *Wai Jiao Bao* 138 (April 8, 1906).
79 Chen Zexian, "1904–1910 Historical Documents of Chinese Laborer Recruitment by England on Behalf of Transvaal," in Chen Hansheng, *A Compilation of Historical Documents*, p. 236.
80 This is a crucial point. Take the example of the first group leaving from Hong King. On May 12, 1904, the 2,300 laborers recruited by local agents gathered in Hong Kong and prepared to depart for South Africa. On May 24, 1,800 showed up at the port. After physical exams by doctors, 1,055 passed the screening. Upon arrival in Port Durban, South Africa, only 1,005 remained, which was not even half of the originally recruited number. See P. Richardson, *Chinese Mine Labour in Transvaal*, pp. 85–86.
81 "Ambassador to England Zhang Deyi's Letter to the foreign minister on the need for a treaty prior to permitting South African Labor Recruitment," October 16, Guangxu 29, in Chen Hansheng, *A Compilation of Historical Documents*, vol. 1, p. 1650.
82 "Minister to England Zhang Deyi's confidential letter to the foreign minister on the need to draft a governing regulation in response to foreign labor recruitment," January 9, Guangxu

29, in Chen Hansheng, *A Compilation of Historical Documents*, vol. 1, pp. 1643–1644.

83   Chen Zexian, "The Popular Indentured Chinese Laborer System in the Nineteenth Century," see esp. Appendix "1800–1925 Estimation Chart of Indentured Chinese Laborers Going Abroad."

84   Most of the Chinese in South Africa claim that their ancestors came from Mauritius.

85   Dominic Dillon and Ron Hunton, *History of Chinese in Réunion*, quoted in Fang Zhigen, *History of Chinese Africa*, pp. 456, 462–463. Chinese laborers in 1844 were from Fujian. See overseas Chinese Economic Yearbook Committee, *Overseas Chinese Economic Yearbook* (Taipei, 1959), p. 725.

86   He Jingzhi, *History of Chinese Réunion*, p. 16.

87   Melanie Yap and Dianne Leong Ma, *Colour, Confusion and Concessions*, p. 13.

88   Slawecki, *French Policy towards the Chinese in Madagascar*, p. 44; Li Zhuofan, *History of Chinese West Indian Ocean*, cited in Fang Zhigan, *History of Chinese Africa*, p. 209.

89   History of Overseas Chinese Compilation Committee, *History of Overseas Chinese*, p. 196.

90   Melanie Yap and Dianne Leong Man, *Colour, Confusion and Concessions*, pp. 14–24; Xiao Ciyi, *Chinese in the African Economy*, pp. 4, 16.

91   Melanie Yap and Dianne Leong Man, *Colour, Confusion and Concession*, p. 38.

92   Philip Snow, *The Star Raft*, p. 46.

93   Melanie Yap and Dianne Leong Man, *Colour, Confusion and Concession*, pp. 38, 180.

94   Dominic Dillon and Ron Hunton, *History of Chinese in Réunion*, cited in Fang Zhigen, *History of Chinese Africa*, p. 475.

95   Chen Zexian estimated that there were 150,000 indentured Chinese laborers shipped to European continent, England, and North Africa during 1900–1925. See Chen Zexian, "The Popular Indentured Chinese Laborer System in the Nineteenth Century," pp. 176–178.

96   Fei Zhengqing, *Cambridge Republic of China History*, vol. 1 (Beijing: China Sociology Press, 1994), p. 27.

Chapter III

1   Overseas Chinese Economic Yearbook Compilation Committee, *Overseas Chinese Economic Yearbook* (Taipei: Author, 1994), p. 922.

2   Larry W. Bowman, *Mauritius: Democracy and Development in the Indian Ocean*, p. 9.

3   Wilson and Thompson, *Oxford History of South Africa*, vol. 1 (Oxford: Clarendon Press, 1969), pp. 65–66, 193; Eric A. Walker, *A History of Southern Africa* (London: 1957), p. 508; R. Elphick and R. Shell, "Intergroup Relations: Khoikhoi, Settlers, Slaves and Free Blacks, 1652–1795," in R. Elphick and H. Giliomee, eds., *The Shaping of South African Society, 1652–1850* (Cape Town: Longman, 1979), p. 145.

4   "Mr. Snow's introduction to the History of Chinese in Africa," *Overseas Chinese Historical*

NOTES — CHAPTER III

Society Communication 2 (1982).

5 Melanie Yap and Dianne Leong Man, *Colour, Confusion and Concessions: The History of the Chinese in South Africa*, pp. 6–9.

6 E. A. Walker, *A History of Southern Africa* (London: Longmans, 1964), pp. 101–102.

7 Melanie Yap and Dianne Leong Man, *Colour, Confusion and Concessions: The History of the Chinese in South Africa*, pp. 5–24; James Armstrong, *Chinese during the Dutch East Indian Company Period (1652–1795)*, cited in Fang Zhigen, *History of Chinese Africa*, p. 35.

8 Wen Guangyi and Cai Renlong, *Indonesian Chinese History* (Beijing: Ocean Press, 1985), pp. 157–163.

9 Melanie Yap and Dianne Leong Man, *Colour, Confusion and Concessions*, pp. 6–9. Some scholars thought the free Chinese and "free blacks" were unrelated. See James Armstrong, *Chinese during the Dutch East Indian Company Period, 1652–1795*, cited in Fang Zhigen, *History of Chinese Africa*, p. 35.

10 Li Zhuofan, *History of Chinese in the West Atlantic Ocean*, cited in Fang Zhigen, *History of Chinese Africa*, p. 228.

11 Melanie Yap and Dianne Leong Man, *Colour, Confusion and Concessions*, p. 177.

12 *South African Law Journal*, vol. 23 (1906), pp. 245–246; Melanie Yap and Dianne Leong Man, *Colour, Confusion and Concessions*, p. 57.

13 Melanie Yap and Dianne Leong Man, *Colour, Confusion and Concessions*, pp. 33–35.

14 Ibid., p. 177.

15 Dominic Dillon and Ron Hunton, *History of Chinese in Réunion*, cited in Fang Zhigen, *History of Chinese Africa*, pp. 456, 480–481. See also Zeng Fanxing, "Searching for Roots," p. 40.

16 Li Zhuofan, *History of Chinese in the West Atlantic Ocean*, cited in Fang Zhigen, *History of Chinese Africa*, p. 120.

17 Ibid., p. 122.

18 Ibid., p. 121.

19 "Announcement Made by Lu Caixin et al., the First Chinese Immigrants, upon Their Arrival in Hong Kong" (Mauritius Archive Z2D/1826); Li Zhuofan, *History of Chinese in the West Atlantic Ocean*, cited in Fang Zhigen, *History of Chinese Africa*, p. 307, 180. "On December 8, 1846, Seven Chinese Holding French passports arrived in Mauritius from Réunion."

20 Li Zhuofan, *History of Chinese in the West Indian Ocean*, cited in Fang Zhigen, *History of Chinese Africa*, p. 154.

21 Slawecki, *French Policy towards the Chinese in Madagascar*, p. 43.

22 Li Zhuofan, *History of Chinese in the West Atlantic Ocean*, cited in Fang Zhigen, *History of Chinese Africa*, p. 173.

23 Chen Ying-Dong, *Chinese in Mauritius* (Taipei: Zheng Zhong Press, 1989), p. 32. Chen had two sons: elder son Chen Ruixing, younger son Chen Longxing; both had outstanding performances among local Chinese.

24 Li Zhuofan, *History of Chinese in the West Indian Ocean*, cited in Fang Zhigen, *History of Chinese Africa*, pp. 51, 114, 160; *Xing Shang Bao* (Mauritius: August 14, 1958). An asterisk (*) indicates that the data come from August Tusson, *History of Mascarene Islands* (Shanghai: Shanghai People's Press, 1977), p. 598.

25 Li Zhuofan, *History of Chinese in the West Atlantic Ocean*, cited in Fang Zhigen, *History of Chinese Africa*, 104.

26 Edith Wong-Hee-Kam, *La Diaspora Chinoise aux Mascareignes: Le Cas de Réunion*, pp. 71–112; Dominic Dillon and Ron Hunton, *History of Chinese in Réunion*, cited in Fang Zhigen, *History of Chinese Africa*, pp. 473, 484.

27 Some Chinese scholars translate the name to Akwon Lawson.

28 On Liu Weno's family tree, see Edith Wong-Hee-Kam, *La Diaspora Chinoise Mascareignes: Le Cas de Réunion*, pp. 449–452; He Jingzhi, *Réunion Chinese History* (Taipei: Overseas Chinese History Compilation Committee, 1965), pp. 75–77.

29 He Jingzhi, *Réunion Chinese History*, 19–20.

30 Regarding the various claims on earliest Madagascar immigrants, see Slawecki, *French Policy towards the Chinese in Madagascar*, pp. 43–44.

31 Hubert Deschamps, *Histoire de Madagascar* (Paris: Edition Berger-Levrault, 1961), p. 216.

32 Slawecki, *French Policy towards the Chinese in Madagascar*, p. 43.

33 Edith Wong-Hee-Kam, *La Diaspora Chinoise aux Mascareignes: Le Cas de Réunion*, p. 93.

34 Xiao Ciyin, *Chinese in Africa Economy*, pp. 125–127. Data hereafter came from this book. See also Chen Tiehun, *History of Chinese in Madagascar Republic* (Taipei: Zheng Zhong Press, 1989), p. 27.

35 Hubert Deschamps, *Histoire de Madagascar* (Paris: Editions Berger-Levrault, 1961), pp. 216, 253, 299; Slawecki, *French Policy towards the Chinese in Madagascar*, pp. 43–49; Li Zhuofan, *History of Chinese in the West Atlantic Ocean,* cited in Fang Zhigen, *History of Chinese Africa*, p. 221. The asterisk (*) indicates the count possibly including the first group of indentured Chinese laborers in Madagascar.

36 Zi Yu, "A Glimpse of Lourenço Marques Chinese in East Africa," *Overseas Chinese Monthly News* (November–December, 1936).

37 Jeanne Marie Penvenne, *African Workers and Colonial Racism: Mozambican Strategies and Struggles in Lourenço Marques, 1877–1962* (Portsmouth: Heinemann, 1995), p. 40.

38 D. J. Soares-Rebelo, "The Chinese Extraction Group in Mozambique," unpublished paper, 1966, cited in Melanie Yap and Dianne Leong Man, *Colour, Confusion and Concessions*, p. 39.

39 Li Zhuofan, *History of Chinese in the West Indian Ocean*, cited in Fang Zhigen, *History of Chinese Africa*, pp. 328–329.

40 He Zinan, "Chinese History in Mauritius Luodili Island," *Jing Bao* (Mauritius: March–April), cited in Fang Zhigen, *History of Chinese Africa*, pp. 64–68.

41 "1948 Seychelles Census Report," Li Zhuofan, *History of Chinese in the West Indian*

Ocean, cited in Fang Zhigen, *History of Chinese Africa*, p. 169.

42 *Wai Jiao Bao* 173 (April 27, 1907).

43 Scholars in China generally translate the name as "A Xin." "A Xian" seems to be a general name given for Mauritius Chinese. Cited in a letter from Mauritius Nanshun Guan president Li Yongtian to Li Anshan dated October 28, 1998.

44 The translated name was cited in Zeng Hanxing, "Searching for Roots," p. 41. The translated name provided by Nanshun Hui Guan president Li Yongtian was Affen Tingjun. For the biographies of Lu Caixin and Affen Tank Wen, see Li Zhuofan, *History of Chinese in the West Indian Ocean*, Appendix 9, cited in Fang Zhigen, *History of Chinese Africa*, pp. 320–325.

45 Li Zhuofan, *History of Chinese in the West Indian Ocean*, cited in Fang Zhigen, *History of Chinese Africa*, p. 128.

46 Ibid., pp. 132–133.

47 Li Zhuofan, *History of Chinese in the West Indian Ocean*, cited in Fang Zhigen, *History of Chinese Africa*, p. 114. An asterisk (*) indicates the amount in the Mauritius rupee, the country's currency.

48 Ibid., pp. 112–113.

49 Dillon and Hunton, *History of Chinese in Réunion*, cited in Fang Zhigen, *History of Chinese Africa*, pp. 480–481. The 1911 Chinese count differs from the aforementioned count by Wong Hee-Kam. See table 3.7 above.

50 Slawecki, *French Policy towards the Chinese in Madagascar*, p. 63.

51 Chen Tiehun, *History of Chinese in Madagascar*, p. 29.

52 This person was a Chinese merchant in Tamatave and owned sixteen stores.

53 French Overseas Archives, Fonds Madagascar, Folder MCE308/778, Immigration: Réglementation de l'Immigration Asiatique et Afrique, Letter, General Pennequin to Minister of Colonies, December 28, 1899, cited in Slawecki, *French Policy towards the Chinese in Madagascar*, pp. 113–114.

54 Melanie Yap and Dianne Leong Man, *Colour, Confusion and Concessions*, pp. 7–8.

55 Melanie Yap and Dianne Leong Man, *Colour, Confusion and Concessions*, p. 83.

56 Karen L. Harris, *Closeted Culture: The South Chinese in Africa*, p. 4.

57 Melanie Yap and Dianne Leong Man, *Colour, Confusion and Concessions*, p. 194.

58 Ibid., p. 66.

59 Ibid., p. 44.

60 Li Zhuofan, *History of Chinese in the West Indian Ocean*, cited in Fang Zhigen, *History of Chinese Africa*, p. 321.

61 Melanie Yap and Dianne Leong Man, *Colour, Confusion and Concessions*, pp. 12–14.

62 Ibid., p. 15.

63 Zeng Fanxing, "Searching for Roots," pp. 40–41. Information on the Nan Shun Society was mostly provided to me by its current president, Li Yongtian. For the organization's introduction within China, readers can consult Xu Zhi, "Introduction to Mauritius Nan

Shun Society," *Hua Sheng Bao*, November 11, 1894; see also Lin Jingzhi, "Mauritius Chinese Societies," *Ba Gui Qiao Shi* 2 (1995).

64 In 1996, Mauritius Chinese celebrated the 125th anniversary of the founding of the Ren He Society. Based on this, the founding year of the Ren He Society should be 1871. Some scholars in China thought 1904 was its founding year, which in reality was the official year it registered with the government.

65 In the member meeting on April 12, 1929, the proposal to merge the two was approved.

66 Information regarding the Ren He Society mainly came from Li Jixiang, "History of the Ren He Society's Establishment"; Wang Huijun, "Study of Mauritius Chinese Societies"; Huang Kunzhang, "The Ren He Society in Mauritius." All of them were published in the "Mauritius Ren He Society 125th Founding Anniversary Special Edition," Port Louis, November 10, 1996. No page number was listed in the original article.

67 Edith Wong-Hee-Kam, *La Diaspora Chinoise aux Mascarengnes: Le Cas de Réunion*, pp. 221–233; He Jingzhi, *Réunion Chinese History*, pp. 51–52.

68 Dominic Dillon and Ron Hunton, *History of Chinese in Réunion*, cited in Fang Zhigen, *History of Chinese Africa*, pp. 487–488.

69 Melanie Yap and Dianne Leong Man, *Colour, Confusion and Concessions*, p. 89.

70 Melanie Yap and Dianne Leong Man, *Colour, Confusion and Concessions*, p. 90.

71 "Pump" means the host commission from weekend and holiday Mahjong games played by society members and their associates. See Ye Xun, "Recalling South Chinese in Africa Situations," *A Compilation of Historical Documents*, vol. 87, p. 83.

72 Melanie Yap and Dianne Leong Man, *Colour, Confusion and Concessions*, pp. 210–238; Ou Tie, *Chinese in the South Africa Republic* (Taipei: Zheng Zhong Press, 1991), p. 64. The single asterisk (*) indicates the earliest documented society leader, while the double asterisk (**) indicates Tan Pak Fah was originally a Singapore Chinese; his English name in London was Bernard Brown.

73 Zeng Fanxing, "Searching for Roots," p. 40.

74 Li Zhuofan, *History of Chinese in the West Indian Ocean*, cited in Fang Zhigen, *History of Chinese Africa*, p. 291.

75 Edith Wong-Hee-Kam, *La Diaspora Chinoise aux Mascareignes: Le Cas de Réunion*, p. 222.

76 Zheng Xiangheng, "Madagascar Chinese," *Qiao Wu Monthly* (Taipei) 166 (June 16, 1967): 25; Fang Zhigen and Li Xiouhua, "History and Current State of Madagascar Chinese"; Fang Zhigen, *History of Chinese Africa*, p. 78.

77 Melanie Yap and Dianne Leong Man, *Colour, Confusion and Concessions*, pp. 86–87.

78 Ibid., p. 54.

79 J. C. Armstrong, *The Chinese at the Cape in the Dutch East India Company Period 1652–1795*, cited in Fang Zhigen, *History of Chinese Africa*, p. 38.

80 Melanie Yap and Dianne Leong Man, *Colour, Confusion and Confessions*, p. 123.

81 Zeng Fanxing, "Searching for Roots," p. 41.

82 "Report of South African Consul Liu Yi to the Ministry of Foreign Affairs on Banning Smoking among Chinese," in Chen Hansheng, *A Compilation of Historical Documents on Chinese Indentured Laborers Abroad*, vol. 1 (IV), p. 1785.

83 Charles van Onselen, *Studies in the Social and Economic History of the Witwatersrand 1886–1914*, vol. 1 (New York: Longman), pp. 146–147.

84 Wen Xian, "Pioneering History of South Chinese in Africa," *Hua Sheng Monthly* (July 1997): 81.

85 Melanie Yap and Dianne Leong Man, *Colour, Confusion and Concessions*, pp. 85–86.

Chapter IV

1 Zeng Fanxing, "Searching for Roots," p. 40; Slawecki, *French Policy towards the Chinese in Madagascar*, p. 42.

2 The second Royal Investigation team received five hundred petitions. See Esnow Barberji, trans. Liang Yi, *A Short History of Mauritius* (Shanghai: Shanghai People's Press, 1973), p. 80.

3 Ibid., pp. 90–92.

4 Davenport, *South Africa: A Modern History*, pp. 214–216.

5 I have read at least the following contracts: "South Africa British Transvaal Recruiting Chinese Mining Laborer Contract," *Wai Jiao Bao* 79; "South Africa British Transvaal Recruiting Cantonese Mining Laborer Contract," *Wai Jiao Bao* 82; "Contract between Chinese Laborer and Employer," *Bei Guo Chun Qiu* 2 (1960). In addition, in the September 17–18, 1904 issue of *Da Gong Bao*, there was an advertisement by Tian Jing Ji Cha Labor Agency, listing recruitment conditions; in the appendix of Chen Da's *Chinese Immigrants with Special Focus on Labor Conditions*, English edition (1923), there are also Transvaal's "Importing Chinese Procedures" and "Service Contracts."

6 Lionel Phillips, *Transvaal Problems, Some Notes on Current Politics* (London, 1905), pp. 110–111, cited in Song Xi, "Chinese Laborers' Contribution towards South Africa's Transvaal Goldmines during the Late Qing Period," pp. 60–61.

7 Xie Zixiu, "South Africa Travel Journal," in Chen Hansheng, *A Compilation of Historical Documents*, vol. 9, pp. 278–289.

8 "Chinese Minister to England Zhang Deyi's Letter to Chinese Ministry of Foreign Affairs on Stipulating Signing a Charter Prior to Permitting South Africa to Recruit Chinese Laborers" (October 16, Guangxu 29), in Chen Hangsheng, *A Compilation of Historical Documents*, vol. 1 (IV), p. 1650.

9 *Annual Report of the Transvaal Government Mining Engineering for 1909–1910*, Tables 2, 10, and 11. L. M. Thompson, *The Unification of South Africa, 1902–1910* (London: Oxford University Press, 1960), p. 498. The symbol "s" is for shilling and "d" is for pence (penny) in the British currency used before decimalization in 1971. As such, a pounds (£) was divided into

twenty shillings or 240 pennies, and a shilling subdivided into 12 pennies.

10 Zhou Peizhi, *Guo Min Jian Jie Lu*, 1906, pp. 20–21, cited in Zhang Zhiliang, "Truth of 1904–1910 South Africa British Transvaal Recruitment of Chinese Laborers," *Beijing University Newspaper* 3 (1956): 92–93. Based on my own research, at the time there were at least four letters from Chinese laborers in South Africa published in the Chinese newspapers and magazines, exposing the misery of Chinese miners in South Africa.

11 The British Parliamentary documents, No. 2819, p. 149, cited in Peng Jiali, "History of British Recruiting Chinese Laborers for South Africa Goldmines during the Late Qing Period," *History Research* 3 (1983): 187.

12 P. Richardson, *Chinese Mine Labour in the Transvaal*, pp. 256–257n5.

13 See Chen Da, *Chinese Immigrants—Devoted to Labor Conditions*, in Chen Hansheng, *A Compilation of Historical Documents*, vol. 4, pp. 74–75.

14 Chen Zexian, "1904–1910 Collection of Historical Documents on the Recruitment of Chinese Gold Miners in Transvaal, British South Africa," in Chen Hansheng, *A Compilation of Historical Documents*, vol. 9, p. 252.

15 "South Africa Consul Liu Yulin's Report to Chinese Ministry of Foreign Affairs on His Detailed Investigation into Chinese Laborer Affairs (June 5, Guanxu 31)," in Chen Hansheng, *A Compilation of Historical Documents*, vol. 1 (IV), pp. 1746–1747.

16 An English Eyewitness, *John Chinaman, on the Rand* (London: R. A. Everett, 1905), p. 74.

17 John Hamill, *The Strange Career of Mr. Hoover under Two Flags* (New York: William Faro, 1931), p. 161. The thirty-first U.S. president Herbert Clark Hoover (ca. 1874–1964) once was a major player in the trading and shipping of Chinese laborers to South Africa. He graduated from Stanford University and came to China in 1899; he was later promoted to the chief engineer of Kai Ping Mining. In July 1900, representing British Bewick, Moreing & Co., along with the representative of the Kai Ping supervisor and Gustav von Detring, he signed "The Contract to Sell Kai Ping Mining" and robbed the mining right with an empty document. In 1901, the mining organization was renamed to Chinese Engineering and Mining Co. Ltd; Hoover became its first general manager.

18 "An Open Letter from South Africa," *Bei Guo Chun Qiu* 2 (1960): 82–83.

19 Xie Zixiu, "South Africa Travel Journal," in Chen Hansheng, *A Compilation of Historical Documents*, vol. 9, pp. 283–284. On tactics to control Chinese laborers, readers can also consult P. Richardson, *Chinese Mine Labour in the Transvaal*, pp. 158–160, 172–175.

20 Melanie Yap and Dianne Leong Man, *Colour, Confusion and Concessions*, pp. 117–119, 125; An English Eyewitness, *John Chinaman on the Rand*, pp. 62–74.

21 British Parliamentary documents, Cd. 2819, Affidavit by A.J. McCarthy, Campbell, Chinese Coolie Emigration, p. 196n3.

22 *Wai Jiao Bao* 106 (April 15, 1905).

23 "A Letter from Defuerre to his Company, July 20, 1762," Li Zhuofan, *History of Chinese in the West Indian Ocean*, cited in Fang Zhigen, *Chinese in Africa History Data Selection*, p. 308.

24 Slawecki, *French Policy towards the Chinese in Madagascar*, p. 102.
25 Chen Tiehun, *History of Chinese in the Madagascar Republic*, p. 29.
26 Dominic Dillon and Ron Hunton, *History of Chinese in Réunion*, cited in Fang Zhigen, *History of Chinese Africa*, pp. 467.
27 An English Eyewitness, *John Chinaman on the Rand*, pp. 77–97; P. Richardson, *Chinese Mine Labour in the Transvaal*, pp. 174–175. The reader can also consult Peng Jiali, "History of British Recruiting Chinese Laborers for South Africa Goldmines during the Late Qing Period"; Zhang Zhiliang, "Truth of 1904–1910 South Africa British Transvaal Recruitment of Chinese Laborers."
28 An English Eyewitness, *John Chinaman on the Rand*, p. 84.
29 Ibid., pp. 95–96.
30 Campbell, *Chinese Coolie Emigration*, p. 209.
31 Richardson once studied the 1905 Chinese laborer strike incident. See P. Richardson, "Coolies and Randlords: The North Randfontein Chinese Miners 'Strike' of 1905," *Journal of Southern African Studies* 2:2 (April 1976): 151–177.
32 An English Eyewitness, *John Chinaman on the Rand*, pp. 57, 82–83.
33 An English Eyewitness, *John Chinaman on the Rand*, pp. 53–54.
34 Campbell, *Chinese Coolie Emigration*, pp. 194–199, 209.
35 Xie Zixiu, "South Africa Travel Journal," in Chen Hansheng, *A Compilation of Historical Documents*, vol. 9, p. 285.
36 Chen Da, *Chinese Immigrants—Devoted to Labor Conditions*, cited in Chen Hansheng, *A Compilation of Historical Documents*, vol. 4, p. 75.
37 Melanie Yap and Dianne Leong Man, *Colour, Confusion and Concession: The History of the Chinese in South Africa*, pp. 119–228; Shen Siyao, *Overseas Anti-Sino History* (Beijing: Chinese Sociology Press, 1980), pp. 145–146.
38 An English Eyewitness, *John Chinaman on the Rand*, p. 95.
39 Li Zhuofan, *History of Chinese in the West Indian Ocean*, cited in Fang Zhigen, *History of Chinese Africa*, pp. 134–135.
40 Ibid., pp. 187–188.
41 *Journal Officiel de Madagascar et Dependences, Tananarive, Madagascar*, New Series 44 (December 12, 1896): 196; Slawecki, *French Policy towards the Chinese in Madagascar*, p. 107.
42 Slawecki, *French Policy towards the Chinese in Madagascar*, p. 111. This system was first implemented in French Indochina, similar to the "group of ten families," a neighborhood watch and defense system in ancient China.
43 Slawecki, *French Policy towards the Chinese in Madagascar*, pp. 112–117.
44 Melanie Yap and Dianne Leong Man, *Colour, Confusion and Concessions*, p. 7.
45 Toward the end of the 1946 issues of *Qiao Sheng Bao*, a lengthy serial article written by Miu Tong, then Chinese vice consul at Johannesburg, titled "Explanations of the Harsh Laws" were published; it gave detailed descriptions of the many South African laws discrimi-

nating against Chinese in the nineteenth century.

46 Li Zhuofan, *History of Chinese in the West Indian Ocean*, cited in Fang Zhigen, *History of Chinese Africa*, p. 259.

47 Miu Tong, "Explanations of the Harsh Laws," *Qiao Sheng Bao* (South Africa: May 4, 1946 until July 30); Xiao Ciying, *Chinese in the African Economy*, pp. 30–37; Li Changfu, *History of Colonial China* (1936; reprint Taipei: Shang Wu Press, 1983), pp. 309–311. Single asterisk (*) indicates nullified in June 1933, while the double asterisk (**) indicates replaced the Gold Legislation from 1898.

48 Melanie Yap and Dianne Leong Man, *Colour, Confusion and Concessions*, p. 73.

49 Li Zhuofan, *History of Chinese in the West Indian Ocean*, cited in Fang Zhigen, *History of Chinese Africa*, pp. 147–148.

50 Ibid., p. 148.

51 Melanie Yap and Dianne Leong Man, *Colour, Confusion and Concessions*, pp. 153–168, 232–237. Ou Tie believed that "Wei Yi She" was formed after "Lian Wei Hui; this claim, however, is at odds with the historical facts. See Ou Tie, *Overseas Chinese in South Africa Republic*, p. 64.

52 There were no trade statistics from 1877; however in 1878, Mauritius's imports from China were 50 rupees and zero from Hong Kong. Li Zhuofan, *History of Chinese in the West Indian Ocean*, cited in Fang Zhigen, *History of Chinese Africa*, p. 112.

53 Ibid., p. 138.

54 He Jingzhi, *Réunion Chinese Journal*, p. 16.

55 Statute Laws of the Transvaal, 1839–1910. "Law no. 3 of 1885, Relating to Coolies, Arabs, and Other Asiatics"; Karen L. Harris, *Closeted Culture: The Chinese in South Africa*, pp. 3–4.

56 Ibid., p. 4.

57 Melanie Yap and Dianne Leong Man, *Colour, Confusion and Concessions*, pp. 65–69.

58 Melanie Yap and Dianne Leong Man, *Colour, Confusion and Concessions*, p. 51.

59 *Wai Jiao Bao* 97 (December 1, 1904) (October 25, Guangxu 31); for the English version of the legislation content, see Melanie Yap and Dianne Leong Man, *Colour, Confusion and Concessions*, p. 63.

60 For content of this legislation, see "Overseas Chinese Journal," *Wai Jiao Bao* 166 (January 9, 1907) (November 25, Guangxu 32).

61 Melanie Yap and Dianne Leong Man, *Colour, Confusion and Concessions*, pp. 171–172.

62 On Chinese in the South Africa nonviolent resistance movement during 1907–1911, readers can consult Melanie Yap and Dianne Leong Man, *Colour, Confusion and Concessions*, pp. 137–168; Li Zhuofan, *History of Chinese in the West Indian Ocean*, cited in Fang Zhigen, *History of Chinese Africa*, pp. 244–254. Readers can also consult Chen Zexian, "1904–1910 Collection of Historical Documents on the recruitment of Chinese Gold Miners in Transvaal, British South Africa," in Chen Hansheng, *A Compilation of Historical Documents*, vol. 9, pp. 243–247; Wo Xian, "South Chinese in Africa Business History," *Hua Sheng Monthly*

(September 1997).

63 Li Zhuofan, *History of Chinese in the West Indian Ocean*, "Article 13, a Petition from Liang Jing to the London Representative of His Highness, Emperor of the Chinese Empire (Explanation of the Decision to Refuse to Obey the Asian Amendment Legislation)," cited in Fang Zhigen, *History of Chinese Africa*, pp. 332–334.

64 *Eastern Magazine*.

65 Melanie Yap and Dianne Leong Man, *Colour, Confusion and Concessions*, pp. 147–149.

66 Li Zhuofan, *History of Chinese in the West Indian Ocean*, cited in Fang Zhigen, *History of Chinese Africa*, p. 246.

67 *Wai Jiao Bao* 208 (May 13, 1908) (April 15, Guangxu 34).

68 Li Zhuofan, *History of Chinese in the West Indian Ocean*, cited in Fang Zhigen, *History of Chinese Africa*, pp. 263–264.

69 Ibid., pp. 335–337.

70 *Wai Jiao Bao* 208 (May 14, 1908) (April 15, Guangxu 34).

71 Melanie Yap and Dianne Leong Man, *Colour, Confusion and Concessions*, pp. 155–159.

72 There were two different views on Liang Zuojun's whereabouts. Li Zhuofan believed that his long jail sentence destroyed his health; "He did not continue running the society, although he continued his concerns for Gandhi's work and frequented Tolstoy Farm (the experimental base built by Gandhi to train leaders for the non-violent struggle)." Li Zhuofan, *History of Chinese in the West Indian Ocean*, cited in Fang Zhigen, *History of Chinese Africa*, p. 254. Ye Huifen believed that he mysteriously disappeared. See Melanie Yap and Dianne Leong Man, *Colour, Confusion and Concessions*, pp. 166–169.

73 The authoritative book on the overseas Chinese policy of the Late Qing government is Yen Chinghwang's *Coolies and Mandarins: China's Protection of Overseas Chinese during the Late Ch'ing Period (1851–1911)*.

74 Wang Tieyai, *A Compilation of Old Foreign Treaties*, vol. 1, p. 145.

75 Ibid., p. 148.

76 Yang Jiancheng, *Overseas Chinese History* (Taipei: Chinese Scholastic College South Ocean Research Center, 1985), p. 134.

77 Wang Tieyai, *Old Foreign Treaties*, pp. 242–246.

78 Zhang Zhiliang, "Truth of 1904–1910 South Africa British Transvaal Recruitment of Chinese Laborers," *Beijing University Newspaper* 3 (1956): 89.

79 On the contribution of Guo Songtao in protecting overseas Chinese, see Liu Hua, "Guo Song-Tao Must be Expelled to Protect Overseas Chinese," *Overseas Chinese History Research* 1 (1998).

80 Yen Chinghwang, *Coolies and Mandarins: China's Protection of Overseas Chinese during the Late Ch'ing Period (1851–1911)*, pp. 335–337. On the content of the petition, see the two attachments of "A Letter from the Chinese Minister in England to the Chinese Minister of Foreign Affairs on Chinese Citizens Being Abused in South Africa," in Chen Hansheng, *A*

Compilation of Historical Documents, vol. 1 (IV), pp. 1732–1733.

81 Melanie Yap and Dianne Leong Man, *Colour, Confusion and Concessions*, p. 109.

82 Wang Tieyai, *Old Foreign Treaties*, Vol. 2, p. 239.

83 Ibid., p. 241.

84 Zhang Zhiliang, "Truth of 1904–1910," p. 90.

85 This is a direct quote from the original document. "Consulate or vice consulate" should have been "consul or vice consul."

86 "A Request from Yuan, Governor of Zhi, to the Ministry of Foreign Affairs on the need to appoint a Consul to protect Labor Recruits in South Africa," *Eastern Magazine* 1:7 (September 4, 1904).

87 "Request to the Emperor by the Ministry of Foreign Affairs on Appointing Liu Yulin as the Consul in British South Africa (September 17, Guangxu 30)," in Chen Hansheng, *A Compilation of Historical Documents*, vol. 1 (IV), p. 1721.

88 "A Letter from Liu Yulin, Consul in South Africa, to the Ministry of Foreign Affairs on Chinese Labor Affairs (November 15, Guangxu 31)," in Chen Hansheng, *A Compilation of Historical Documents*, vol. 1 (IV), pp. 1766–1767. This negotiation effort produced no outcome.

89 *Wai Jiao Boa* 166 (January 9, 1907) (November 25, Guangxu 32).

90 Melanie Yap and Dianne Leong Man, *Colour, Confusion and Concessions*, p. 142.

91 Ibid., p. 461 n9.

92 Yen Chinghwang, *Coolies and Mandarins*, pp. 343–346.

93 Melanie Yap and Dianne Leong Man, *Colour, Confusion and Concessions*, pp. 172–173.

94 "A Report from the Consul General Liu Yi to the Ministry of Foreign Affairs on Banning Chinese Smoking (July 1, Guangxu 34)," in Chen Hansheng, *A Compilation of Historical Documents*, vol. 1 (IV), pp. 1785–1787.

95 Ai Zhouchang and Mu Tao, *History of Sino-African Relations*, pp. 182–183.

INDEX

Aden, 25, 36, 43
Affen Tank Wen, 103, 108, 116, 124-25, 152
African colonies, 5, 12, 61, 84, 87, 91, 114, 142, 150, 165
African laborers, 72, 132, 136-37
African regions, 10, 50, 51, 78-85, 99, 107
Agents, 60, 63, 76, 89
Ai Zhouchang, 6, 80
Alexandria (Egypt), 19-20, 31, 46
Altars, 122, 124
AmaXhosa (South Africa), 78
Ambergris, vii, 31-32, 34, 44, 47
Americas, the, 57-58, 60, 74
Ancestors, 47, 56, 91, 96, 105, 122-23, 127-29
Arabs, 26, 53, 150-52
Artifacts, 26-27, 35
Asia, 7, 9, 12-14, 22, 33, 39-40, 53, 64-65, 70-71, 73, 86, 88, 96, 111-12
Asian immigrants, 63, 86, 148-49, 162
Asian Legislation Amendment, 152, 156-58, 161-62, 167-69
Asian resistance movement, 160-61
Asians, 7, 13-14, 111, 113, 145, 148-52, 154-55, 157, 159-61, 165
Association system, 148-49
Atlantic Slave Trade, 57-58, 65
Australia, 60, 74

Badi Niort Company, 73
Barawa, 41-43, 45
"Barbarian servants" (*fan-hsiao-ssu*), ix
"Barbarian slaves" (*fan-nu*), ix
Batavia, 1-2, 51, 56, 96-98
Beijing, 36, 40, 77, 165, 168
Belgium, 76
Bibaluo, 23-24, 30, 32, 45
Bilateral relationship, 54
"Black servants" (*hei-hsiao-ssu*), ix
Bobali Kingdom, 23-24, 30
Boers (Dutch farmers), 79, 83, 133, 144, 165
Britain, 3-4. *See also* England.
British East India Company, 12, 15, 65-66
British government, 11, 14, 59, 79, 98, 114, 140-41, 155, 158, 161, 164-66, 168
British protected area, 166
British South Africa, 3, 5, 9, 84, 90, 167
British territory, 158, 163, 165-66
British West Africa, 75-75, 85, 87, 89, 92
Building of railroads, 72, 91

Camels, 30-31, 34
Cape Colony, 1, 78-79, 89, 96-99, 114-15, 121, 156-57
Cape of Good Hope, 2, 47, 49, 51, 53, 78, 115
Cape Town, 4, 9, 15, 49, 51, 56, 89,

96-100, 112, 114, 121-22, 124-25, 151, 169
Capitalism, 57
Cattle, 24, 31, 33-34
Ceng Yaoluo, 33-34
Chen Da, 4, 146
Chen Hansheng, 3, 80
Chen Xingxiong, 21, 27
Chen Zexian, 5, 64, 69, 80, 85, 137
China and Africa, viii, 17, 28, 36, 54
Chinaman, John, 15, 144
Chinese business, 109, 111-14, 126
Chinese citizens, 77, 163, 167
Chinese consul(ate), 6-7, 147, 157, 162, 168-70
Chinese government, 61, 145, 157, 165-66, 170
Chinese immigrants, 13-14, 63, 93, 97-101, 103, 106, 108, 114, 158, 162, 168
Chinese in Cape Colony, 115, 157
Chinese in Madagascar, 56, 67, 104, 110-11, 120
Chinese in Mauritius, 10, 56, 102, 110, 116-18, 123, 147
Chinese in South Africa, 8, 10, 13, 85, 97, 99-100, 112, 114-15, 120-21, 126, 153, 156, 158-59, 165, 167, 170
Chinese laborers, 2-3, 14, 52-57, 60-71, 73-91, 93, 96, 98, 105, 115, 124, 131-54, 162-69
  contracted, 2, 61, 165
  indentured, 54, 56-57, 60-65, 67-69, 71, 73, 78, 83-93, 96, 102, 105, 114, 124, 132-33, 142, 144, 148, 156, 162, 164-65
  recruited, 14, 60, 72, 75, 77, 91, 167
Chinese merchants, 11, 26, 97, 105, 112, 114, 125-26
Chinese miners, 74-75, 124, 137

Chinese minister in England, 155, 157-58, 161, 167
Chinese scholars, iii, ix, 20, 27, 37, 80
Chinese shops (stores), 109-10, 112-13, 125, 152, 154
Chinese workers, 61-63, 66, 76
Christianity, vi, 51, 124-25
Colonial governments, 64, 68-70, 73-75, 79, 88-89, 99, 105, 112, 114, 125, 128, 132, 142, 147-49, 152, 154-55
Congo Free State, 76-77, 84, 87, 89, 91-93
Coolies, 60-64, 67, 71, 80, 99, 101-03, 110, 112, 135, 145, 150-52, 163
Crops, 34-35, 53, 66, 142
Customs (cultural), vi-viii, 23, 30, 32, 34-36, 38, 40-41, 44, 49, 52, 110, 134, 138

Da Gu, 80-81
Da Qing Kingdom, 166
Da Xia, 18
Dakar (Senegal), 12, 72-73, 88
Dakar-Saint Louis Railroad, 73, 88
Dao Yi Zhi Lue, 28, 33
Dashi, 22-23, 25, 29, 31, 34
"devil-slaves" (*kuei-nu*), ix
Diplomatic ties, 37-39, 54
Discrimination policies, 129, 132, 147
Du Huan, 22
Duan Chengshi, 22-24
Dutch colonialists, 1, 49, 97-98
Dutch East Indian Company, 96

Early Chinese in Africa, 129, 131
East Africa, i-x, 10, 23-25, 28, 30-38, 40, 43, 47-50, 52, 60, 70-72, 78, 87, 89, 90, 99-100, 106, 169
Egypt, 18-20, 23-24, 26, 28-29, 31, 33,

35-37, 41, 43-46, 49-50, 53
Emperor Ming Cheng Zu, 39-42
Emperor Ming Tai Zu, 38
England, 53, 55, 58-59, 65, 75, 79-80, 84-85, 87, 131, 143, 155, 157-61, 165, 167, 170. *See also* Britain.
Enslaved Africans, 26, 48, 57, 63, 65, 112
Enslavement, x, 79. *See also* slavery.
Envoys, 37-39, 41-42, 48
Ethiopia, 18, 20-21, 23, 35, 37
Eunuch Zheng He, 38, 40-41. *See also* Zheng He.
European powers, 5, 49, 53-54, 57, 60, 165

Fabrics, 31, 34, 41, 44, 47, 111, 154
Fan Shouyi, 49, 51
Fei Xing, 38, 40, 42-44, 47
Feng Chengjun, 33
Feng Ziyou, 8
Foreign News (publication), 3, 5
France, 12, 58-59, 63, 67, 72, 163
francs (French currency), 64, 69, 73, 76, 102, 148-49
Free immigrants, 56, 61, 85, 96-97, 100, 125, 148, 165
French government, 12, 64, 67, 72-73, 163-64
French Madagascar, 85, 87
French merchants, 52, 72, 88, 109, 111, 163-64
French North Africa, 91, 93
French West Africa, 12, 72-73, 85, 87-88
Fu Zhou, 65, 69
Fujian, 56, 65, 86, 88, 102-03, 105, 107, 116, 118, 122, 142, 152

Gambling, 123, 125, 146, 156
Gandhi (Mohandas Gandhi), 120, 160-62
General Smits, 168
German colonies, 5
Germans, 35, 70-72, 85, 87, 91
Gervase Mathew, vii
Ghana government, 13
Gifts, 26, 40-41, 44, 47-48, 117
Giraffe, viii-x, 19, 33, 42, 47
Gold, 15, 31, 44, 47, 55, 58, 60, 75, 79, 99, 139
Gold Coast (present-day Ghana), 12, 14-15, 74-75, 89
Goldmines, 83, 89, 99, 102, 114, 124, 133-34, 138, 142-43, 145-46
Grains, 22-23, 29, 34, 44, 47, 154
Guan Yu, 122, 127-28
Guandi temple(s) 115-16, 122-23, 127-28, 152
Guangdong, 105-06, 116, 118-21, 123, 145
Guangfu, 56, 114, 116, 121-23, 152-53
Guangxu (period), 71, 167
Guangzhou, 8-9, 19, 22, 25, 36, 53, 62, 65-66, 72-73, 76, 88-89, 98, 102, 107, 163

Han Dynasty, 1, 17-18, 20-21
Handcuffing, 139-40
Harsh laws, explanations of, 158-59, 161-62
Hong Kong, 1, 53, 71, 76-77, 80, 89, 91, 107, 109-10, 154
Horses, 22, 41-42, 139
Huan Jiao, 34
Huo Huiduan, 115, 160

Ibn Battuta, 35-36, 38
Immigrants. *See* Chinese immigrants.
Imports, 47, 91, 109, 114, 154, 169
Indentured Chinese laborers. *See* Chi-

nese laborers.
India, vii, 21, 23, 31, 36, 41, 60, 63-66, 87, 153, 158, 161
Indian Ocean, i-ii, viii, 21, 38, 40, 43, 51, 53-54, 60, 63-64, 107
Ivories, 30-31

Java, 41, 70
Jia Jiang Menli, 33, 35, 46
Johannesburg, 5-8, 71, 79, 112-13, 120, 124-25, 147, 155, 160-61

Kankan-Conakry Railroad, 73, 88
Kejia, 56, 100-03, 116-23, 152-53
Kenya, 23-24, 27, 33, 35, 45, 47, 72
Kidnapping, iv, 61, 163
Kunlun Zengji Kingdom, 30, 46

Labor recruitment, 6, 63, 76, 84, 91, 163-64
Labor shortage, 57, 63, 74, 87
Lashing(s), 139
Late Qing Period, 102, 169-70
Laws, 9, 14, 22, 59, 74, 78, 147-48, 150-52, 156-68
Legislation, 90, 97, 101, 114, 120, 141, 144, 147-69
Legislation, discriminatory, 7, 155, 157
Legislation (regulations), harsh, 3, 7, 9, 120, 158-62, 168
Li Xuan, 19
Li Zhuofan, 63, 86, 109, 153
Liang Zuojun, 115, 131, 158-62
Liu Yi, 4, 125, 162, 167-69
Liu Yulin, 4-5, 80, 147, 157, 167-68, 170
London, 75, 84-84, 121-22, 138, 141, 155, 157, 165, 167
Lourenço Marques, 7, 90, 106-07

Ma Huan, ii, 38, 41-44
Macau, 48, 51, 67, 71, 76-78, 87, 89, 91, 100, 106
Madagascar, 10, 12-13, 30, 35-37, 46, 52-56, 60-63, 66-69, 85, 87-93, 103-06, 110-11, 120, 123, 126, 132, 142, 148-49, 156
Maghreb, 23, 29, 35
Maldives, 36, 43
Malindi, viii-x, 23, 33-34, 41, 45
Maritime routes, 29, 36, 43, 47
Mauritius, 1-2, 7-1, 43, 51, 56, 59, 61-67, 85-86, 89-92, 97-111, 115-18, 122-26, 132, 142, 147, 152-56
Mei Xian, 100, 102, 105, 119, 122
Merchants
    African, 33, 35-36
    Arab, ii, x, 26
    Asian, 149
    Dutch, 112
    European, 56, 113, 126
    Foreign, iv, 23, 39
    French, 52, 72, 88, 109, 111, 163-64
    Indian, 111
    Muslim, 154
Ming Dynasty, ii, 33, 37-38, 43, 47-48, 54, 162
Mining, 6, 9, 74, 79-80, 82, 124-25, 134, 137, 165, 169
Ministry of Foreign Affairs (China), 2-6, 9, 125, 167
Missionaries, 35, 47, 49, 69
Mobile vendors, 109-10, 112
Mogadishu, 27, 40-45, 47
Molin, 22-23
Morocco, 23, 29, 35, 46, 73
Mozambique, 7, 10, 25, 33, 35, 46-47, 51, 78, 89-90, 106
Mulangpi Kingdom, 29-30, 46

Nan Shun Society, 116-17, 120
Natal (South Africa), 15, 81, 89, 99-100, 114, 122, 151, 155
North Africa, 18, 23, 29, 33, 36, 47-48, 50, 53, 87, 90-93

Oceanic voyages, 20, 33, 39, 41-42
Opium (smoking), 4, 91, 125, 146, 156, 169
Oppression, 132, 146
Overseas Chinese communities, 91, 95-129
Overseas Chinese policy, 162

Passive sabotage, 142, 145
Peng Jiali, 80
Petition, 97, 110, 112-13, 115, 132, 154-55, 157-58, 161, 165, 167-68
Plantation economy, 58-60, 87
Plantation owners, 63, 108, 132
Plantations, sugarcane, 108, 110, 126, 142
Police, 71, 125, 133, 143, 149, 156-57
Porcelains, 21, 27-28, 31, 35, 47, 52-53, 100
Port Louis, 62, 101, 109, 115, 117, 125, 152
Portugal, 51, 55, 77, 84
Portuguese, 2, 5, 7, 14, 34, 47-48, 57, 60, 63, 65, 76-78, 89-90, 97, 106
Prisoners, iv, 1, 56, 96-97, 112
Products, ii, 21, 23, 28-29, 32-34, 36, 44, 57, 75, 100, 106, 109, 111-13, 126
Prostitution, 125

Qi Ying Hao (ship), 53
Qing Dynasty, 1-2, 4, 9, 49, 51, 53-56, 69, 99, 116, 125, 134, 159, 162-66, 169-70
Qing government, 62, 76, 132, 161-62, 164, 168, 170

Racial discrimination, 113, 115, 120, 150, 153, 170
Railroads (railways), 12, 14, 19, 60, 71-74, 77, 85, 91. *See also* building of railways.
Recruitment, 3-11, 60-66, 69-71, 76, 81-84, 88, 91, 99, 138, 163-67
Religion, v, vi, 31, 35, 52, 128, 160
Resistance, 9, 63, 98, 120, 132, 141-44, 146, 153, 158-61
Resistance, passive, 142, 144, 162
Réunion, 10, 12-13, 53, 60, 64-65, 67, 69, 73, 86-88, 91-93, 100-05, 110, 118-19, 123, 142, 147, 155-56
Reunion government, 63-65, 86, 88
Rice, 31, 47, 135, 153-54

Saint Helena Island, 15, 49, 53, 65-67, 98, 115
Salt, 34, 52, 111
Sanlang Kingdom, 25-26
Senegal, 60, 72-73
Seychelles, 107, 126
Shantou, 1, 70-73, 76, 87-89
Sheng Fuwei, 18, 40
Shungwaya, vi-vii
Silk fabric, 19, 44, 47
Silver, 34, 44, 47, 64, 67
Singapore, 63, 70-71, 86, 102, 164
Sino-African relations, 21, 27-54, 61
Sino-African trade, 26, 47-48, 53
Slavery, 58, 61, 77, 87
Slavery, abolition of, 57, 59, 64, 79, 88, 108, 147
Slavery, modern-day, 131, 133, 146
Socotra Island, 32, 36, 42, 45
Somalia, 23-27, 35-36, 41, 43, 45-46
Song Dynasty, 23, 28, 35, 37
South Africa, 1-15, 47, 51, 56, 60, 78-93, 96-103, 107, 112-15, 120-26, 132-38,

141-47, 150-70
Southeast Asia, 26, 40, 44, 56, 60, 62-64, 86-88, 96, 99, 101, 108, 155
Spain, 29, 46, 51, 59, 77, 84
Sumatra, 41, 43

Taipei, 27
Tamatave, 67, 69, 88, 104-05, 111-12, 120, 123, 149
Tang Dynasty, i, 1, 17, 19, 21-22, 26, 27-28, 35-36
Tanganyika (Tanzania), 24-25, 70-72, 85, 92. *See also* Tanzania.
Tanzania, 24-26, 32, 35-35, 47,
Temples, 42, 115, 121-24, 127-29, 147, 155
Torture, 56, 84, 132, 140-41, 145, 165
Transvaal, 4-7, 9, 11, 14-15, 79, 83, 90, 99-102, 113, 121-22, 125, 134, 137, 139, 143-45, 150-55, 157-58, 160-61, 167-69
Transvaal Chinese Association, 153, 158, 161
Transvaal government, 80, 125, 139, 150-51, 156-57, 159-61, 163-67, 169
Treaty, 5, 59, 79, 84, 160, 163-68
Tu Huan, iii, viii
Tuopandi, 29-31, 46

United States, 1, 3, 60, 167

West Africa, 12, 60, 72-73, 74-78, 89, 92
West Indian Ocean, 54, 60, 63-64, 107
Western Zone, 17-19, 42
Whipping, 15, 139-41
Women, iv-v, viii, 23-24, 34-35, 44, 52, 65, 72, 125
Worship, 22, 116, 122, 129
Wusili Kingdom, 24, 46

Xia Men, 64, 86

Xiao Ge Lang, 43
Xie Qinggao, 49-51
Xie Zixiu, 5, 8, 81, 134-35, 139, 145

Yuan Dynasty, 28, 33, 36-37,
Yong le (Yung-lo) Emperor, ii, v, 39-42, 47

Zanzibar, 27, 30-31, 35-36, 59
Zeng Fanxing, 62
Zhang Deyi, 49-50, 84, 165
Zhang Junyan, 18
Zhang Tiesheng, 43
Zhang Xingliang, 18, 20-26, 29
Zhang Zhiliang, 166
Zhao Rushi, 28, 30-31, 33
Zheng He (Cheng Ho), ii, 38-45, 47-48. *See also* Eunuch Zheng He.
Zhongli Kingdom, 31-33, 45
Zhu Fang Zhi, 23, 28, 31, 33, 45
Zhubu, 40-41, 44-45, 47

www.ingramcontent.com/pod-product-compliance
Lightning Source LLC
Chambersburg PA
CBHW071959290426
44109CB00018B/2076